CLASSIQUE COVER ART FOR CLASSICAL MUSIC

gestalten

Content

PART TWO

PART THREE

Preface

This book is dedicated to a cultural artifact that has served the friends of classical music as one of the most important sound-carrying media – the long-playing record. It was succeeded by the digital Compact Disc, whose ascent began in the early 1980s. Particularly in the initial years after its launch, the CD was accused of having a 'cold' and sterile sound. For many listeners, this disadvantage was apparently irrelevant, since it was compensated for by the easier handling and a playback that was free of hissing and crackling. To date, there are only still very few music-lovers who have remained true to the LP. In particular, like me, they are the owners of large record collections. I quite agree that the sound quality of the LP is, in comparison, at least on par with that of the CD – providing that they are played on a very good record player. I can still remember the shellac records of my youth, when LPs were put on the market. At that time we sneered at those music-lovers who still listened to shellac records. Today, those who have remained true to the LP are the ones who are sneered at. But new market developments in 2007/2008 indicate a welcome increase in sales of long-playing records. Even the versatility of what is being offered and record player sales are on the rise again.

The LP was introduced to the market in the USA in 1948, when Columbia America presented the first long-playing records with so-called microgrooves. In Germany, the long-playing record was launched in 1950. At least as far as popular music was concerned, shellac records were still produced for a few more years, since singles in microgroove format had not yet been developed. I first heard Bill Haley's *Rock Around the Clock* in 1955 on a shellac record. The parallelism of two systems repeated itself, when in the early 1960s, the development of the stereo record had reached market maturity. Simultaneously, mono and stereo versions became available. The long-playing record was unrivaled for a period of 30 years and was not even seriously threatened by the tape cassette.

The industry noticed quite early on that interesting covers had a sales-boosting effect. Columbia America was the first manufacturer to act on this realization. It has been reported that sales soared after the graphic artist Alex Steinweiss was hired as Art Director and started designing the covers for the classical records from 1940 onwards, when they were still shellac records. An attractive cover grabs the customer's attention and has sales appeal. And so, this book also serves as a homage to all the graphic artists and designers who, with visual means, prompted this attention to establish musical associations to composers or to the work.

How does one come up with the idea to create a book about the cover culture of classical long-playing records? To begin with, I have always had a weakness for an attractive cover, as well as for the abundantly illustrated manufacturer catalogues. Ultimately, a cover should wow you into buying. When I had the idea for this book, I already owned three illustrated books on the cover art of jazz records and the book *The Classical Long Playing Record: Design, Production and Reproduction* from the Dutch record antiquary, Jaco van Witteloostuyn. Along with other themes, the author devotes around 100 pages to the cover culture from the 1950s to the 1980s. He focuses, however, on continental European productions. British, American and Eastern European manufacturers are decidedly underrepresented. These, though, make up the majority of productions worldwide. Particularly Mercury and RCA from the USA, along with Decca and EMI from Great Britain, have produced long-playing records that are the most coveted among today's vinyl-collectors. This resulted in the idea of documenting the most inspiring covers from my international classical LP collection in an illustrated book, in which more than half of all the covers documented are from both of these aforementioned countries. They include many legendary recordings, with the provision that they have covers that are either interesting or typical for that epoch.

In the second part of this book, I provide an international overview of record producers with information on their repertoires. This includes sought-after record labels for the audiophile classical collector. These round labels, pasted in the center of the album, are not of such great artistic importance, but their design is significant to the collector, who recognizes in them historically significant information about a specific producer. *Shaded dogs* from RCA, Decca *Wide bands*, *Tulips* from Deutsche Grammophon and Command Classics *Gold* are all coveted collectors' items.

Dr. Horst Scherg
Sandhausen, February 2008

PART ONE
THE COVER CULTURE OF THE CLASSICAL LP

Introduction

Older music-lovers will remember of the record shop where they used to go. There, thousands of them could be found, the classical long-playing records, packed in cartons that were 30 by 30 centimetres in size, printed with romantic landscapes, conductors in heroic pose, a graceful ballerina, a handsome, young female pianist at the grand piano or a musically-related illustration that awakened the curiosity of the viewer. Printed on them, the names of famous artists and composers. How often have we been drawn to an album, while rummaging through a stack of records, only because we liked the cover? Attracting attention – that's been the job of the record cover since the late 1950s. Up until then, records were hidden on shelves behind the sales counter with only a view of the four millimetre-wide spine. There wasn't much to be seen, either – mostly just a standard cover with the contents printed in a standardized layout. Purchasing one was not possible without consultation and the assistance of a salesperson. There was no self-service, at least not in Europe. When the album covers started becoming more colourful and elaborate, due to improved printing techniques, the means of presentation also changed. The previous high, inaccessible shelves gave way to containers of standard table height, where the albums, which were placed slightly inclined towards the back of the container, could be "leafed through", as is the procedure with today's CDs. For those who required it, there was still sales assistance. And another thing: it was possible to listen to the album in a soundproof booth with hi-fidelity loudspeakers. This was offered, for instance, in the Heidelberger Hauptstraße at the PHORA company – which is long extinct.

The culture of the album cover has survived, however. The stylistic devices of graphic arts were to catch attention and awaken buying interest. The printed information was linked to the visualization and as it were transferred into sound in the mind of the potential buyer. The development of cover art reached its peak in about the mid-1970s. It only changed minimally up to the end of the LP era. Cover art was continued on the CD booklet, the seductive effect was lessened, though, as was the accuracy of the illustration, due to the smaller format. Externally, the CD became a miniature version of the long-playing record.

The purpose of this book is to reincarnate the culture of the album cover: from the mono era in 1950 up to the nineteen eighties, where there were still LPs, but the layout had already been customized to fit the CD, which was offered simultaneously. Cover art had actually been around since the 1940s. Alex Steinweiss, who designed the covers for Columbia Records in the USA – at that time still for shellac records – was a trailblazer in this field. Up until that time, Columbia had been selling classical music shellac records in a box, with a cover layout that was reminiscent of a tombstone. This book shows a series of covers designed by Alex Steinweiss, albeit from the LP era. For those who want to marvel at Steinweiss' artistic qualities, I recommend the book by Jennifer McKnight, which he co-authored, which presents covers from the age of the shellac records. These also include many classical music covers. The covers from Alex Steinweiss can also be seen in a book by Eric Kohler, which deals with the period of time from 1940 to 1960, and which acknowledges many other artists: Jim Flora, Robert Jones, Rudolph de Harak, David Stone Martin, Burt Goldblatt, Reid Miles and others. Both books are certainly worth seeing and reading. As a matter of fact, the covers of the shellac records in the 1940s and 1950s, at least those from the USA, were by far more interesting and designed with more care than those done at a later date.

The development of the record industry, following the introduction of the long-playing record and the artistic and technical further development of the cover design for pop and jazz records, is presented in an illustrated book from Nick de Ville titled "Album Style and Image in Sleeve Design". Here, tribute is also paid to many illustrators from the Forties, Fifties and Sixties. Many similarities can be seen in the development of both the popular and classical music sectors, whereby the most conspicuous is the replacement of hand drawn or graphically designed artwork with the use of photos. These, on the other hand, made it easy to depict the artists, whether rock singers or conductors, in striking photographic portraits.

Another book about pop and jazz covers from Barry Miles, Grant Scott and Johnny Morgan, carries the ambitious title "The Greatest Album Covers of All Time". It starts off in the Fifties and goes on to the year 2000, whereby it is structured according to the defining musical styles of the corresponding decades and artists.

And finally, we come to the book from Jaco van Witteloostuyn, which I referred to in the preface. The cover culture only constitutes a part of this book. It also comprises an international manufacturer and order number registry of classical long-playing records classified according to time period, and provides rich background knowledge regarding the development of the LP and the related production and recording techniques. The section on cover culture concentrates mainly on continental European producers. The work has also given me inspiration for my own book.

A list of all the books introduced here, together with additional books, can be found in the literature section.

I started buying classical long-playing records in 1966. I had just heard Beethoven's "Pastoral" and "Prélude à l'après-midi d'un faune" from Debussy for the very first time. Both works have a programmatic character and I found this especially exciting, since I was thereby able to connect images or stories to the music. I am no longer certain about which classical records were the first ones that I ever bought. But I am sure that they included Respighi's "Pines of Rome" and "Fountains of Rome", conducted by Frühbeck de Burgos, and Arlésienne and Carmen suite from Bizet conducted by Cluytens. Smetana's cycle "My Country", the "Nights in the Gardens of Spain" from Manuel de Falla and Schumann's "Rhenish" symphony were also part of the collection. Later, the standard symphonic works of great composers like Beethoven, Brahms, Chopin and Dvorak followed. I was particularly fond of the Romantics at this time.

During a work residency in England in 1971, I attended a symphony concert in Birmingham, where I heard music from the English composers Frederick Delius and Edward Elgar (Walk through the Paradise Garden und Sea Pictures), through which I was able to perceive an entirely new musical ambience. This led to my love of the English late Romantic period and soon thereafter to composer Ralph Vaughan-Williams. In the following years, there were many other subsequent discoveries: American composers such as Samuel Barber, Aaron Copland, Charles Ives, William Schuman and Russian composers such as Alexander Scriabin, Sergei Rachmaninov, Nicolai Rimksy-Korsakov, Alexander Borodin, Dimitri Shostakovich and the many nearly unknown composers from the former Soviet Republics. Many of these works couldn't be bought in Germany. So I had to import them – the Russian ones as English licensed editions or as originals from English importers, the American ones from the USA and the English ones as original pressings from England.

The musical focus of the collection is on the symphonic music beginning with Haydn. The only conductors that were specifically collected were Fritz Reiner and Sir Thomas Beecham. The RCA stereo recordings from Reiner are nearly complete. The same holds true for the EMI stereo recordings with Thomas Beecham. Well-represented are also the recordings with Eugene Ormandy and Leonard Bernstein on Columbia, Ernest Ansermet and Georg Solti on Decca and Karel Ančerl on Supraphon. The country focus is established by the works from England, the USA, former Russia and the former Soviet Union. I have even systematically collected records from specific producers. These include Russian Melodiya records and albums from the US companies Capitol Records, Command Classics and Everest. Nearly comprehensive here is the English His Master's Voice collection from EMI and albums from the companies Decca, Lyrita and Mercury Golden Imports, the latter as reissues of the legendary Mercury recordings.

The collection is international. Only every sixth album comes from Germany. It also contains a great number of Soviet Melodiya albums from various republics of the Soviet Union with a focus on the 20th Century. Every eighth album in the collection is from the now extinct Soviet Union. In addition, there is a large number of albums from former Communist East European countries.

I first acquired a majority of the collection when LPs were only still available in second hand shops. I obtained them primarily from abroad: from England, the USA and from Hungary. Many of the albums that I was able to acquire in this manner are from the years 1955–1965, when I didn't even own one single classical album. In the year 2000, I realized that I would not be able to pay due attention to the music if I pursued my collecting passion. So I stopped collecting. In the meantime, my collection had grown to nearly 4,000 long-playing records.

In contrast to the afore mentioned book by Witteloostuyn, the LP covers in this presentation are not categorized according to time periods, but rather in terms of design and theme – in other words, according to the element used to catch the eye. These are primarily photos, paintings, complex typographical fonts and illustrations. They also include portrayals of conductors and soloists, whereby the latter have often been catapulted to stardom through their visual presentations over the past 30 years. And there are even original and expressive examples amongst these. Alongside these characterisations, paintings with artwork done at the time of origin of the composition are an appropriate way of illustrating the musical content for the record buyer. Therefore, a vast album collection is like a gallery full of famous masterpieces. But it isn't the artwork alone that makes an aesthetic record cover – it's also the integration of the artwork in the record cover, the geometric arrangement, the typographic embellishment and the contrasting background.

Basically, I call all visual presentations that are made specifically for the album – with the exception of photos – illustrations. For the viewer of the record cover, illustrations are the most significant category. Just as movie advertising was painted on posters until well into the Sixties, there were also special production procedures for album covers. Graphic artists illustrated the composers, artists or scenes, expressing musical content with colour pencils or colours. This technique is used by many record companies, most notably though by the US companies RCA and Capitol Records. Differentiations according to other criteria are made in the picture section. I can recommend using the Table of Contents for an initial overview.

Creating the groups and categories to present the covers was a long process. Essentially, the procedure involved determining categories for the covers that were similar to each other under certain aspects, and to then assign these categories to groups. These groups constitute the chapters of this book. For example, while reviewing the covers, I found some for which the category names "Proud America", "English Countryside" and "American Idyll" seemed appropriate. I allocated these to a group which I named "Themes". I had already established the categories "Magnificent Operas" and "Immortal Ballet". Initially, I intended to assign these to a group named "Musical Content". One doesn't exactly have a visual association for every music genre, such as a symphony. That's why I decided to drop the group "Musical Content" and also assign the aesthetic opera and ballet covers to the "Themes" group. I had already photographed two covers where "folk heroes" were artistically depicted, but I knew that there were others. So, I took photos of these too making them enough to create the category "Knights and Folk Heroes" and to then assign these to the group "Themes" as well. The theme group was thus created in a dynamic process. The covers were assigned to categories, but they could change categories, too. A painting of a folk hero can be assigned to the group "The Art Gallery in the Record Cabinet", but it also fits in its own category. Ultimately, priority for the category determination depended predominantly on which category was more typical for the cover. This was the process for all categories and groups.

The covers shown in this book are, with only a few exceptions, all from my collection. Of the 3,304 record covers, I have classified about every fifth one as being artistically and historically significant and photographed them. For about 50 of the covers, I have either borrowed them to photograph them, or I have acquired the photographs from another source. The book presents a total of 777 covers.

I'm sure that the covers will inspire some readers to buy the recording as a CD. Many of the recordings are now available, reissued on CD or in other formats. For this reason, I have listed the Internet addresses of the record companies presented in the book in such a manner that the recordings that are now available on other labels, can be located as well. No guarantee is given for the completeness of this list.

Notes on the Presentation

The image section has been arranged in 13 groups or chapters, of which the majority is again subdivided into categories. Only the first two groups (mono era and the early stereo era) and Group XII (Three Decades of Typical Picture Illustration) have a temporal aspect. The rest of the groups have all been arranged according to design-related aspects. The order of the presentation of the groups does not follow any particular logic. The Table of Contents illustrates the structure of the presentation.

I have attempted, with this presentation, to also name the artist or graphic artist who designed the cover, in addition to discography data such as label, catalogue number, country of production and year of release. This information was not always printed on the record cover. If the specifics are missing, either the graphic studio of the producer or their in-house photographer were generally responsible for the cover design. Most of the cover producers furnish this information on the reverse side of the cover. With paintings, obviously, the title of the picture, the year of origin and the gallery is stated. All discography and artistic data are printed in a separate legend field on the same double page as the cover. Additions in brackets are from the author.

The countries of origin of the record companies have been abbreviated as follows:

AUS	Australia
BRASIL	Brazil
BULG	Bulgaria
CAN	Canada
CS	Czechoslovakia
GDR	German Democratic Republic
GFR	German Federal Republic
EU	Europe (CBS and Philips)
F	France
FIN	Finland
GB	Great Britain
HU	Hungary
ISR	Israel
JAP	Japan
N	Norway
NL	Netherlands
NZ	New Zealand
POL	Poland
PORT	Portugal
RUM	Rumania
S	Sweden
SU	Soviet Union

In the notes to the cover, the following abbreviations are used: Ph for photo, CA for cover art (an illustration or painting created especially for the cover by the artist), CD for cover design (in regard to the arrangement of text and art), DPAD Decca Publicity Art Department.

Russian names are written according to English transliteration rules. An alphabetic register of producers is located in the Appendix.

COLUMBIA. Set MX-203, USA 1943, CA: Alex Steinweiss

COLUMBIA. Set MM-653, USA 1947, CA: Alex Steinweiss

— Two covers designed by Alex Steinweiss in the 1940s for Columbia Records. They illustrate how creative and innovative these covers were at that time. The covers have been taken from the book from Jennifer McKnight-Trontz and Alex Steinweiss (see literature).

1.0 The Nostalgic Charm of the Fifties

The long-playing record was introduced in Europe in 1950, then only in mono sound. At that time, in addition to the long-playing record (LP) with 30 cm diameter, there was also the somewhat smaller medium play (MP) record with 25 cm diameter and shorter playing time (see note in the remarks). I first heard Ravel's Bolero on this type of "MP" record. The format was available up until the mid-1960s.

In comparison to the shellac record, the launch of the LP in Europe featured the beautification of the "packaging". During this period, cover art in Europe was not as sophisticated as it would become only a few years later. With their technical simplicity, many of the covers presented in Category A extensively differ from those that illustrated records either simultaneously or a few years afterwards. In the 1950s, more technically advanced examples already existed in the USA, such as categories 1.3 (Urania), 1.4 (Mercury) and 1.5 (Remington) and as shown according to the examples produced by Capitol and RCA records in the second half of the Fifties. Elaborately wrought multicoloured prints (i.e. for book illustrations) had already been produced at the end of the 19th Century. In this context, record packaging was behind by about several decades.

Most of the covers presented in this chapter are photographs that I have made of covers from the estate of a Heidelberg record antiquary, or they have been acquired from other collectors as finished picture files. The progress made in cover art is well illustrated by four of the presented covers of the Philips company (1, 2, 21, 22) or Columbia America (6, 14, 15, 16). Even in the age of the shellac record in the 1940s, Columbia had already recognized the sales-boosting effect of interesting record covers. The designer Alex Steinweiss was an absolute pioneer here. He designed covers 15 and 16 and later we will see samples of his art from covers produced by Remington and Everest. On covers 15 and 16, we can see the ornate writing developed by Steinweiss in 1939 – the so-called "Steinweiss Scrawl".

1.1 Covers in "Poster Style" (1–19)

These covers were created with few colours – only two or three – and a minimum of artistic effort. They seem flat and plain. To some extent, they make use of modern style elements. Typical for this period are the covers from Philips (1–3) and the cover from Telefunken (5). Others dispense with using modern elements of style such as the four covers from the producer Decca (7–10) or American-based Columbia (6, 14–16). Included in this category are the covers which were then already routine, with photos of conductors or artists (17–19), which mostly have a conservative look.

1 PHILIPS. N00640R (25 cm), NL 1950s
2 PHILIPS. A00687R (25 cm), NL 1950s
3 PHILIPS. A01173L, NL 1956
4 TOPS. L924 (25 cm), USA ca 1950
5 TELEFUNKEN. TW30155 (25 cm), D 1950s, CA: Eng

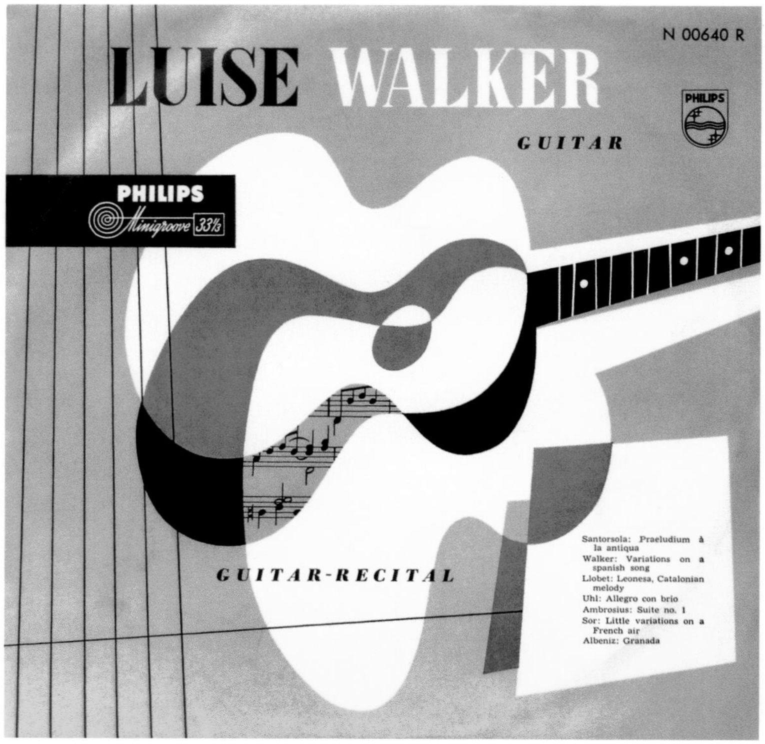

1

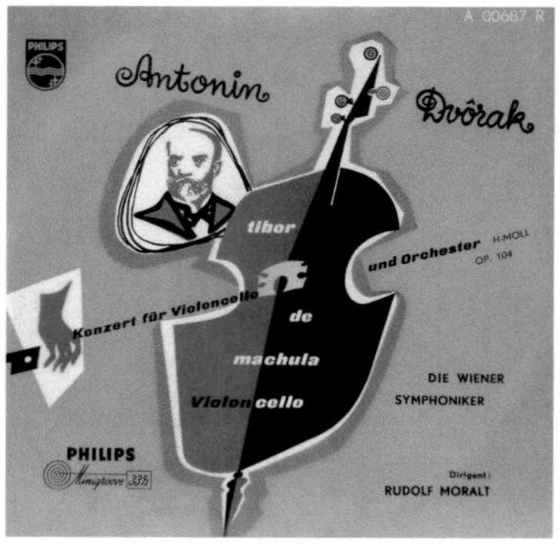

2

3

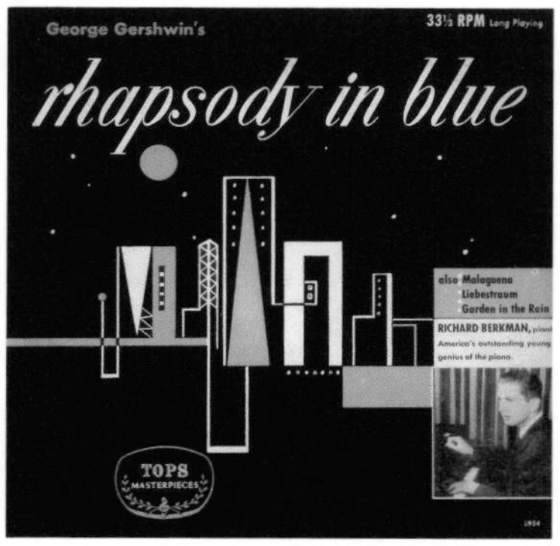

4

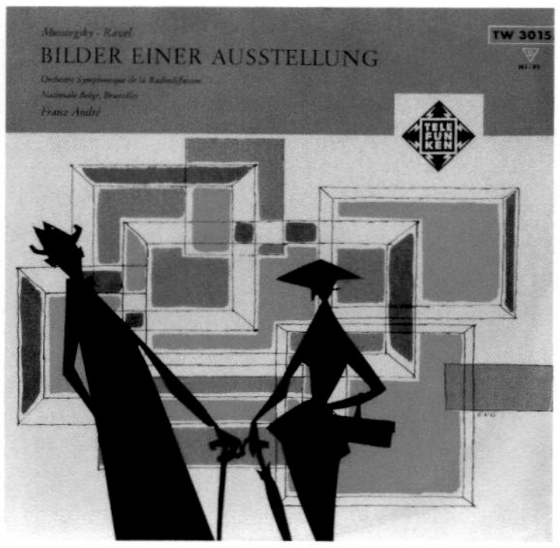

5

6

7

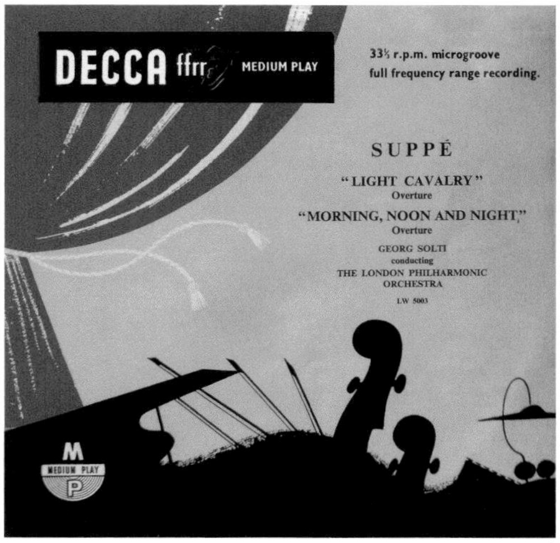

8

9

10

6 COLUMBIA. ML2128 (25 cm), USA 1950
7 DECCA. LW5109 (25 cm), GB 1954
8 DECCA. LW5003 (25 cm), GB 1954
9 DECCA. LXT2751, GB, 1950s
10 DECCA. LW5136 (25 cm), GB 1950s
11 DGG. LPE17020 (25 cm), D 1956, CA: Atelier du Cret
12 DGG. LPE17105 (25 cm), D 1959

11

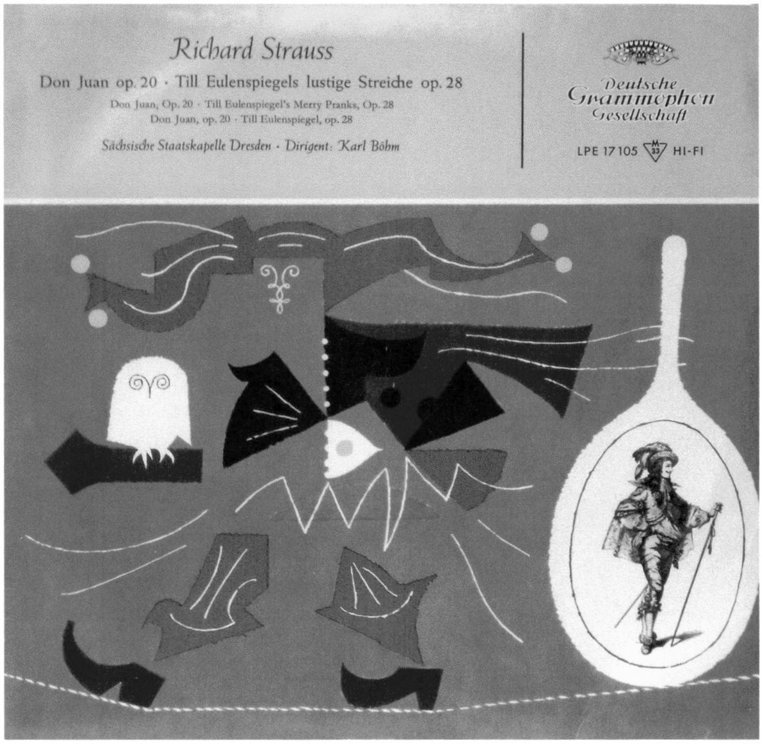

12

13

14

13 PLYMOUTH. P-10-7 (25 cm), USA 1952
14 COLUMBIA. ML2203 (25 cm), USA 1951, CA: Stanley
15 COLUMBIA. ML2167 (25 cm), USA 1951, CA: Alex Steinweiss
16 COLUMBIA. ML4287, USA 1950, CA: Alex Steinweiss
17 EMI. CLP1032, GB 1950s
18 EMI-COLUMBIA. 33CX1067, GB 1952, F: Chidnoff
19 EMI-COLUMBIA. 33CX1046, GB 1950s

15

16

17

18

19

20

1.2 The Early Illustrative Style (20 - 28)

These covers are less bold and to some extent, they present a better printing technique and have more colours. The opulently designed Prokofiev record from Philips is an impressive example of this (22).

— Typical for this more advanced illustrative style is a record from New Zealand (23). This style can also be found in the advertising of that period.

— The covers 26 and 27 are mono records from the American company RCA, which were simultaneously also produced as a stereo version with an identical cover.

— The Capitol record from the mono period (28) advertises the longer playing time of the long-playing record album (LP) as opposed to medium play (MP).

Les Cloches
de Corneville
opéra-comique en 3 actes
Musique de :
Robert PLANQUETTE
Texte d'adaptation phonographique
de Pierre HIEGEL
Germaine : Martha ANGELICI
Serpolette : Nadine RENAUX
Henri : Michel DENS
Grenicheux : Joseph PEYRON
Le bailli : THIRACHE
Le Père Gaspard : Pierre HIEGEL
CHŒURS RAYMOND SAINT-PAUL
ORCHESTRE de L'ASSOCIATION des CONCERTS LAMOUREUX
direction : JULES GRESSIER
Pathé
33 DTX 107
Longue durée 33 1/3 microsillon
BELL

21

22

20 PHILIPS. 825509AY, GB 1957, CA: Calet
21 PATHÉ. 33DTX107, F 1950s, CA: Bellorgeot
22 PHILIPS. A00670R (25 cm), NL 1950s
23 KIWI. LD3, Aus CD: Raymond Boyce

23

24

25

26

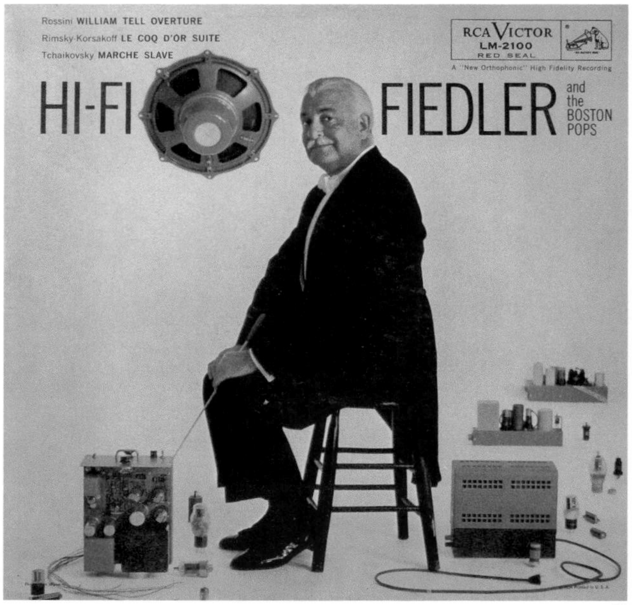

27

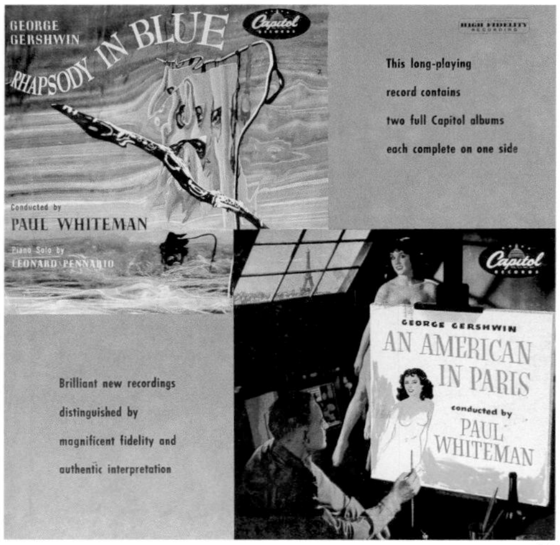

28

24 RCA. LSC1807, USA 1950s
25 TELEFUNKEN. LGX66018, B 1955, CA: bla
26 RCA. LM2292, USA 1950s
27 RCA. LM2100, USA 1950s, CA: Moller
28 CAPITOL. T303, USA 1957

29

31

30

29 URANIA. URLP5002 (25 cm), USA 1951,
CA: Robert Galster
30 URANIA. URLP7126, USA 1954, CA: Rado
31 URANIA. URLP7015, USA 1951, CA: Robert Galster
32 URANIA. URLP7122, USA 1954, CA: Meyers
33 URANIA. URLP7121, USA 1954, CA: Robert Galster

1.3 Urania, USA (29–33)

Urania was an American company in the mono era. The recordings were made mostly in post-war Germany. The cover of the cantata "Battle and Victory" from Carl Maria von Weber (30) is literally shocking. The cantata was the first major success for the composer. Today it has almost disappeared into oblivion. It is not suited to our present time.

32

33

34

1.4 Mercury Records, Mono, USA (34 - 43)

With only one exception (picture 39) all of the covers presented here are courtesy of the Japanese Mercury record collector Kohji Matsubayashi. There is a wealth of information about Mercury on his website (see literature and websites). As is true of so many of the American covers created in the 1950s, they are graphically interesting and lovingly designed, particularly cover 35. The reference to the music is obvious in most cases.

— The Moldau River flowing through Prague in Picture 38 refers to *Smetana's Moldau* and Mozart's *Prague Symphony.*

— Charles Griffes composed *The Pleasure Dome of Kubla Khan* and *The White Peacock* displayed on Cover 40.

— Cover 43 shows a peacock and a Mandarin, portraying the music.

35

36

34 MERCURY. MG50004, USA 1952, CA: Maas
35 MERCURY. MG50009, USA 1952, CA: Maas
36 MERCURY. MG80004, USA 1953

38

39

37

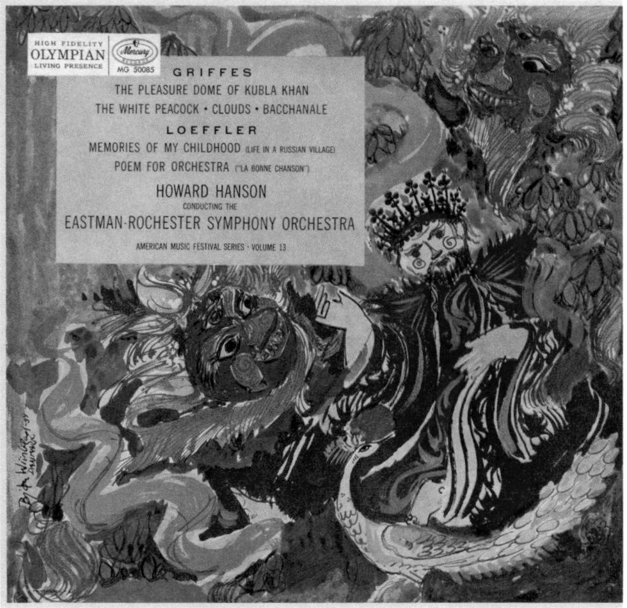

40

37 MERCURY. MG50006, USA 1952, CD: Maas
38 MERCURY. MG50042, USA 1953
39 MERCURY. MG50046, GB 1955, CD: Eugene Bermann
40 MERCURY. MG50085, USA 1953, CA: Björn Wiinblad
41 MERCURY. MG50071, USA 1958, Ph: Henry Ries
42 MERCURY. MG50026, USA 1953
43 MERCURY. MG50038, USA 1954, CA: Maas

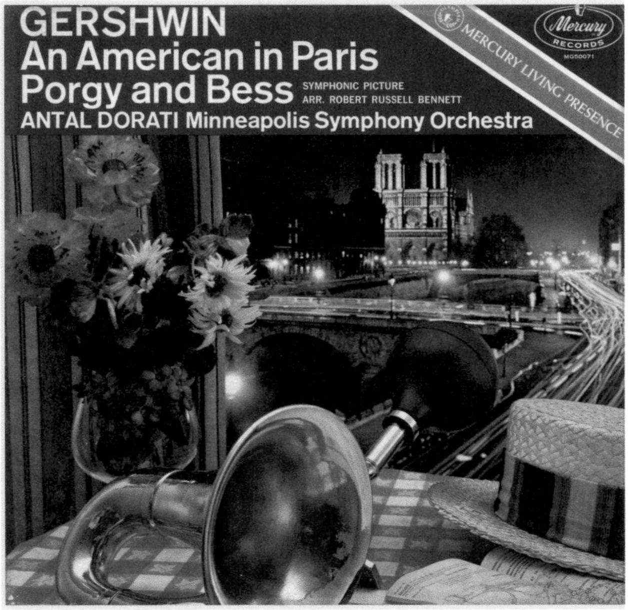

41

42

43

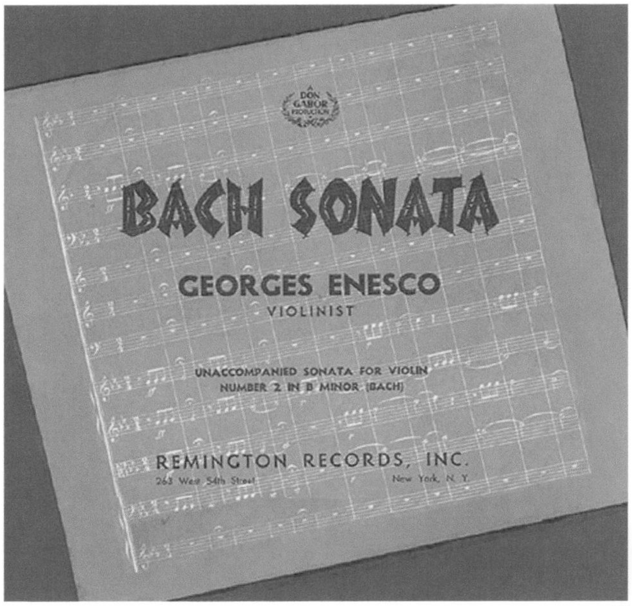

44

45

44 REMINGTON. PL-1-149 (25 cm), USA 1950s
45 REMINGTON. R-199-25, USA 1950s
46 REMINGTON. R-149-20 (25 cm), USA 1950s
47 REMINGTON. R-199-78, USA 1952, CA: Curt John Witt
48 REMINGTON. R-199-75, USA 1952

1.5 Remington, USA (44 - 58)

The recordings were produced in the 1950s mainly in Germany and Austria. Remington records were cheaply priced and of inferior quality. This is not evident when you look at the covers. They were stylish and as good as those from the major producers. The selection shown here gives an insight into the stylistic development of the covers, even though the designers varied. It starts with covers 44, 45 and 46 and ends with 52, 54 and 58. This category also includes some covers designed by the founder of cover art, Alex Steinweiss. Collectors who are interested in Remington records and their artists should refer to the extensive and informative website by Rudolf A. Bruil (see literature and websites). He supplied me with the photos of the 12 Remington covers shown here.

46

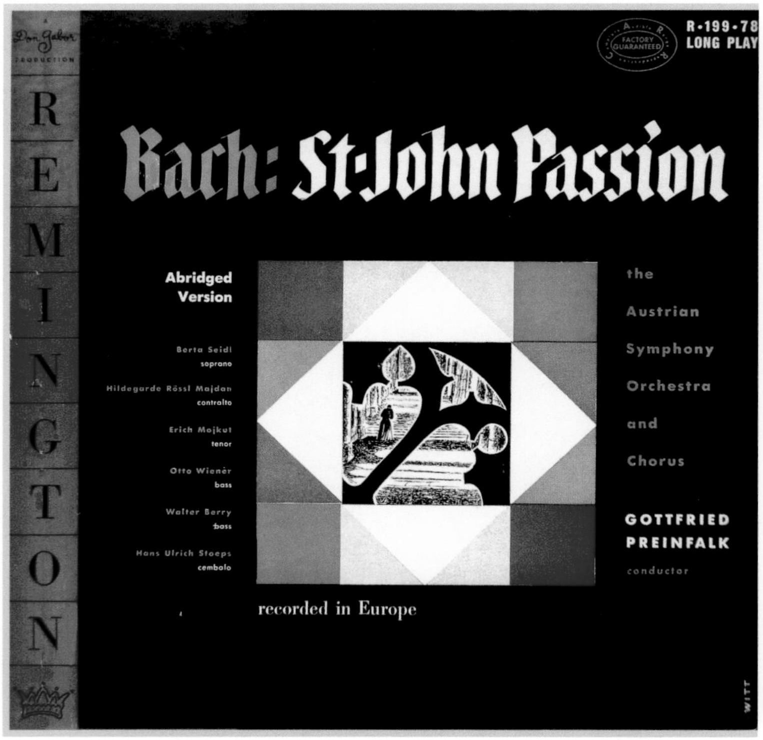

47

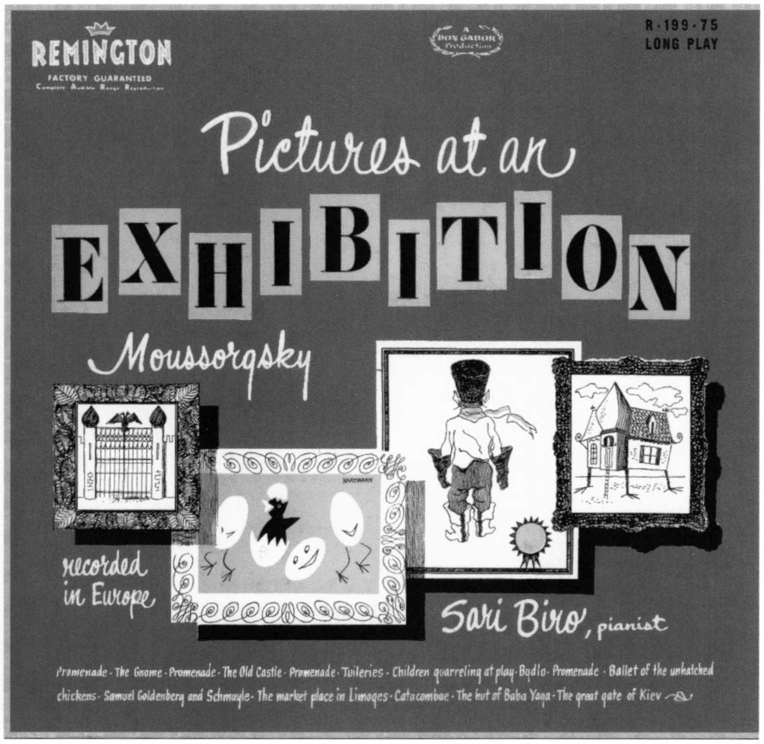

48

49

50

51

52

49 REMINGTON. R-199-131, USA 1953, CA: Alex Steinweiss
50 REMINGTON. R-199-21, USA 1950s
51 REMINGTON. R-149-48, USA 1953, CA: Curt John Witt
52 REMINGTON. R-199-176, USA 1950s, CA: H.K. Albitz

53

54

53 REMINGTON. R-199-13, USA 1951, CA: Einhorn
54 REMINGTON. R-199-178, USA 1950s, CA: Rado
55 REMINGTON. R-199-166, USA 1955, CA: H.K. Albitz
56 REMINGTON. R-199-136, USA 1953, CA: Alex Steinweiss
57 REMINGTON. R-199-133, USA 1953, CA: Alex Steinweiss
58 REMINGTON. R-199-191, USA 1950s

55

56

57

58

2.0 Covers to the Mid-Sixties

This is the period that has produced the records with the highest collectors' value – not because of their beautiful covers, but due to their naturally-sounding recordings with high fidelity, making them LPs for *audiophile* collectors. This especially holds true for records from Decca, RCA and Mercury.

2.1 Capitol Records, USA (59 - 78)

Capitol has presented wonderfully illustrated record covers, all of them specially made for records since the mid-Fifties. Few companies have maintained this tradition so extensively. The special production of the covers also guarantees a particularly close connection to the musical content. Not all of the covers were as successful as the ones shown here. I have only picked out the most interesting ones. Many others are illustrated with photographies, of which two are shown (75, 77). In fact, the majority of the Capitol records from this time are designed with photos. Some of the covers with recordings from England were probably adopted from the English original (59, 64, 67, 69, 70). This is certainly the case with Cover 71.

59

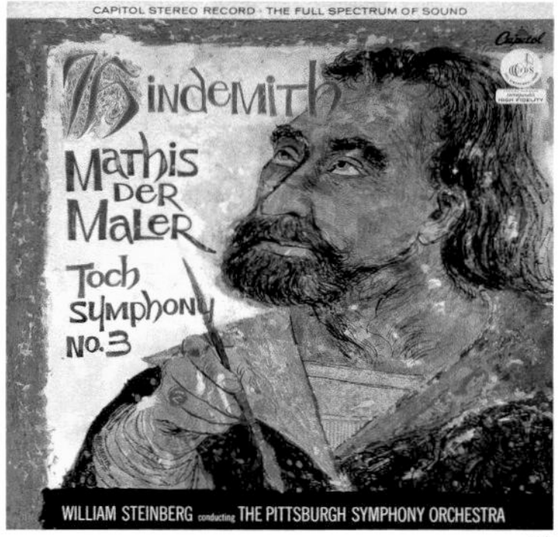

60

59 CAPITOL. SG7103, USA 1958
60 CAPITOL. SP8364, USA 1957, CD: Kelly Seltzer
61 CAPITOL. SP8583, USA 1962, CD: Frank Page
62 CAPITOL. SP8537, USA 1960

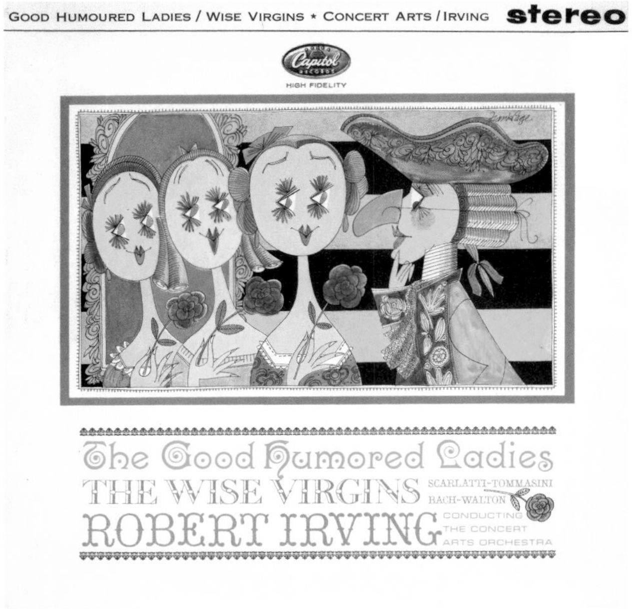

61

62

63

64

65

66

63 CAPITOL. SP8441, USA 1958, CD: Boyle
64 CAPITOL. SG7130, USA 1958, CD: Grant
65 CAPITOL. SP8549, USA 1960, CD: Boyle
66 CAPITOL. SP8508, USA 1960

67 CAPITOL. SG7244, USA 1960
68 CAPITOL. SP8619, USA 1962
69 CAPITOL. SG7214, USA 1959, CD: Schweikert
70 CAPITOL. SG7183, USA 1959, CD: Frank Page

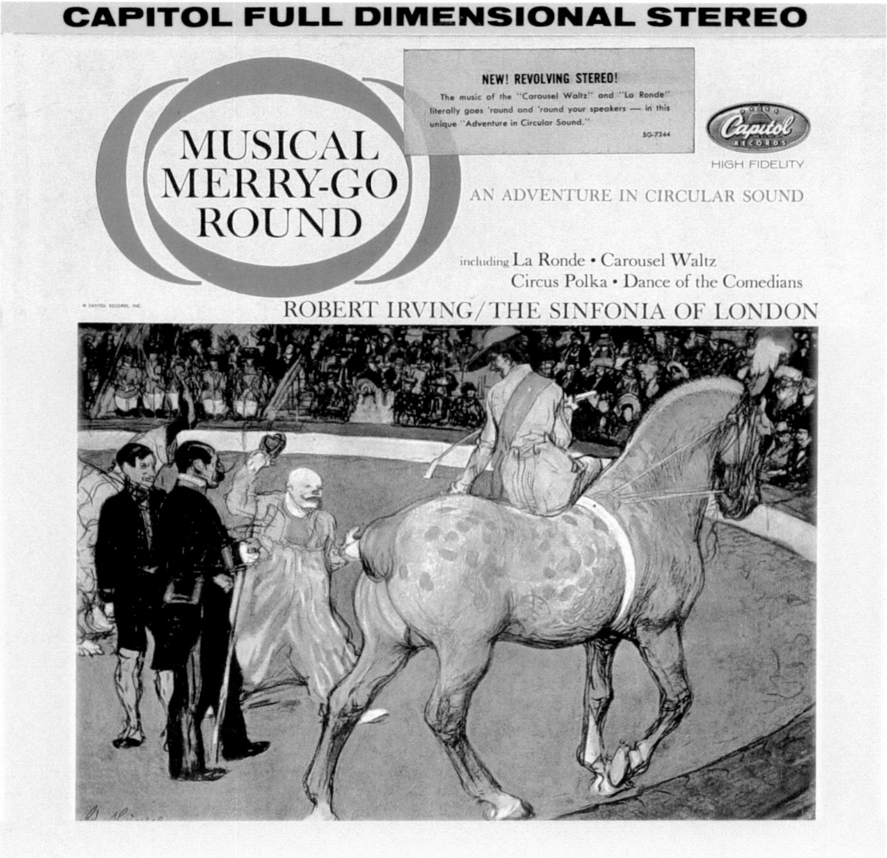

67

68

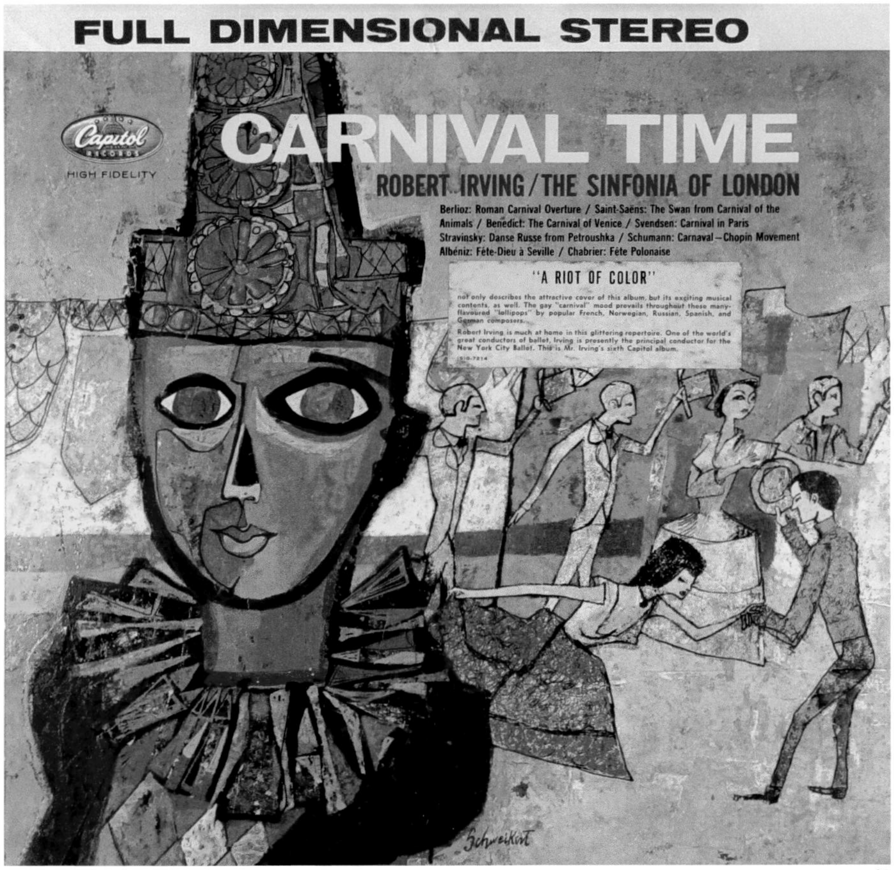

69

70

FULL DIMENSIONAL STEREO
RUSSIAN OVERTURES
TCHAIKOVSKY / ROMEO AND JULIET / FANTASY OVERTURE
RIMSKY-KORSAKOV / RUSSIAN EASTER FESTIVAL / OVERTURE
GLINKA / RUSSLAN AND LUDMILLA / OVERTURE
MOUSSORGSKY / PRELUDE FROM KHOVANTSCHINA
ARTUR RODZINSKI / THE ROYAL PHILHARMONIC ORCHESTRA
Capitol
HIGH FIDELITY

71

71 CAPITOL. SG7182, USA 1959
[Design as original EMI ASD288]
72 CAPITOL. SP8524, USA 1960, CD: Boyle
73 CAPITOL. SP8540, USA 1960
74 CAPITOL. SP8342, USA 1957

CAPITOL STEREO RECORD · THE FULL SPECTRUM OF SOUND
stereo
RACHMANINOFF
Third Piano
Concerto in D minor
Leonard Pennario
The Philharmonia Orchestra
conducted by Walter Susskind
Capitol
HIGH FIDELITY

72

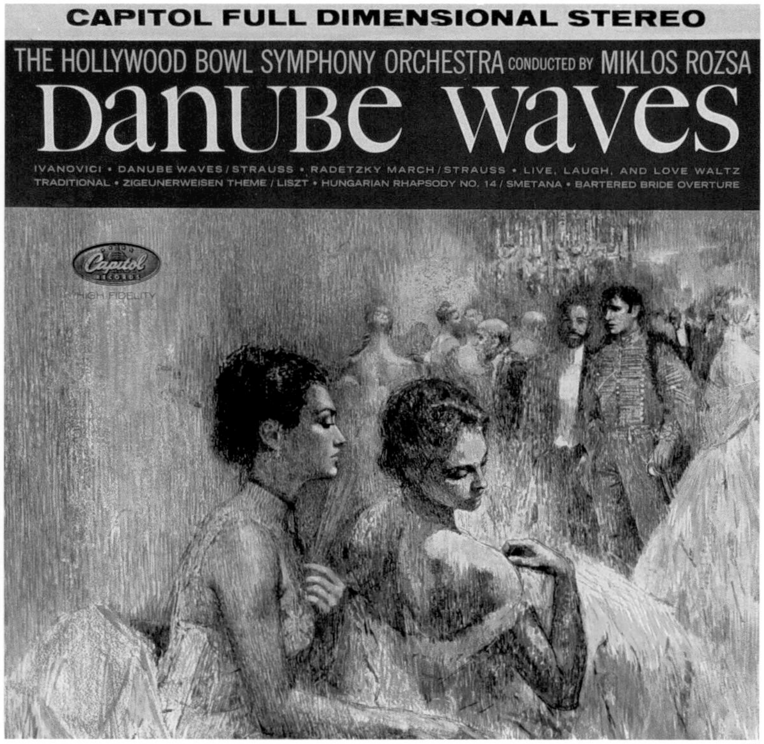
CAPITOL FULL DIMENSIONAL STEREO
THE HOLLYWOOD BOWL SYMPHONY ORCHESTRA CONDUCTED BY MIKLOS ROZSA
Danube waves
IVANOVICI • DANUBE WAVES / STRAUSS • RADETZKY MARCH / STRAUSS • LIVE, LAUGH, AND LOVE WALTZ
TRADITIONAL • ZIGEUNERWEISEN THEME / LISZT • HUNGARIAN RHAPSODY NO. 14 / SMETANA • BARTERED BRIDE OVERTURE
Capitol

73

75

76

74

74 CAPITOL. SP8342, USA 1957
75 CAPITOL. SP8373, USA 1958
76 CAPITOL. SP8405, USA 1958
77 CAPITOL. P8314, USA 1957
78 CAPITOL. SP8576, USA 1962

77

78

2.2 Columbia, USA (79 - 83)

Columbia Records is the parent company of the European CBS and the second largest US producer after RCA. I have only selected some typical examples. Many covers from this period seem to fit better in other categories in this book (see Index). Not to be overlooked is the new stereo recording technique at the time, boldly printed on the upper periphery. All covers reflect their musical reference. Cover 81 is painted.

2.3 Command Classics, USA (84 - 89)

Command Classics used an innovative recording process on 35 mm film track, which is indicated in the upper left corner of the cover. A reference to the music is only revealed on covers 85, 87 and 88.

83

79

79 COLUMBIA. MS6070, USA 1959, Ph: George Jacobs
80 COLUMBIA. MS6235, USA 1961, Ph: Bettmann Archives
81 COLUMBIA. MS6148, USA 1960
82 COLUMBIA. MS6036, USA 1958, CA: Courtesy French Institute, N.Y.C.
83 COLUMBIA. MS6743, USA 1965, Ph: Norman Mishimura

80

81

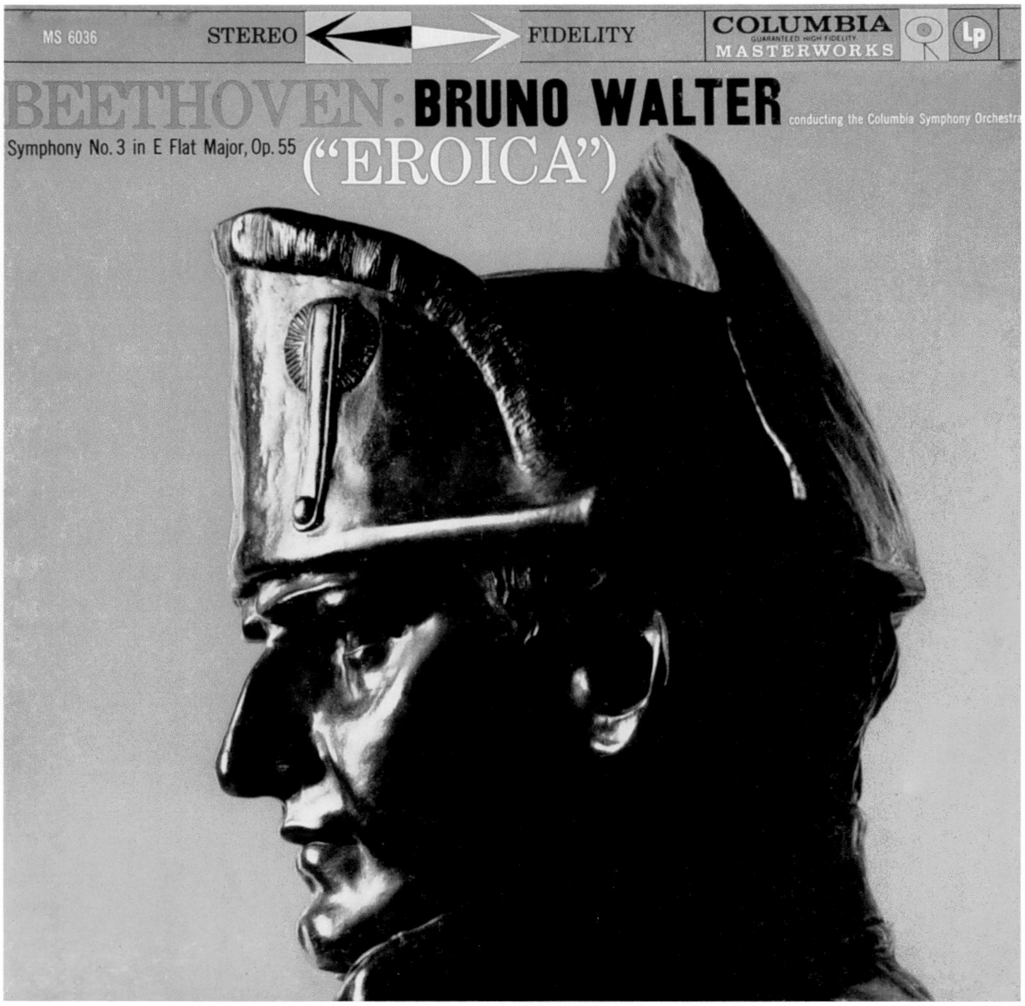

82

84

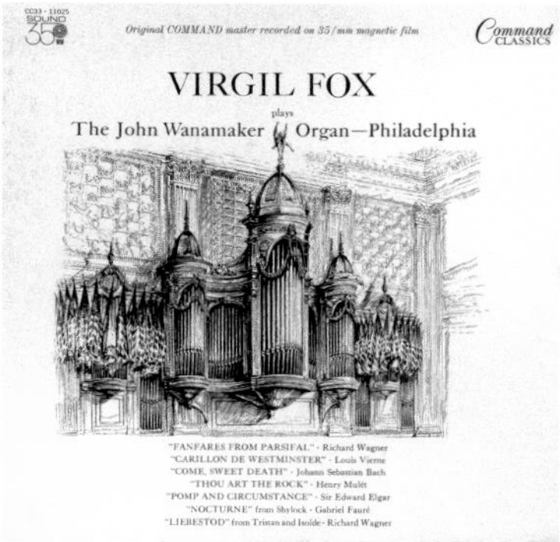

85

86

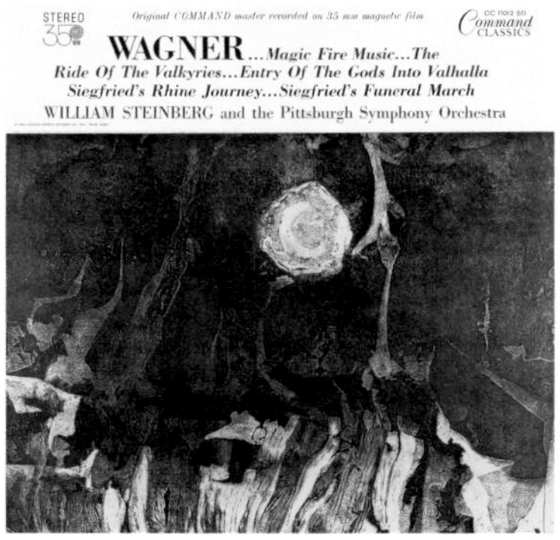

87

88

89

84 COMMAND. CC11034SD, USA 1964, CA: Duevell
85 COMMAND. CC11025, USA 1964, CA: Charles E. Murphy
86 COMMAND. CC11027SD, USA 1964, CA: Charles E. Murphy
87 COMMAND. CC11012SD, USA 1962, CA: Charles E. Murphy
88 COMMAND. CC11038SD, USA 1964, Ph: Bridget Del Forno
89 COMMAND. CC11004SD, USA 1961, CA: Charles E. Murphy

2.4 English Decca (90 - 100)

Four of the covers still have the charm of the 1950s (90, 91, 93 and 99). The remainder uses the stylistic devices that we still find in later productions, namely photos, special printing techniques and illustrations that have been produced especially for the record in question. The covers 97, 99 and 100 communicate the musical content particularly clearly.

2.5 English EMI (101 - 112)

In comparison with the covers from English Decca, some examples are much more advanced. The graphic design of the cover for Peer Gynt (101) from 1957, is surprisingly elaborate for this period. All of the covers reflect the musical content – to a greater or lesser extent.

90

91

92

90 DECCA. SXL2252, GB 1960
91 DECCA. SXL2218, GB 1960 [back cover]
92 DECCA. SXL2197, GB 1960
93 DECCA. SXL2177, GB 1959
94 DECCA. SXL2196, GB 1960
95 DECCA. SXL2091, GB 1959

93

94

95

96

97

98

96 DECCA. SXL6000, GB 1960
97 DECCA. SXL2260, GB 1960
98 DECCA. SXL2062, GB 1960
99 DECCA. SXL2212, GB 1960
100 DECCA. SXL2296, GB 1960

99

100

101

102

103

104

105

106

101 EMI. ASD0258, GB 1957, CD: M.G. Loizides
102 EMI. ASD0326, GB 1958
103 EMI-COLUMBIA. SAX2364, GB 1961
104 EMI. ALP1667, GB 1958
105 EMI. CSD1533, GB 1964, Ph: MIRA
106 EMI-COLUMBIA. SAX2367, GB 1961, Ph: Camera Press & Lotte Meitner-Graf

107

108

109

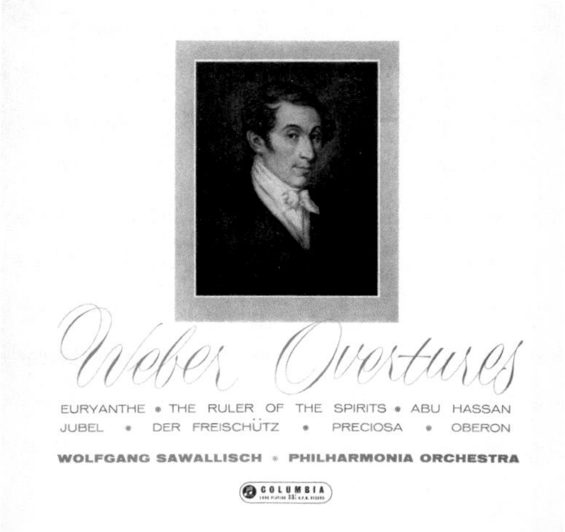

110

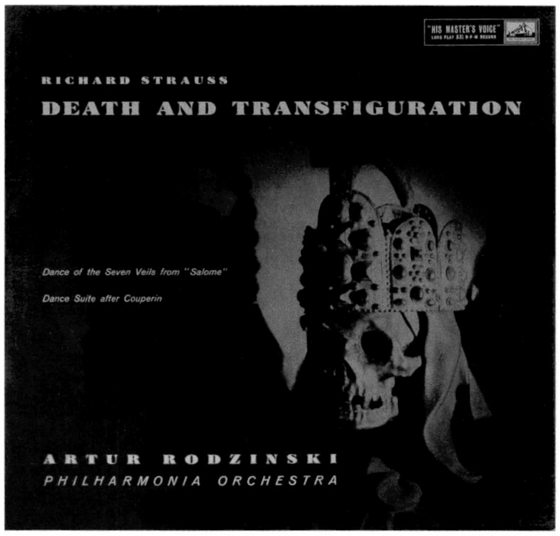

111

112

107 EMI. CSD1444, GB 1962, Ph: British Travel & Holidays Association (Royal Shakespeare Theatre, Stratford upon Avon)
108 EMI. ASD0525, GB 1963, Ph: Harry Weber
109 EMI. ASD0388, GB 1959, Ph: Brian Dagleish
110 EMI-COLUMBIA. SAX2343, GB 1959
111 EMI. ASD0270, GB 1958, Ph: Anton Macku (Death's-head from the sarcophagus of Charles VI in den Imperial Crypt of the Capuchin Church, Vienna)
112 EMI. ASD0347, GB 1960, Ph: Hugo Rodenberg

113 EVEREST. SDBR3029, USA 1959
114 EVEREST. SDBR3032, USA 1959
115 EVEREST. SDBR3003, USA 1958
116 EVEREST. SDBR3034, USA 1959, CD: Alex Steinweiss
117 EVEREST. SDBR3022, USA 1959, CD: Alex Steinweiss
118 EVEREST. SDBR3016, USA 1958, CD: Alex Steinweiss

2.6 Everest Records, USA (113 - 129)

Nearly all of the Everest records are from 1958 and 1959. At Everest, a lot of effort was put into the design of the covers – although the records were only in the medium price range. Picture 123 presents an elaborately handcrafted artistic work. It corresponds perfectly to the programme on the record, and this can also be said for the majority of the other covers. Some of the covers are designed with photos, either posed or as a montage. Quite noticeable here is the somewhat kitsch content, designed by none other than the "inventor" of album cover art, Alex Steinweiss. Evidence that he was also capable of designing more aesthetic covers for Everest can be seen on cover 116 (without reference to the content) and 126. Uirapurú (118) is a legendary enchanted bird. Additional Everest covers are portrayed under numbers 238 and 514. Everest records were still available beyond 1980.

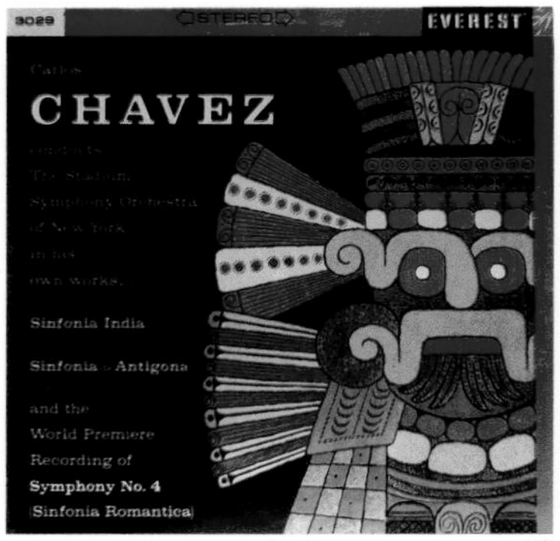

113

115

116

114

117

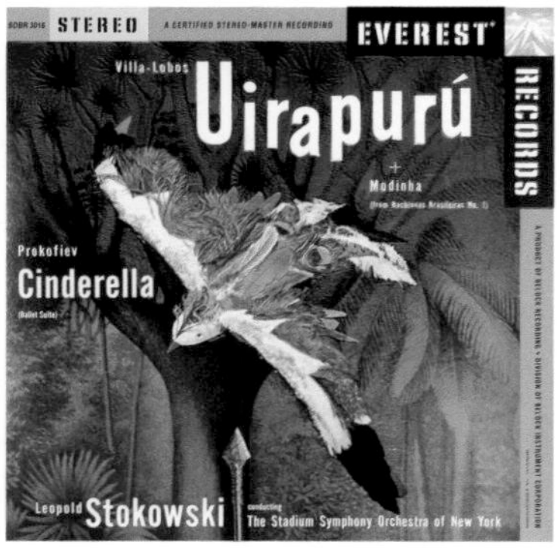

118

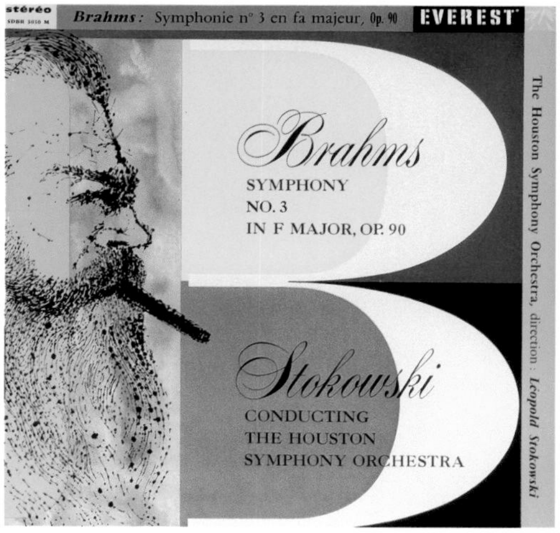

119

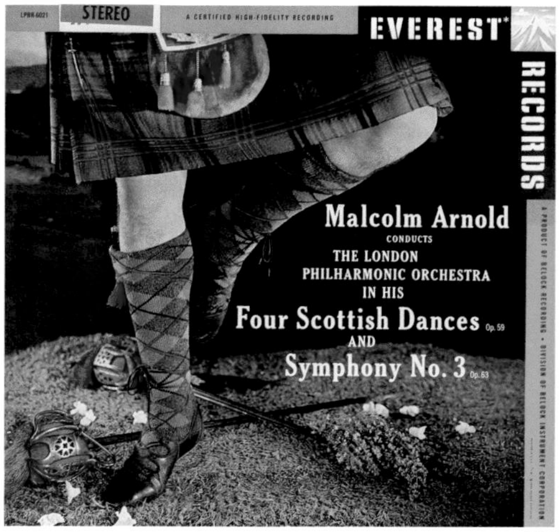

120

121

123

122

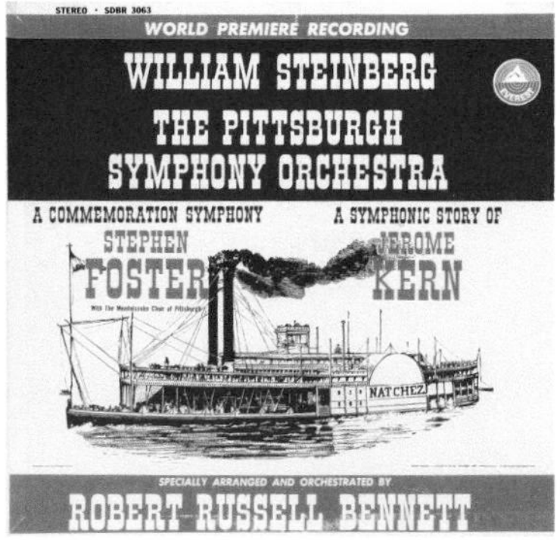

124

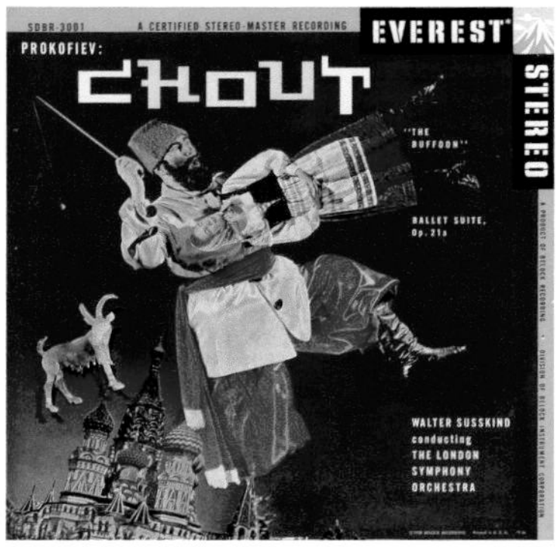

125

119 EVEREST. SDBR3030, USA 1959
120 EVEREST. SDBR3021, USA 1959, CD: Alex Steinweiss
121 EVEREST. SDBR3013, USA 1958, CD: Alex Steinweiss
122 EVEREST. SDBR3251, USA, CD: Edwin Francis
123 EVEREST. SDBR3108, USA 1961, CD: Studio Five
124 EVEREST. SDBR3063, USA 1960, CA: Bettmann Archive
125 EVEREST. SDBR3001, USA 1958, CD: Alex Steinweiss

126 EVEREST. SDBR3009, USA 1958, CD: Alex Steinweiss
127 EVEREST. SDBR3015, USA 1958, CD: Alex Steinweiss
128 EVEREST. SDBR3041, USA 1959
129 EVEREST. SDBR3018, USA 1959, CD: Alex Steinweiss

2.7 London Records, USA (130-135)

The records are from English Decca. In the USA, sale was not permitted under the name Decca, due to the fact that an American company, which was previously owned by Decca in London, still carried the name. The records already received the London label in the English stamping plant and in the USA they were given the American-made cover. Perhaps the idea behind this was to take American tastes into account. As with Everest, the covers that were designed with photos were in the event pure kitsch (132, 133). The "Stereophonic" references really stand out. Stereo was something quite new then and boosted sales. For more London records from this period, see covers 571, 572, and 668. The musical reference is indicated on all covers.

126

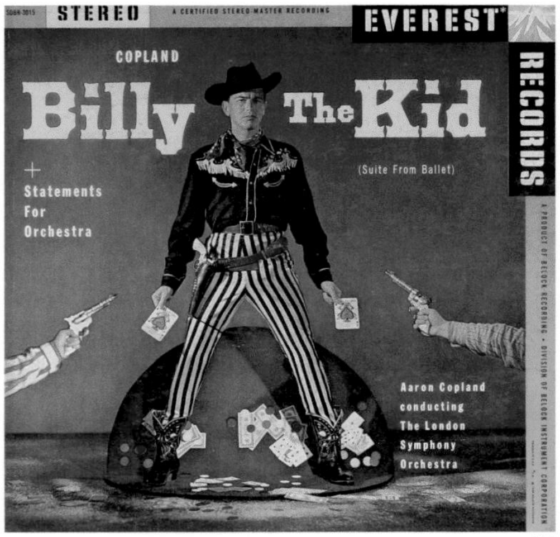

127

128

129

130

131

132

133

134

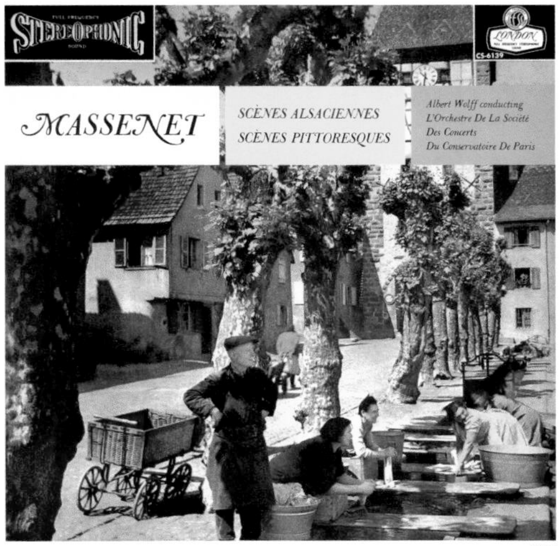

135

130 LONDON. CS6060, USA 1958
131 LONDON. CS6201, USA 1961, CA: Iarusso
132 LONDON. CS6012, USA 1959
133 LONDON. CS6036, USA 1959
134 LONDON. CS6013, USA 1957, Ph: Shostal
135 LONDON. CS6139, USA

136

2.8 Mercury Records, Stereo, USA (136 – 146)

On these Mercury records from the stereo era, design with background photos was already dominant. The covers 34-43, early mono editions shown in category 1.4, are more lovingly executed and artistically more interesting. Cover 138 is a reissue of the Eastman Rochester Archives (ERA) using the original motif. This recording was never released by Mercury in stereo format. Original stereo albums from Mercury are coveted collectors' items. For the covers 141, 144 and 145, the reference to the musical content is missing. Other covers from Mercury from the same period can be seen in pictures 180, 220, 701, 740 and 748.

137

138

139

140

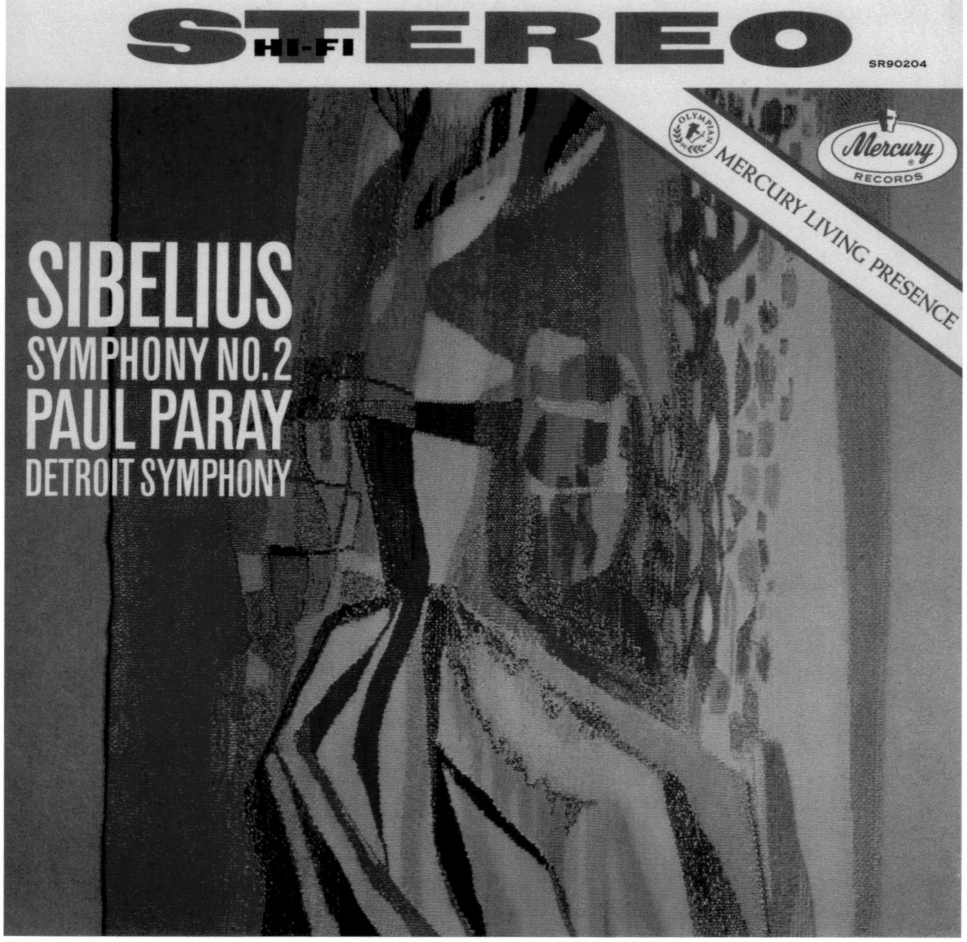

141

136 MERCURY. SR90002, USA 1957,
Ph: Ewing Krainin (lettering by Alex Steinweiss)
137 MERCURY. SR90137, USA 1956
138 EASTMAN ROCHESTER ARCHIVES. ERA1002, USA 1957,
Ph: Radford Bascome [Design as original MG50114]
139 MERCURY. SR90156, USA 1957, Ph: Henry Ries
140 MERCURY. SR900043, USA 1958, Ph: Henry Ries
141 MERCURY. SR90204, USA 1959, Tapestry by
Eva Antilla, courtesy Finnish National Travel Office

142

143

144

145

146

142 MERCURY. SR90190, USA ca 1958
143 MERCURY. SR90006, USA 1957, Ph: Inge Morath, Magnum
144 MERCURY. SR90285, USA 1960, CA: Metalwork Gold, Frankish VII Century, The Metropolitan Museum of Art, Gift wof J Pierpont Morgan, 1917
145 MERCURY. SR90223, USA 1959
146 MERCURY. SR90224, USA 1957, CA: Jane Wilson; Ph: Louis Goldman, RG

2.9 RCA, USA (147 - 166)

147 RCA. LSC2369, USA 1960, CA: Joseph Hirsch
148 RCA. LSC2370, USA 1960
149 RCA. LSC2374, USA 1960, CA: Dick Dodge
150 RCA. LSC2251, USA 1958

The logo on the upper perimeter of this legendary RCA Living Stereo series simply can't be overseen. Following the tradition at the time, the covers were mainly still painted, but photos were also quite common (160, 162, 164). All covers refer to the music in an illustrative manner – rather beseechingly on the three covers 153–155, with the symphonic music for the TV documentary "Victory at Sea", about maritime warfare in the Pacific during World War II. For additional RCA covers from this period, see pictures 178, 223, 248, 284, 511, 543, 670 and 744.

147

148

149

150

151

152

153

154

155

156

151 RCA. LSC2400, USA 1960, CA: Thomson
152 RCA. LSC2234, USA 1958
153 RCA. LSC2335, USA 1959, CA: Victor Colin
154 RCA. LSC2226, USA 1958, CA: Victor Colin
155 RCA. LSC2523, USA 1959
156 RCA. LSC2450, USA 1960, CA: Eugene Korelin

157

158

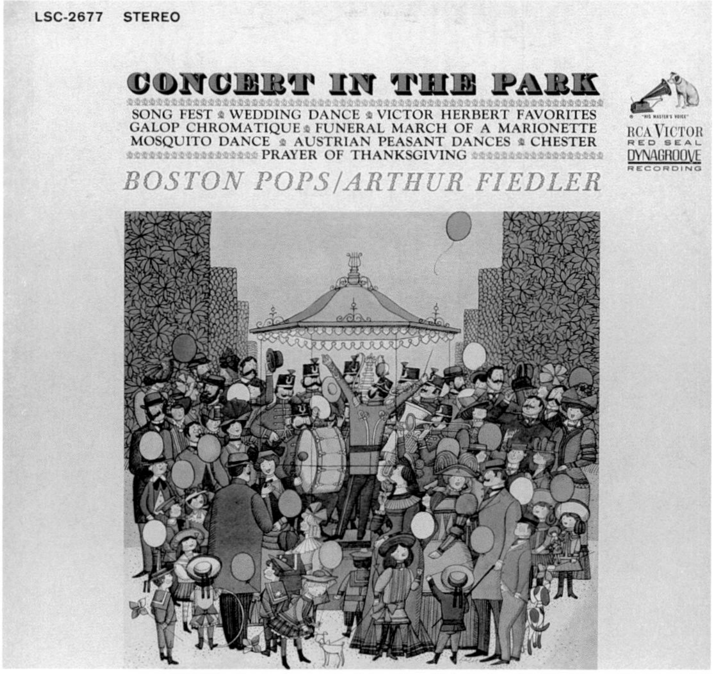

159

160

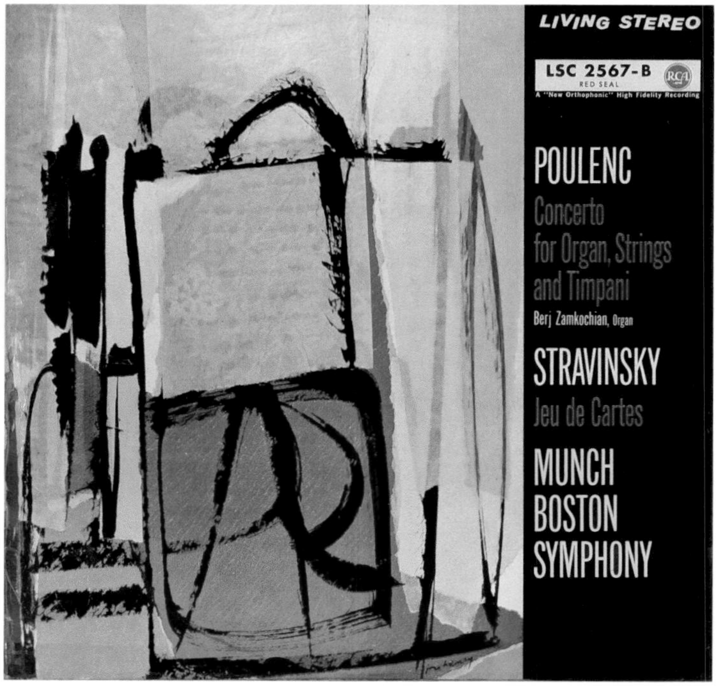

161

157 RCA. LSC2670, USA 1963
158 RCA. LSC2298, USA 1959, CA: Dick Dodge
159 RCA. LSC2677, USA 1963
160 RCA. LSC2201, USA 1958
161 RCA. LSC2567, USA 1962

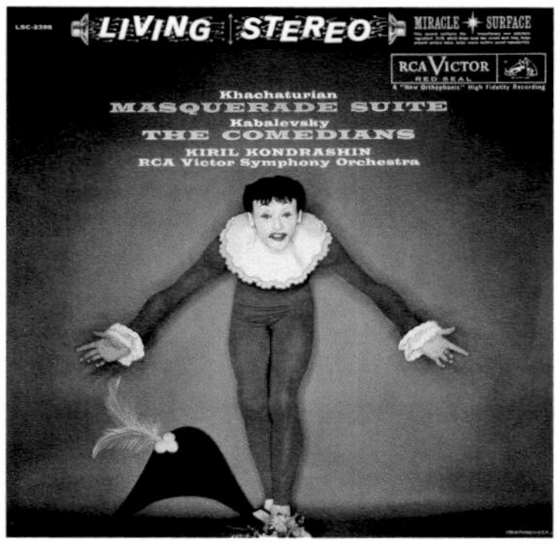

162

163

164

165

166

162 RCA. LSC2398, USA 1960
163 RCA. LSC2586, USA 1962
164 RCA. LSC2322, USA 1959, Ph: David Hecht
165 RCA. LSC2418, USA 1960, CA: Ysobel
166 RCA. LSC2532, USA 1961

2.10 Deutsche Grammophon Gesellschaft (167 - 176)

In comparison with the major non-German producers such as RCA, Decca and EMI, the most significant German producer is under-represented in this documentation. My collection contains only a few records from this producer from the early days of the long-playing record. And there's a another reason for that: at DGG, an interesting cover design did not have priority. All the more dominant was the huge company logo with summary. Still – with its simplicity, cover 174 awakened nostalgic associations, covers 172 and 175 refer expressively to the composition. The musical reference is revealed on all covers.

167 DGG. 138973, GFR 1965
168 DGG. 138658, GFR 1961
169 DGG. 138922, GFR 1964
170 DGG. 138692, D 1961

167

168

169

170

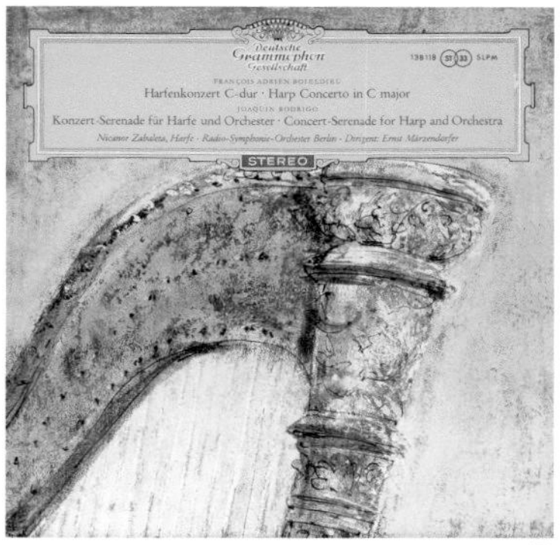

171

172

171 DGG. 138118, GFR 1960, CA: Gerhard Noack
172 DGG. 138873, GFR 1964
173 DGG. 136226, GFR 1961
174 DGG. 138638, GFR 1964
175 DGG. 136474, F ca 1965
176 DGG. 136400

173

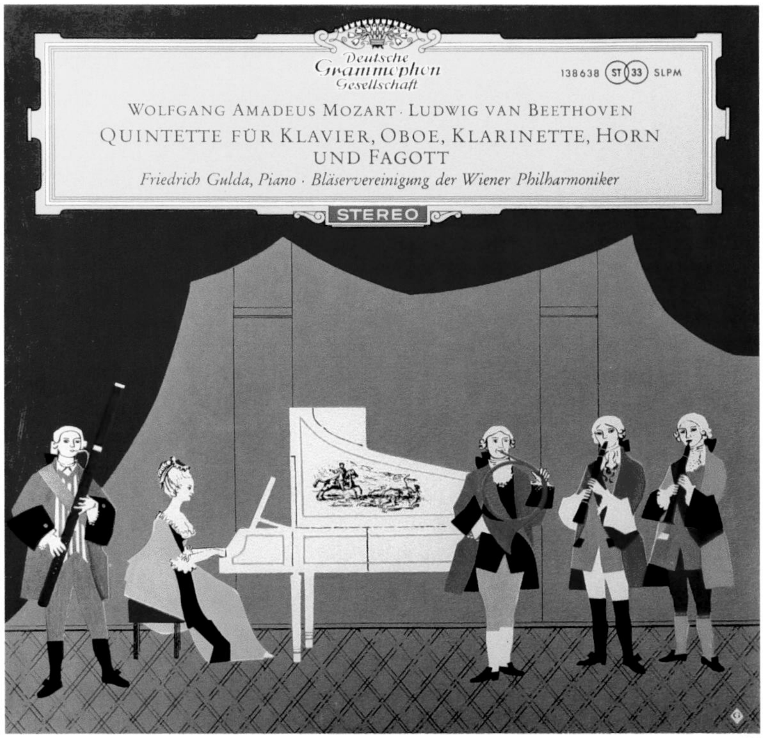

174

175

176

3.0 Recognition of Typical Label Forms

This group is a supplement to previous groups. Its purpose is to illustrate the layout traditions that present themselves in lines, fields and logos for the design of first editions and reissues. Also included here are covers from series of specific music genera, such as early music, chamber music, etc.

3.1 Originals (177 - 193)

Each of the covers shown is typical for the producer at the respective time or for a specific series, music genre or recording process.

— The logos of the Columbia record and the RCA *Living Stereo* record, shown respectively on the upper margin, are typical of the early stereo editions of these major US companies (177, 178)

— The division into segments of the Philips record with Mozart music is typical for the 1960s (179).

— Mercury (180) attracted attention with the remark about its 35 mm magnetic film recording.

— The Columbia and EMI albums (181, 183) are examples of quadraphonic records made by these producers in the early 1970s. For stereo editions, the respective gold frame or the obvious SQ logo were omitted.

— Picture 186 presents the logo of the *Phase 4 Stereo* series from English Decca. Phase 4 Stereo was a special recording technique, which was particularly favoured by conductor Leopold Stokowski.

— Argo produced a series with contemporary music *(Calouste Gulbenkian Foundation series)*, each correspondingly adorned with a modern artwork from the collection of the foundation (182).

— Covers 184 and 185 are examples from chamber music series released by Philips and L'Oiseau-Lyre. The series *Archiv* (DGG) and *Das Alte Werk* (Telefunken) were dedicated to works from the pre-classical era (187, 188), always with a similar design.

— The DGG illustrated Mozart's piano concertos with corresponding city and palace views from Mozart's time (189).

— Lyrita had identical covers in different colour tones for the symphonies by Bax (190). The DGG used the same style to design the Bruckner edition with Karajan (191).

— Decca's Dvorak symphonies with conductor Istvan Kertesz always show pictures by Pieter Bruegel (192, see also picture 288).

— Orchestral works by Tchaikovsky on Philips all had a similar layout in the Sixties (193), which resembled a picture frame.

177

178

179

180

181

177 COLUMBIA. MS6079, USA 1959, Ph: Herb Snitzer
178 RCA. LSC2217, USA 1958
179 PHILIPS. 835256LY, GB 1964, CD: Studio H.B.M.
180 MERCURY. 130525MGY, USA 1962, Ph: Price Somers
181 COLUMBIA. MQ32159, USA 1973, CA and Design: Virginia Team

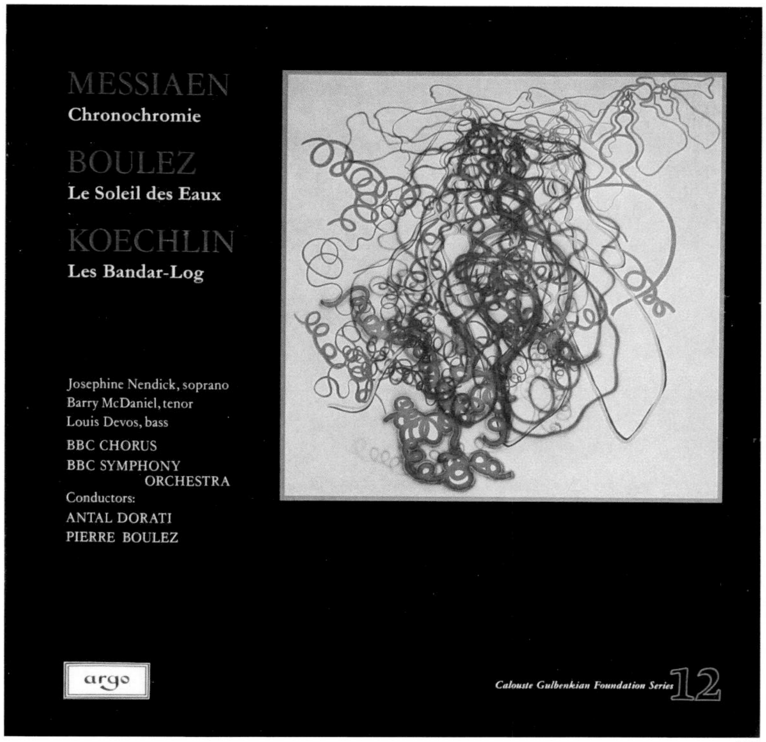

MESSIAEN
Chronochromie
BOULEZ
Le Soleil des Eaux
KOECHLIN
Les Bandar-Log
Josephine Nendick, soprano
Barry McDaniel, tenor
Louis Devos, bass
BBC CHORUS
BBC SYMPHONY ORCHESTRA
Conductors:
ANTAL DORATI
PIERRE BOULEZ
argo
Calouste Gulbenkian Foundation Series 12

182

QUADROPHONIE
HERBERT VON KARAJAN | PETER TSCHAIKOWSKY
Berliner Philharmoniker | Sinfonie Nr. 6
EMI

183

184

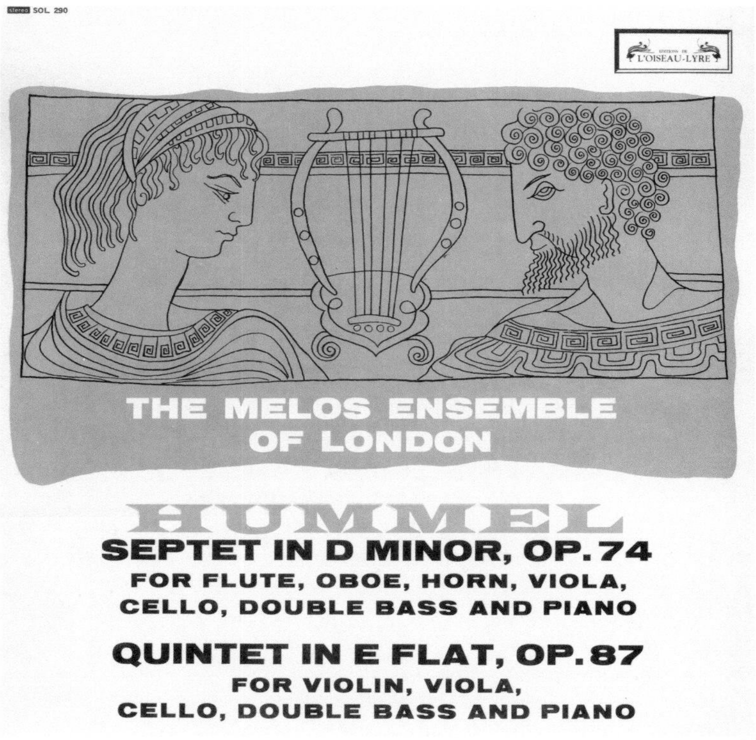

stereo SOL 290
L'OISEAU-LYRE
THE MELOS ENSEMBLE OF LONDON
HUMMEL
SEPTET IN D MINOR, OP. 74
FOR FLUTE, OBOE, HORN, VIOLA, CELLO, DOUBLE BASS AND PIANO
QUINTET IN E FLAT, OP. 87
FOR VIOLIN, VIOLA, CELLO, DOUBLE BASS AND PIANO

185

186

182 ARGO. ZRG756, GB 1975, CA: Bernard Cohen *"Mist"* (1963)
183 EMI. C065-02307, GFR 1972
184 PHILIPS. 839795LY, EU 1969
185 OISEAU-LYRE. SOL290, GB 1966
186 DECCA. PFS4189, GB 1969

187

188

189

190

191

192

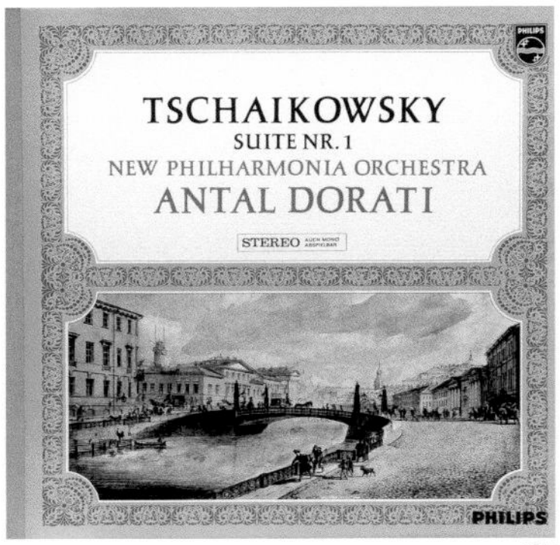

193

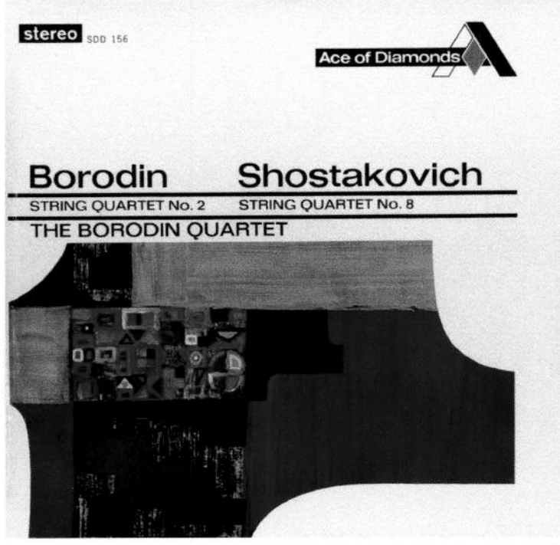

194

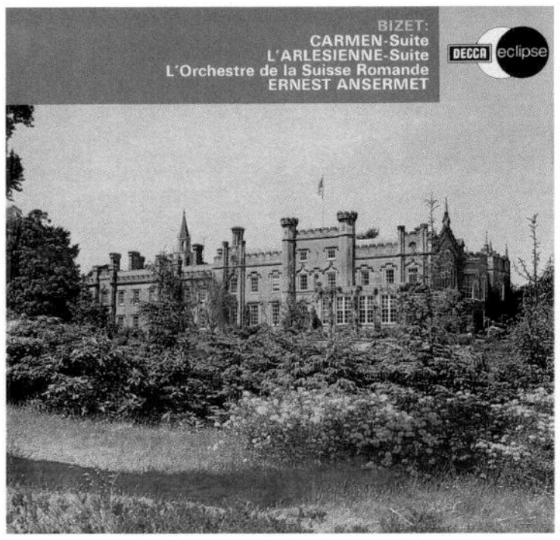

195

196

187 ARCHIV. 198272, GFR 1960
188 TELEFUNKEN. SAWT9541, GFR 1968, CA: Oudry *"La attribute de la musique"*
189 DGG. 139453, GFR 1970, CA: Canaletto *"Palais des Fürsten Liechtenstein"* (Fürstlich Liechtensteinsche Gemäldegalerie)
190 YRITA. SRCS053, GB 1971, CD: Keith Hensby
191 DGG. 2707085, GFR 1976, CD: Holger Matthies
192 DECCA. SXL6044, GB 1963, CA: Pieter Bruegel *"Bauerntanz"* (Kunsthistorisches Museum Wien)
193 PHILIPS. 802788LY, EU 1968
194 DECCA. SDD156, GB 1967, CD: DPAD
195 DECCA. ECS755, GB ca 1974, Ph: John Thomson
196 LONDON. STS15025, USA ca 1970

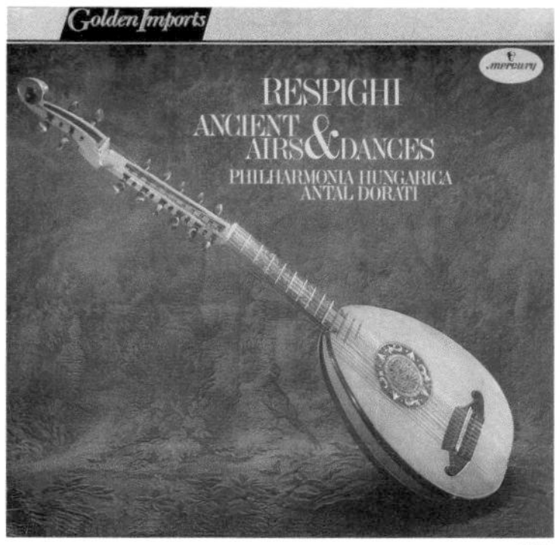

197

198

199

200

201

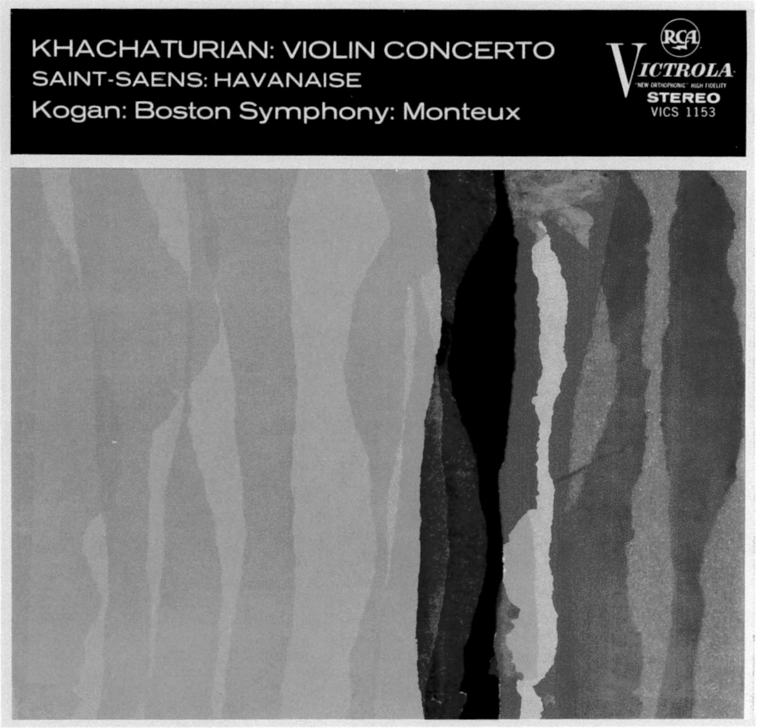

203

202

197 MERCURY. SR175009, EU, Photo as on original SR90199
198 EMI. SXLP20031, GB 1967, Ph: Transworld Airlines (Bavarian Alps near Ramsau)
199 EMI. SXLP30197, GB 1975, CA: Goya *"The Puppet"* (Prado Museum, Madrid)
200 EMI. ESD7009, GB 1976
201 SERAPHIM. S60032, USA ca 1967
202 SERAPHIM. S60104, USA before 1976
203 RCA. VICS1153, GB 1966
204 RCA. GL25058, GB 1977

3.2 Re-issues (194 - 204)

Re-issued recordings from the early days of stereo have been pressed at a later time often sound better than the originals. This is especially true for the early stereo recordings from Decca. Pictures 194–196 show examples for *Ace of Diamonds, Eclipse* and the *Stereo Treasury series.* Cover 197 is a Mercury release that was reissued as a European production by Philips (*Golden Imports* series). *His Master's Voice Concert Classics* was the most significant reissue series by EMI in England (198 and 199; see also 521, 527 and 528). This was later followed by the *Greensleeve* series (200). In the USA, the label Seraphim (201, 202) released English EMI recordings. RCA published older recordings under the *Victrola* label (203) and later under the *Gold Seal* label, shown here in its European layout (204).

204

4.0 Designing with Photos

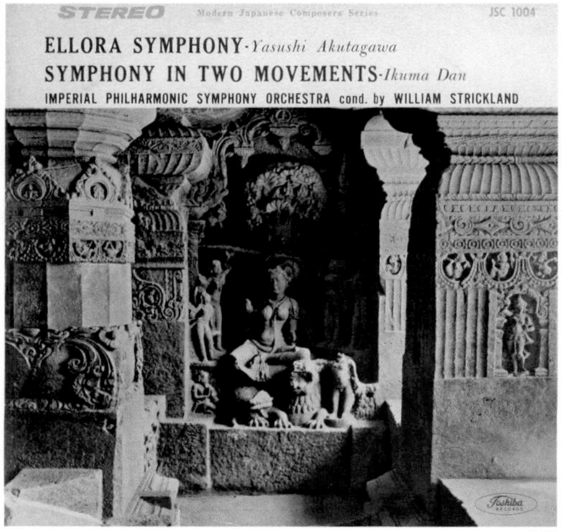

205

206

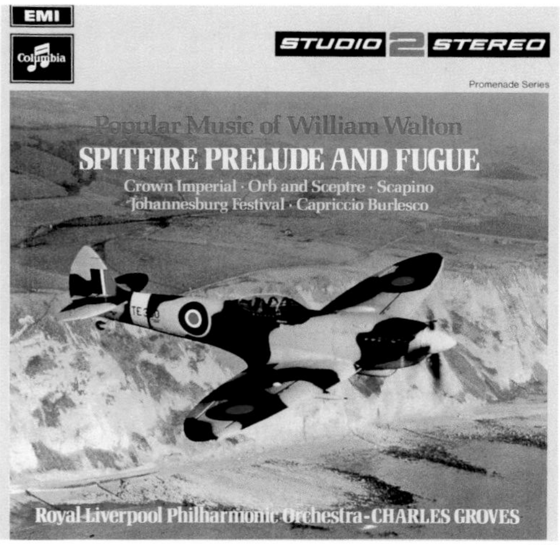

207

The option of illustrating covers with colour photos became more widely-used than the more elaborate composition with a graphic design. In most cases, the photo serves as a general background picture – as a portrait of landscape and artist. Several other applications are also shown here.

4.1 The Large Format Photograph (205 - 225)

Nearly all of the photos shown here bear reference to the musical content, even if only in a geographical sense. Some, though, still require some explanation.

— The photo in picture 213 illustrates the *Souvenir de Florence* sextet by Tchaikovsky.

— The Decca covers with recordings from the English composer and conductor Benjamin Britten (picture 217) depicts *The Malt,* a former malting plant which converted into a concert house, where Britten organized numerous festivals.

— The light burst in picture 218 is clearly designed to create an association with the musical title *Ionisation.*

— The modern pergola in picture 219 makes reference to the contemporary musical content.

Additional large format photos are presented in the next category (Nature Photography) and later in the category "English Countryside" in Chapter IX.

208

205 TOSHIBA. JSC1004, J
206 PHILIPS. 6500812, F 1974, Ph: Oronez (La Tour *"La Giralda"*, Alcazar, Sevilla)
207 EMI-COLUMBIA. TWO272, GB 1969
208 PHILIPS. 6580012, GB 1969
« (opposite page)

209 RCA. SB6727, GB 1967
210 EMI. ASD2593, GB 1970, Ph: Lev Ustinov (courtesy Soviet Life Magazine)
211 COLUMBIA. M2S322, USA 1965, Ph: USSR Magazine from Sovfoto
212 EMI. SLS897, GB 1974, Ph: Memorial to 600,000 Russian dead in the Piscaryov Cemetery Leningrad
213 EMI. ASDF794, F 1963, Ph: Mercure Ed. Paris - Atelier Joubert

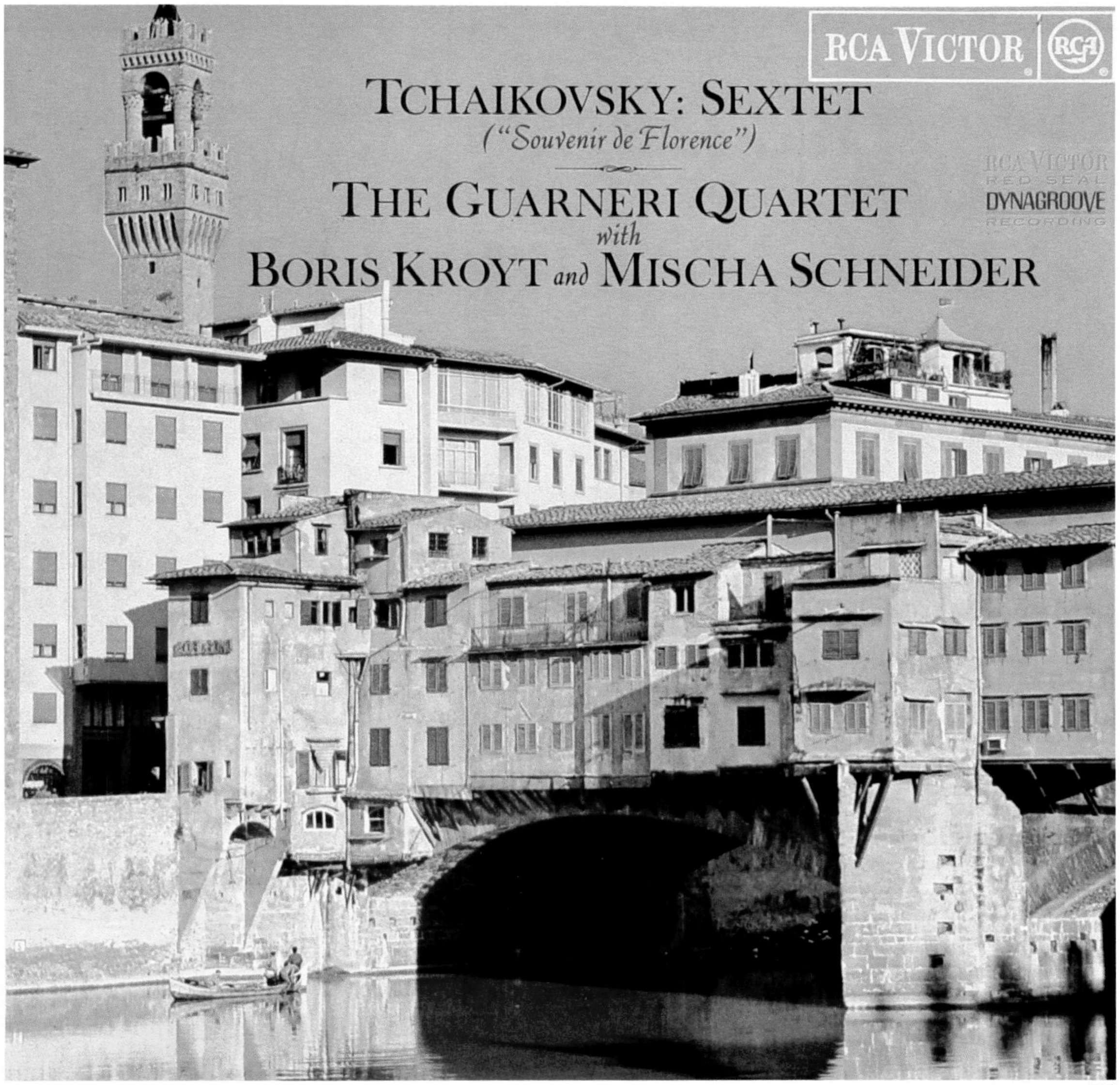

209

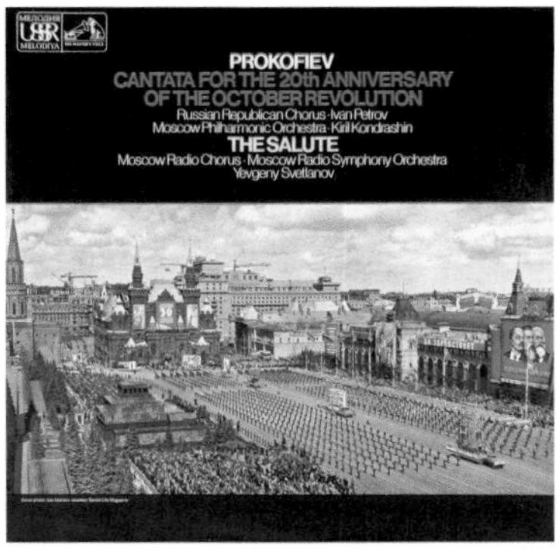

210

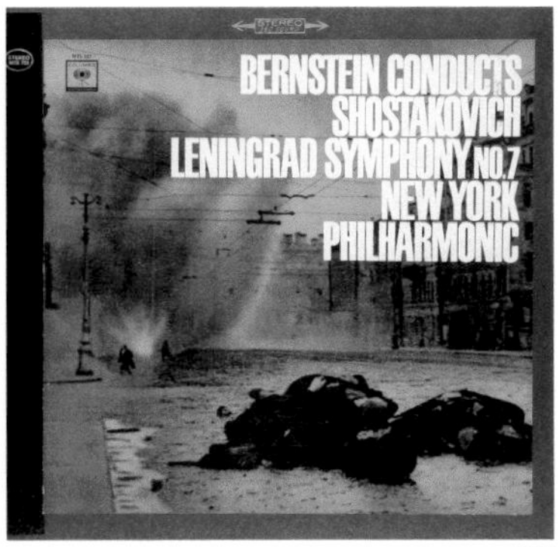

211

212

213

214

215

216

217

218

214 EMI. ASD2435, GB 1968, Ph: Irish Tourist Board
215 ANGEL. S36329, USA 1966, Ph: Stadtverkehrsbüro Salzburg
216 EMI. ASD0541, GB 1963. Ph: Trond Hedström
217 DECCA. SXL6405, GB 1969. Ph: Hans Wild (The Maltings, Snape)
218 DECCA. SXL6550, GB 1972, Ph: Suzette Stephens
219 EMI. SXLP30138, GB 1972

219

220

221

222

223

220 MERCURY. AMS16027, USA 1959, Ph: George Pickow
221 PHILIPS. 839775LY, F 1969, Ph: Peter Schütte
222 PHILIPS. 835517AY, F 1957, Ph: Lipnitzki
223 RCA. LSC2150, USA 1958, Ph: Ben Rose
224 PHILIPS. 835483LY, F ca 1966, Ph: Wiezniak, Decor: Odette Adias
225 MERCURY. 90177, F 1958, Ph: Herman Leonard

224

225

4.2 Nature Photography (226 - 234)

These are the most beautiful and artistic nature photos in my collection. The Melodiya record with the *Mindia* opera by the Georgian composer Taktakishvili shows a mountain scene in the Caucasus, the setting of the opera (picture 227). Geographical references to the music are also conveyed by pictures 226, 230, 231 and 232. The latter shows the rural environment that is home to the North West Chamber Orchestra of Seattle. Covers 227 and 228 should trigger associations with modern musical content. Cover 233 sets the fitting nocturnal mood for *Notturni et Alba.*

4.3 From the Photographic Studio (235 - 240)

Objects are arranged in the studio and photographed. The reference to the musical content is particularly pronounced in cover photos 235 and 240. The cover from the Columbia record (236) has a powerful effect. The instruments of the soloists illustrate the works of Debussy and Honegger. The locomotive is reminiscent of Honegger's composition *Pacific 231.* Covers 237 and 238 are designed to establish a reference to the "modern" compositions of the 20th Century.

4.4 Photo Collages (241 - 246)

The illustration on the Villa-Lobos album (picture 244) is actually a single picture. It seems, however, to be a collage, and that is why it is presented here. In Picture 245, there are two explicit references to music. The portrait of President Lincoln bears reference to the composition "Lincoln Portrait" by Aaron Copland with Gregory Peck as the narrator. The second photo motif recalls the racial disturbances in the USA in the 1960s, corresponding to the composition *Contextures: Riots – Decade '60* by William Kraft.

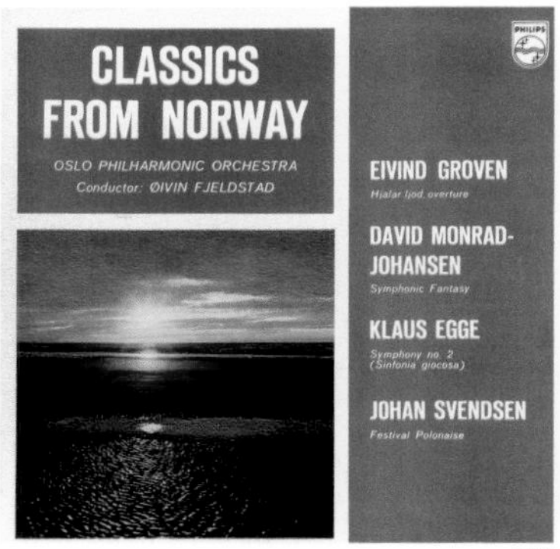

226

227

228

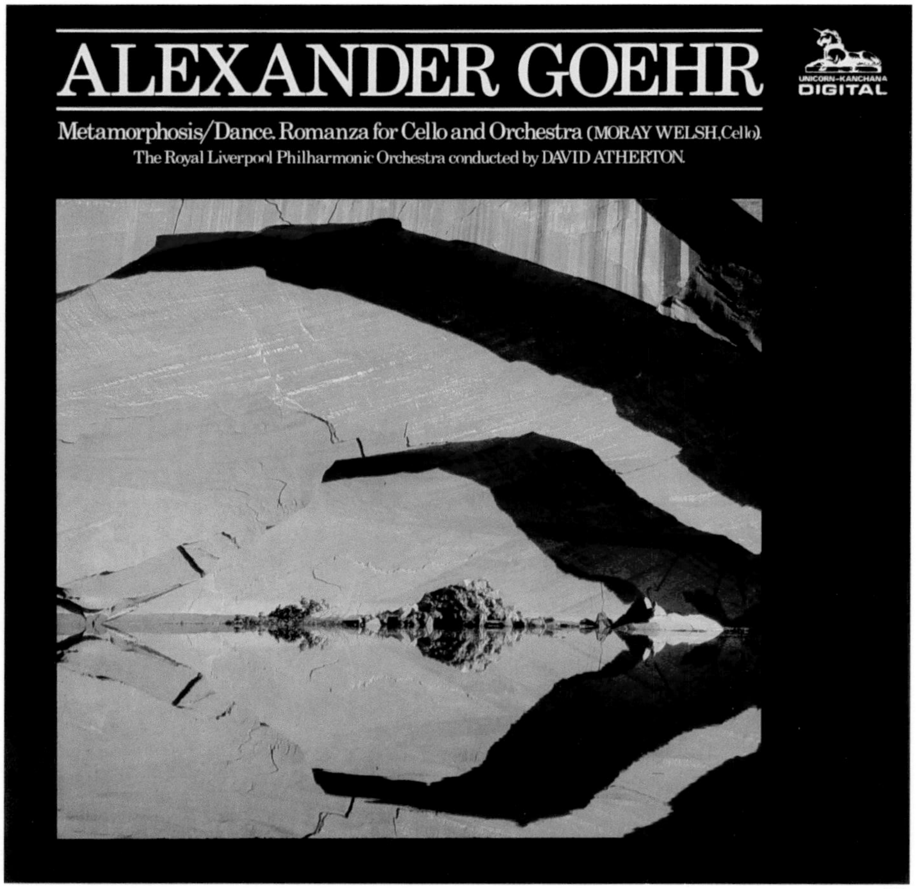

229

230

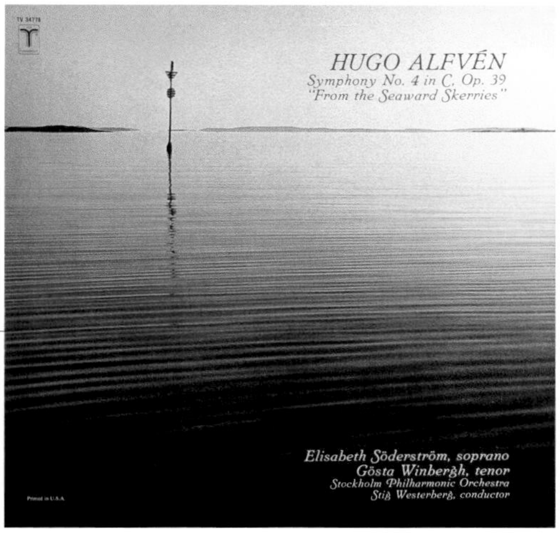

231

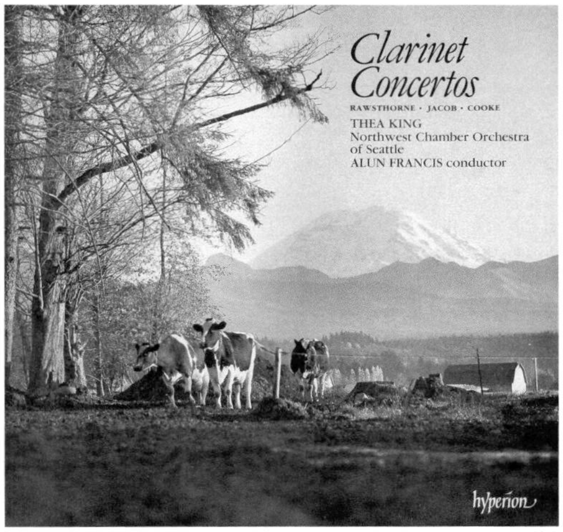

232

233

234

226 PHILIPS. 838052AY, N 1976, Ph: Cussac
227 MELODIYA. C00705, SU 1984. Ph: I. Raskina
228 ORIEL. ORS1002, GB 1981, CD: MIKEITH design;
Ph: Bill Craig (Submerged wreck in Rhosili Bay, Gower)
229 UNICORN. DKP9017, GB 1981, Ph: Philip Hyde
(Rising Waters in the Escalante Region, Utah)
« (opposite page)

230 RCA. LSC2923, GFR
231 TURNABOUT. TV32778, USA 1982, Ph: Jan Borgfelt
232 HYPERION. A66031, GB 1981, Ph: M.G. Rees
(Sun Top Farm, Washington State)
233 EMI. ASD2904, GB 1973
234 COLUMBIA. MS7242, USA 1969, CD: Lloyd Ziff;
Ph: Don Hunstein & Nicholas

235

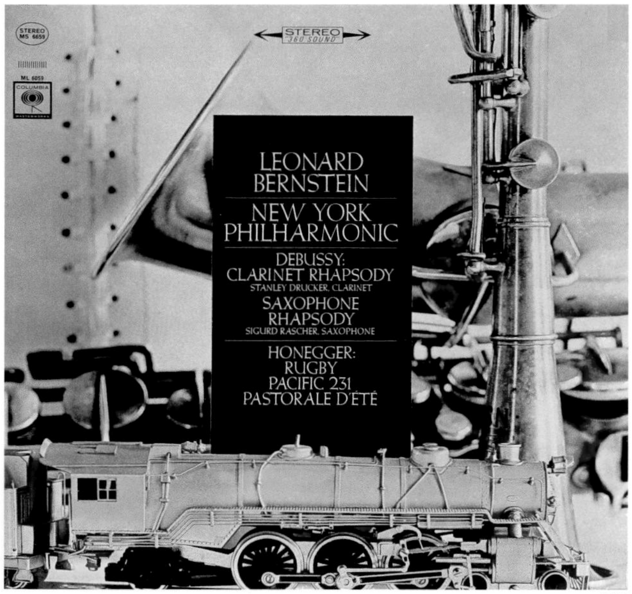

236

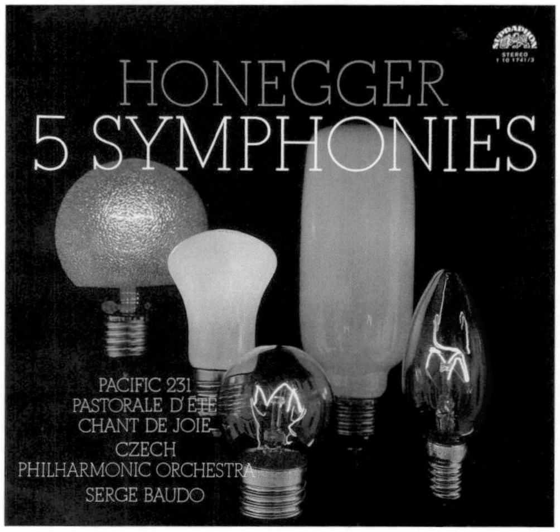

237

238

239

240

235 DECCA. SXL6119, GB 1964
236 COLUMBIA. MS6659, USA 1964, Ph: Bob Cato
237 SUPRAPHON. 1101741/43, CS 1977, CD: Jaroslav Oseck; Ph: Jaroslav Oseck
238 EVEREST. LPBR6020, USA 1950, CD: Alex Steinweiss
239 PHILIPS. A02454L, EU 1965, Ph: Bart Mulder
(Toys from the collection of the Museum *"De Waag"*, Deventer, NL)
240 RCA. VICS1079, GB 1968

241

242

241 DECCA. SXL6757, GB 1975
242 RCA. RL12320, GB 1976. Collage: Carol Wald
243 COLUMBIA. MS7431, USA 1971, CA: Virginia Team
244 UNITED ARTISTS. UAS5506, USA,
CD: Ron Wolin; CA: Laurence Dreiband
245 DECCA. SXL6388, GB 1968
246 LONDON. STS15293, USA 1976, Collage: Rob Cobuzio

243

244

245

246

4.5 Photo Arrangements (247 – 256)

With the exception of the first two examples (247 and 248), where the reference to the music is clearly communicated, and cover 256, the covers are rather uninteresting even though they are initially intriguing due to their detailed arrangement. The picture series on cover 249 is designed as a portrayal of film strips, since the album is a recording of film music.

4.6 A Microcosm of Nature (257 – 261)

Exotic birds adorn the Brazilian complete edition of *Bachianas brasileiras* by Villa-Lobos, Volume 2 shown here (258). On the Mercury cover, both of the Respighi works are represented, whereby the *Brazilian impressions* are illustrated by the parrot. Although the record is a reissue, the photo has been taken from the original (259).

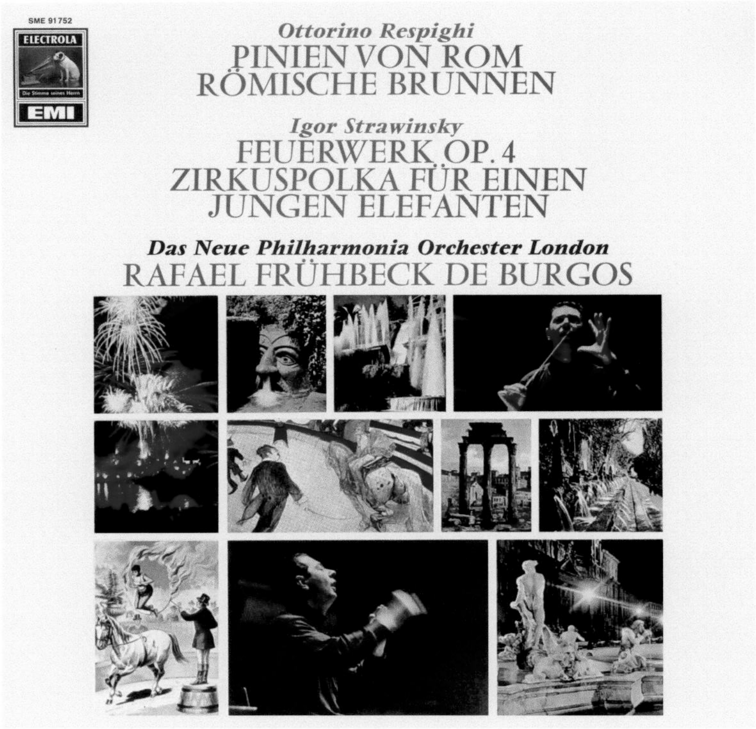

247

248

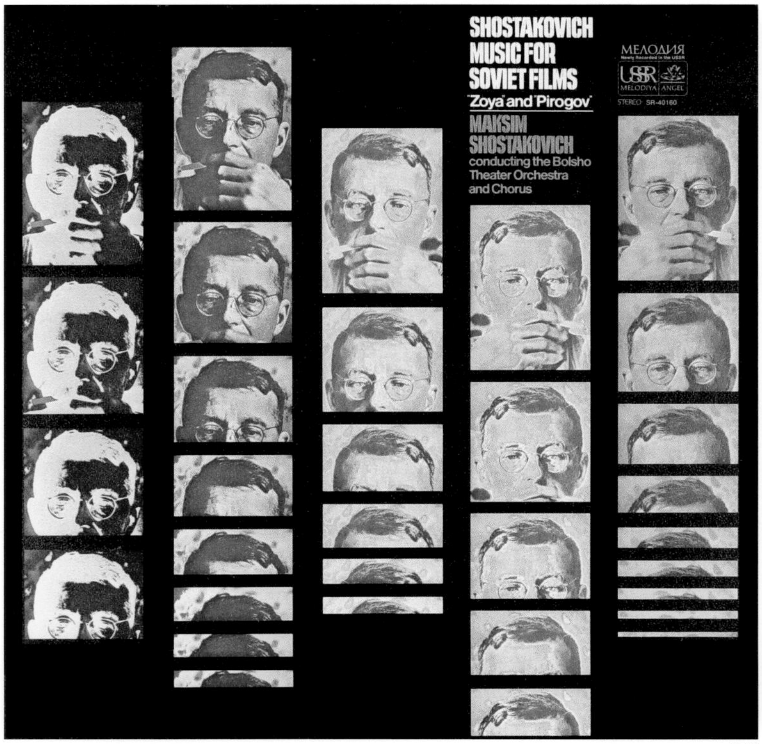

249

250

251

252

247 EMI. SME91752, GFR 1969
248 RCA. LSC2436, USA 1960, Ph: F.P.G
249 ANGEL. SR40160, USA 1975
250 ANGEL. S36984, USA 1973, CD: Marvin Schwartz
« [opposite page]

251 COLUMBIA. MS6062, USA 1959, Ph: Gjon Mill
252 ODYSSEY. Y32224, USA 1973, CD: Henrietta Condak
253 ANGEL. S36009, USA 1967 [Design as original EMI-Columbia SAX5275]
254 COLUMBIA. M31241, USA 1972, CD: John Berg; Ph: Tetsu Okuhara
255 CAPITOL. SG7255, USA 1961, Ph: George Jerman
256 COLUMBIA. MQ32232, USA 1973, CD: Karenlee Grant; Photo of Sérgio and Eduardo Abreu: Don Hunstein; Other Photos: New York Public Library Picture Collection

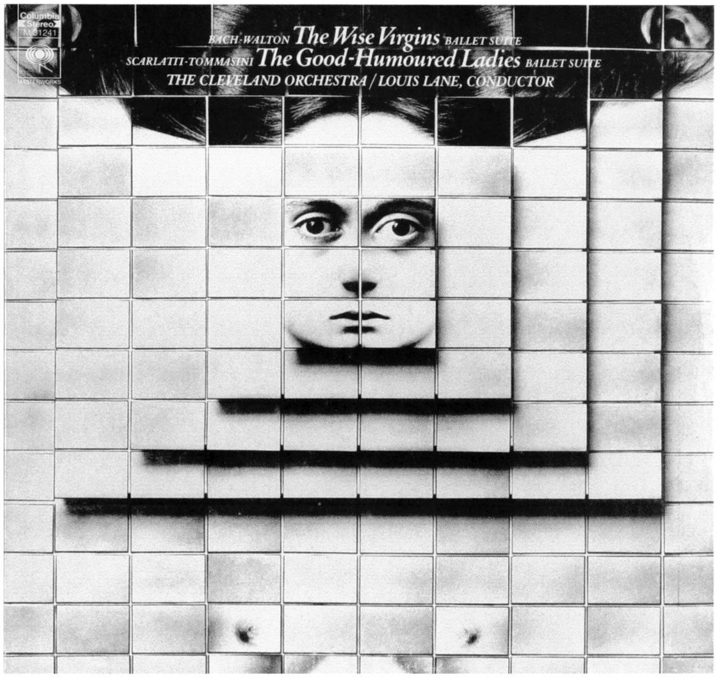

253

254

255

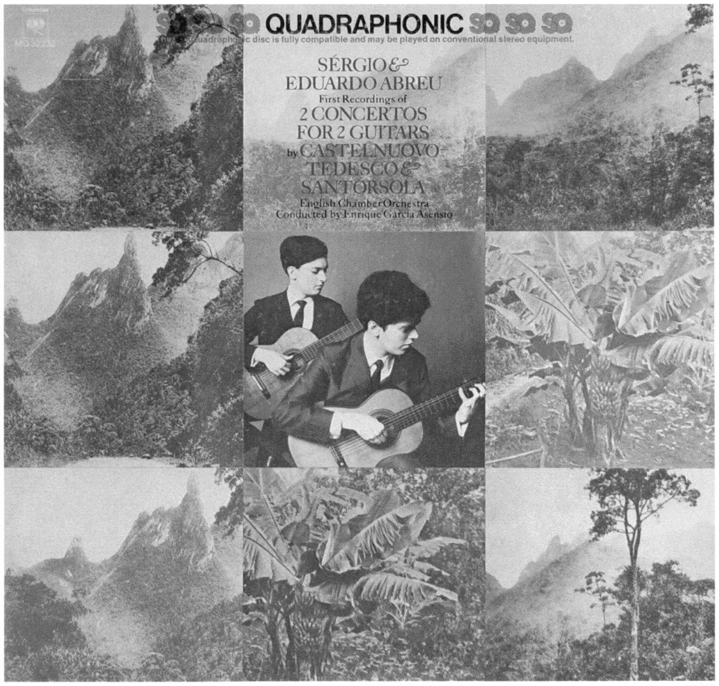

256

257

258

259

260

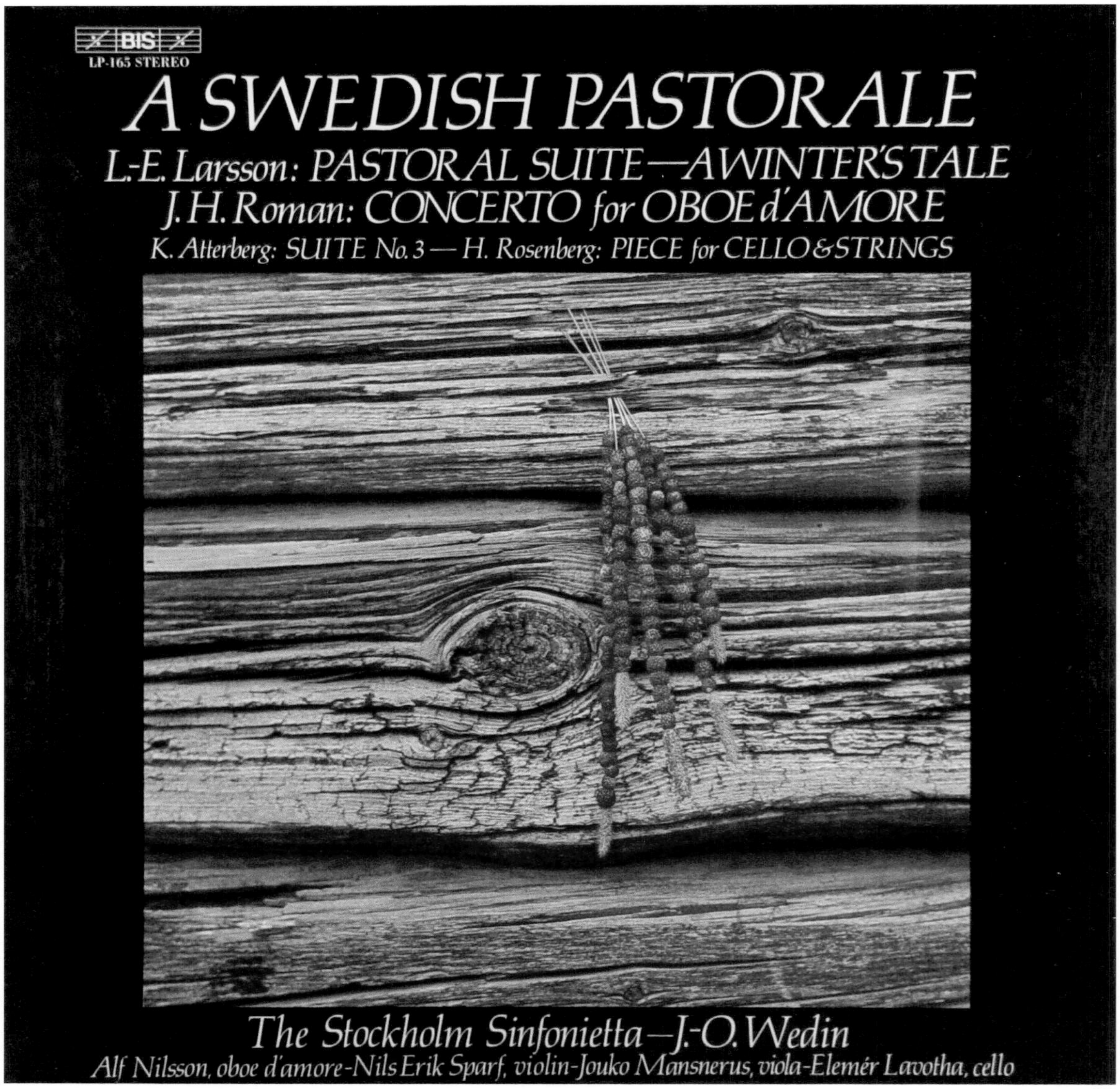

261

257 RCA. SB6868, GB 1973
258 ANGEL. S3CBX493, Brazil 1964
259 MERCURY. SRI75023, EU before 1976
260 RCA. LSC2614, USA 1963
261 BIS. LP165, S 1980, Ph: Ari Laitinen

5.0 Maestros and Other Musical Artists (262 - 285)

RECORD IMPORTED FROM ENGLAND
LONDON
CS6997
PHILHARMONIC SOLO!
Soloists and Members of the
LOS ANGELES PHILHARMONIC ORCHESTRA
ZUBIN MEHTA
Haydn·Trumpet Concerto Weber·Clarinet Concertino Vivaldi·Piccolo Concerto
Wieniawski·Polonaise de Concert & Scherzo-Tarantelle
Thomas Stevens, Trumpet Michele Zukovsky, Clarinet Miles Zentner, Piccolo Glenn Dicterow, Violin

262

Covers with soloists and conductors, whether painted or photographed, are always an advertising label. There are some presented here which are particularly expressive. The identity of the persons portrayed is generally written up in the title. This makes comments relatively superfluous. The following are an exception:

— Cover 263 shows, next to the flautist Elena Durjan, Eric Fenby, friend and trustee to the estate of English composer Frederik Delius.

— Two covers with the conductor George Weldon (266, 267) catch one's eye with his obvious preference for fast cars.

— We can even see the beautiful Brazilian pianist Christina Ortiz twice (270, 272), followed by her Georgian colleague Marina Khvitia on a trilingual cover in Cyrillic, Georgian and Latin writing (273).

— The "dominating" lady seated next to the conductor Sir John Barbirolli is his wife, Evelyn Rothwell (275).

— English conductor Sir Adrian Boult is depicted twice (274 und 285).

— Jazz musician Benny Goodman is a soloist in the clarinet concert by the Danish composer Nielsen (277)

— The Melodiya record (278) shows the Russian conductor Mravinsky together with the composer Shostakovich. This is one of the very few painted Russian covers.

— On the horizon of a Caucasian mountainscape, the monumental James Galway raises his flute to his lips (280). The Caucasus is the homeland of the composer, Khachaturian.

— Both pianists on cover 283 remind one of Simon and Garfunkel – and floating above them, the composer Max Bruch appears on the horizon.

262 LONDON. CS6997, USA 1974, Ph: London Records
263 EMI. ASD3688, GB 1979, Ph: G. Hammond
264 PHILIPS. 6582017, GB 1977, Ph: Paul-André Duvoisier
265 EMI. ASD0345, GB 1959

263

264

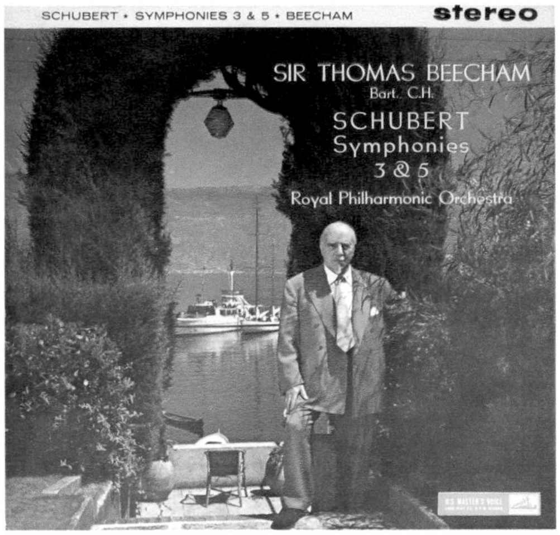

265

266

267

266 EMI-COLUMBIA. SCX3499, GB 1963, Ph: Edgar Brind
267 EMI. CSD1503, GB 1963, Ph: Edgar Brind
268 CRYSTAL. S323, USA 1975, Ph: Abraham Sternick
269 CBS. 72861, GFR 1971
270 EMI. ASD3081, GB 1975

268

269

270

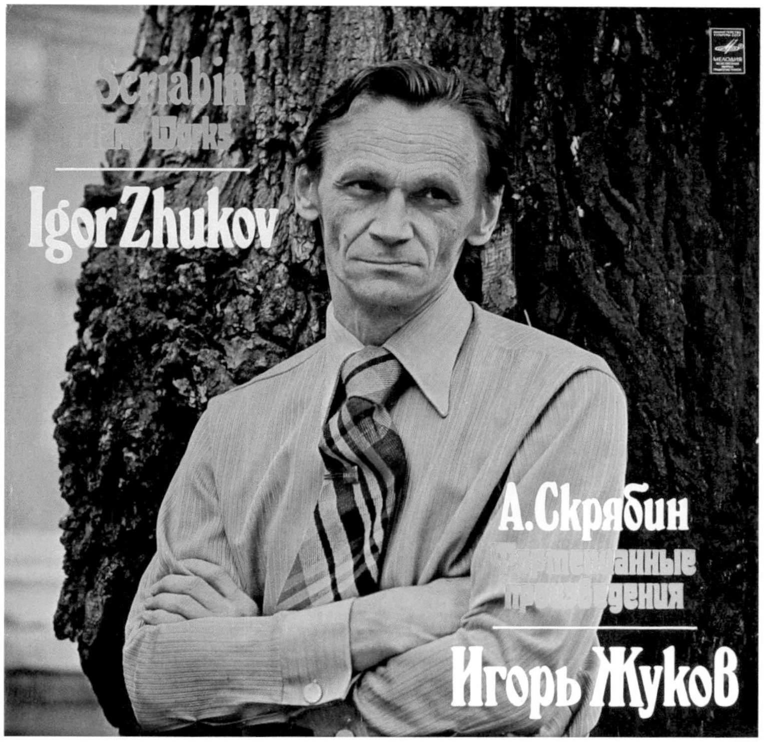

271

272

273

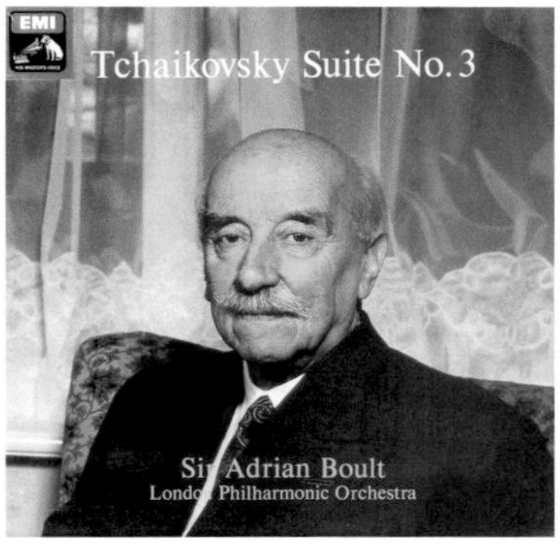

274

271 MELODIYA. C14931, SU 1982, Ph: V. Pishchalnikov
272 EMI. ASD3197, GB 1976
273 MELODIYA. C29875, SU 1990
274 EMI. ASD3135, GB 1975, Ph: Reg Wilson
275 EMI. ASD2496, GB 1969

275

276

277

276 EMI. ESD7065, GB 1978
(on the left the composer Malcolm Arnold)
277 RCA. SB6701, GB 1966, Ph: Elis Högh-Jensen
278 MELODIYA. C02857, SU ca 1975. CA: O.L. Lomakin
279 RCA. ARP1-4443, J 1983,CA: Susan Obrant
280 RCA. HRC1-7010, GB 1985, CA: Owl Graphics Limited

278

279

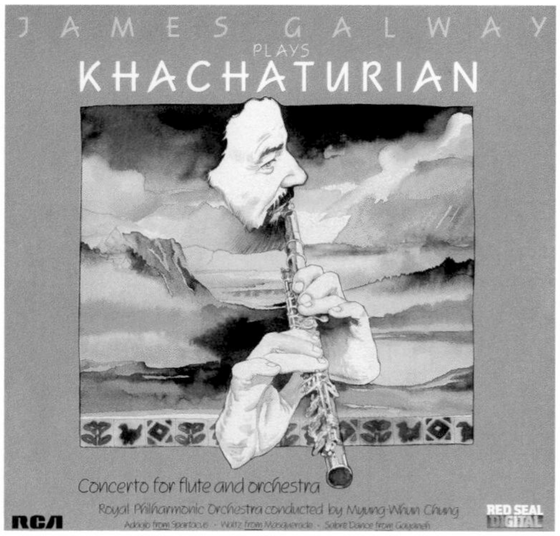

280

281

282

283

284

285

281 RCA. AGL1-1278, USA 1975, CA: Gary Bralow
282 RCA. AGL1-1275, USA 1975, CA: James Barkley
283 ANGEL. S36997, USA 1974, CD: Richard Drayton
284 RCA. LSC7037, USA 1965
285 LYRITA. SRCS084, GB 1978. CD: Keith Hensby; CA: Joy Finzi

6.0 The Art Gallery in the Record Cabinet

The selection here is vast. But how should artwork from so many centuries be arranged? By the style of the art, by the theme? This is not intended to be a chapter about painting. For this reason, categories A–D are roughly arranged according to period. Art styles such as Romanticism or Impressionism should also not be regarded as such in a strict sense. Included here are related tendencies towards a similar style or even several styles at once. Themes are the focus of categories 6.5 and 6.6.

6.1 Romanticism, Classicism and Previous (286 - 318)

Direct references to the musical content can be found only in the Mozart records 290 and 310, with *Harold in Italy* from Berlioz (289), the harpist (297), Mendelssohn's Scottish Symphony (300, with a view of Edinburgh), Charpentier (301) and Debussy (316).

6.2 Impressionism and Related (319 - 330)

Reference to musical content is only shown in pictures 328 and 329, although the music of Ravel and Debussy (322, 325, 326 327, 330) are both inspired by Impressionism. Throughout LP history, works by Ravel and Debussy have as a preference been illustrated with Impressionist paintings.

6.3 Art Nouveau and Related (331 - 336)

Only the covers for Vaughan Williams (333) and Schönberg (335) bear reference to musical content. For the other covers in this category, there is only a temporal reference.

286

287

288

286 UNICORN. RHS331, GB 1974, CD: Neal Boyd;
CA: The Dragon Arum from Thornton's *"Temple of Flora"*
287 MELODIYA. C09303, SU ca 1975
288 DECCA. SXL6288, GB 1967,
CA: Pieter Bruegel *"The Tower of Babel"*

289

290

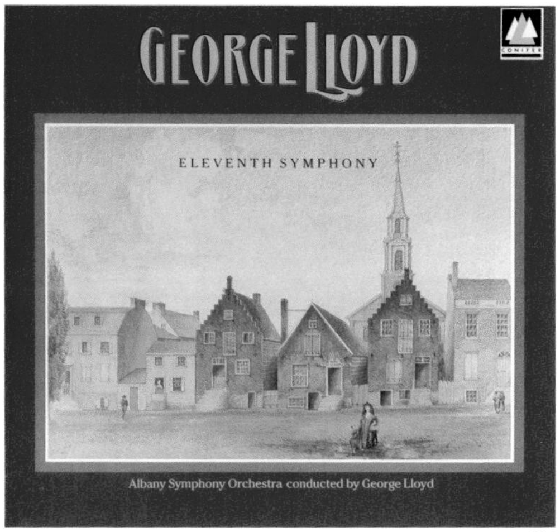

291

292

289 EMI. ASD 537, GB 1963, CA: Quaglio *"The Rocks of San Leone"*
290 ANGEL. S36129, USA 1963, CA: A. von Saar *"Ansicht von Prag"* (Staatsmuseum Wien/Mercure Ed. Paris – Atelier Joubert)
291 CONIFER. CFC144, GB 1986, CA: James Eights *"Albany-North Peace St-Westside-from Maiden Lane North"* 1814 (Albany Institute of History and Art)
292 ANGEL. S37099, USA 1975, CD: Marvin Schwartz; CA: Fritz d'Allemand *"Centenary order of the Maria Theresia"* (Kunsthistorisches Museum Wien)

293

293 KIWI. SLD48, NZ 1976, CD: Trevor Plaisted; CA: John Buchanan *"Milford Sound, looking north-west from Freshwater Basin"* 1863 (used by permission of the Hocken Library, Dunedin)
294 PHILIPS. 6500927, F 1975, CA: William Turner *"Norman Castle, Sunrise"* (The Tate Gallery, London)
295 EMI. ASD2826, GB 1973, CA: J.F. Millet *"Gardeuse du moutons"* (Musée Fantin Latour, Grenoble)

TRÉSORS CLASSIQUES
SUPER ARTISTIQUE-STÉRÉO
6500 927
PHILIPS
Lalo
Symphonie en sol mineur
Rapsodie norvégienne
„Le Roi d'Ys"- Ouverture
Orchestre National de l'Opéra de Monte-Carlo
Antonio de Almeida

294

EMI
Victoria de los Angeles
Songs of the Auvergne
(Canteloube)
Poème de l'amour et de la mer
(Chausson)
The Lamoureux Orchestra(Paris) · Jean-Pierre Jacquillat
J-Baptiste Millet.

295

296

296 KIWI. SLD57/58, NZ 1981, CD: Murray Vincent; CA: George O'Brien
"View of Otage Heads and Port Chalmers" 1866 (used by permission of the Hocken Library, Dunedin)
297 EMI-COLUMBIA. SAXF1031, F 1965, CA: Joseph Israels
"La Joyeuse de Harpe" (Mesdag Museum, La Haye); Ph: Scala, Florence
298 ARGO. ZRG696, GB 1972, CA: John Constable *"The Cornfield"*
(reproduced by kind permission of the Trustees of the National Gallery, London)

297

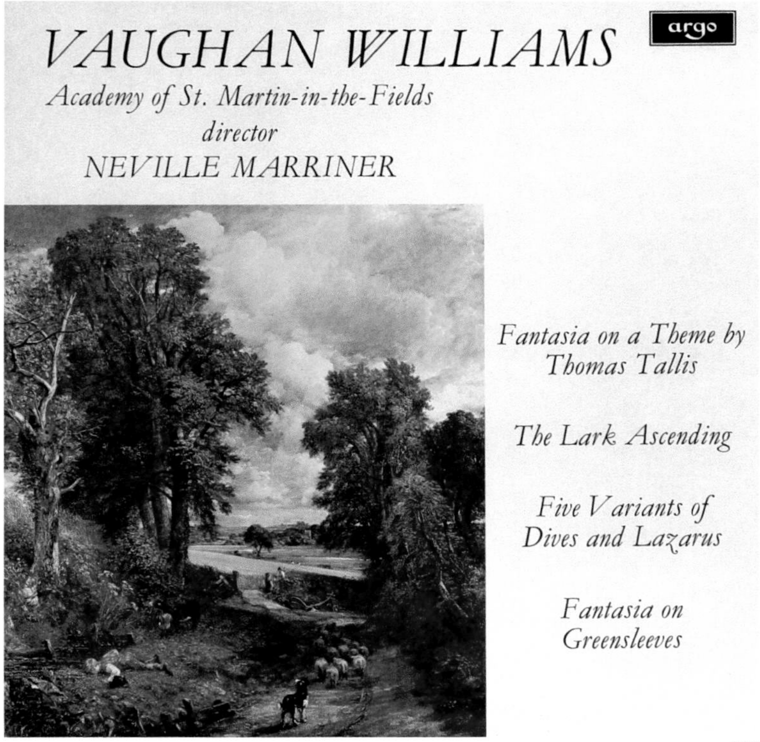

298

299

300

301

299 LYRITA. SRCS070, GB 1973, CD: Keith Hensby;
CA: William Turner *"Storm Clouds: Sunset"*
(reproduced by kind permission of The Tate Gallery, London)
300 EMI-COLUMBIA. SAX2342, GB 1961, CA: drawn by
William Turner, engraved by George Cooke (Edinburgh)
301 LONDON. STS15117, USA 1974

JOHAN HALVORSEN
FOSSEGRIMEN op. 21
MASCARADE-suite
SOLIST: SIGBJØRN BERNHOFT OSA, HARDINGFELE
KRINGKASTINGSORKESTRET, OSLO
DIRIGENT: ØIVIND BERGH

302

JOHAN SVENDSEN
SYMFONI NR.1 D DUR, OP. 4
FILHARMONISK SELSKAPS ORKESTER, OSLO, DIRIGENT MILTIADES CARIDIS

304

303

305

302 NORSK. Kulturfond NKF30029, N 1978, CA: Theodor Kittelsen *"Nokken pa land"* 1898 (Billedgalleria, Bergen)
303 NORSK KULTURFOND. NKF30011, N 1976, CA: Johannes Flintoe *"Fra Jotunheimen"* 1822-1835 (National Gallery, Oslo)
304 NORSK KULTURFOND NKF30001, N 1974. CA: Lars Hertervig *"Fra Borg ya"* 1867 (Nasjonalgalleriet Oslo)
305 NORSK KULTURFOND. NKF30009, N 1975, CA: Nicolai Astrup *"Kollen"* 1906 (Rasmus Meyers Samlinger, Bergen)

306

307

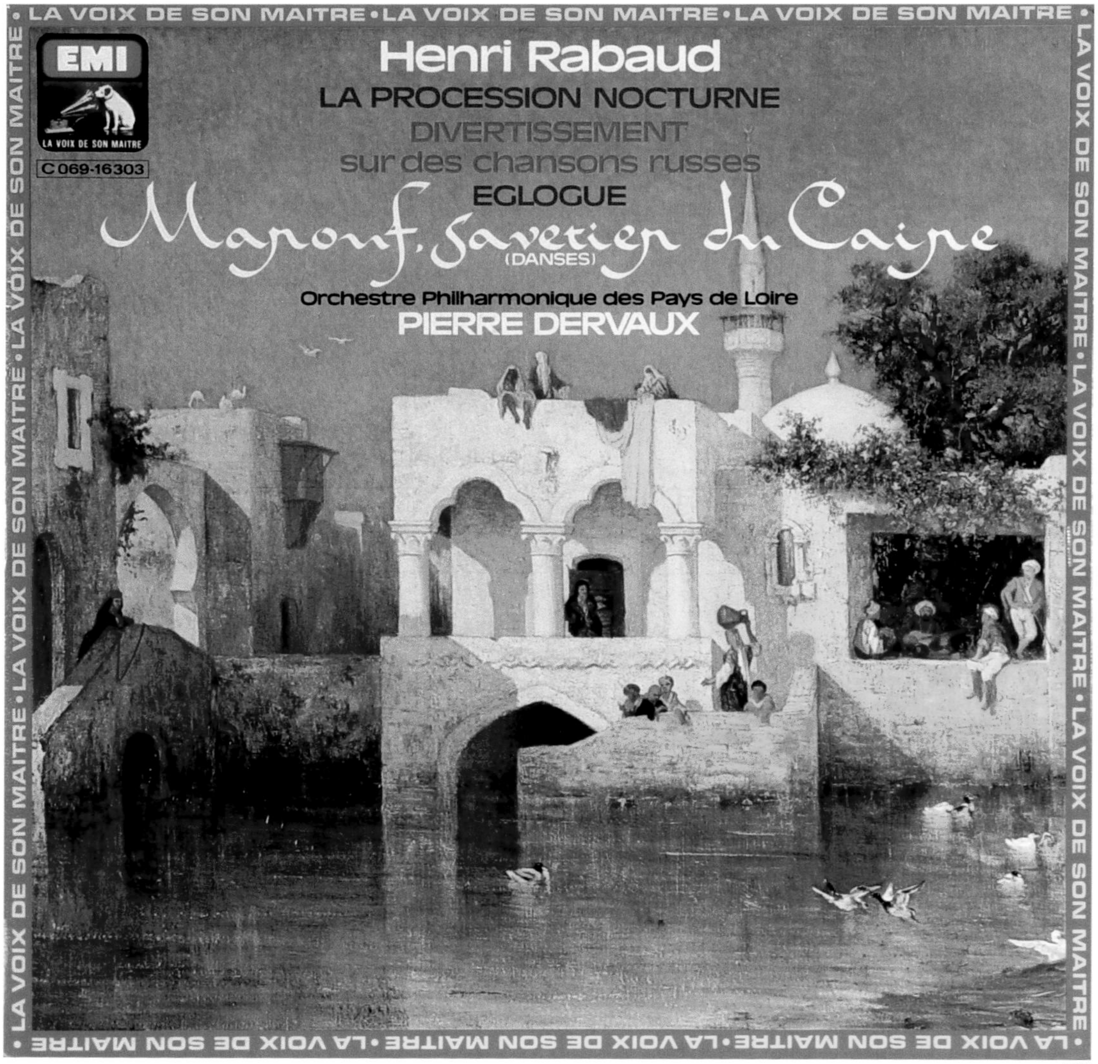

308

306 EMI. ASD3154, GB 1976, CA: Cavendish Morton
"The Moot Hall, Aldebourgh"
307 EMI. SLS867, GB 1973, CA: C.D. Friedrich
"Das große Gehege bei Dresden"
(Gemäldegallerie Neue Meister, Dreden);
Ph: Gerhard Reinhold, Leipzig-Mölkau
308 EMI. C069-16303, F 1978,
CA: Charles-Emile Tournemine
"Habitants près d'Alia"
(Musée du Louvre, Paris); Ph: AGRACI

309

310

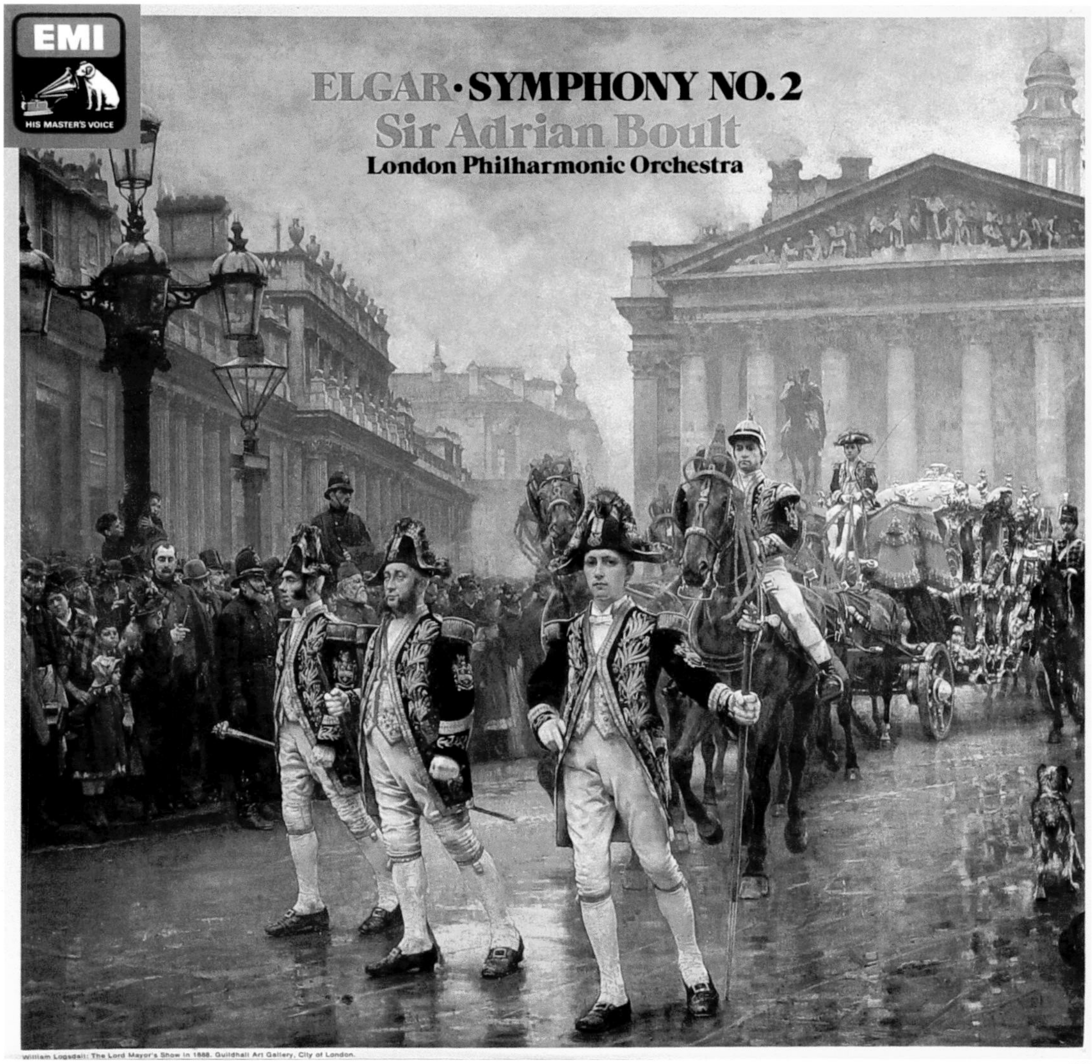

311

309 SWEDISH SOCIETY DISCOFIL. SLT33161, S 1964, CA: Hugo Alfven *"Anacapri"* 1922
310 EMI. SAN193, GB 1968, CA: C.D. Friedrich *"Kreuz im Gebirge"* 1808 (Staatliche Kunstsammlungen, Dresden)
311 EMI. ASD3266, GB 1976, CA: William Logsdail *"The Lord Mayors Show"* 1888 (Guildhall Art Gallery, City of London)

312

313

312 LYRITA. SRCS106, GB 1979, CA: William Turner
"Scene on the Thames" (reproduced by courtesy of the Trustees of the British Museum)
313 RCA. LRL1-5133, USA 1976, CA: Curot
(reproduced by courtesy of the Trustees, The National Gallery, London)
314 ANGEL. S36415, USA 1967, CA: William Turner
"Windsor Castle from the Meadows" (The Tate Gallery, London) [Design as original EMI ASD2698]

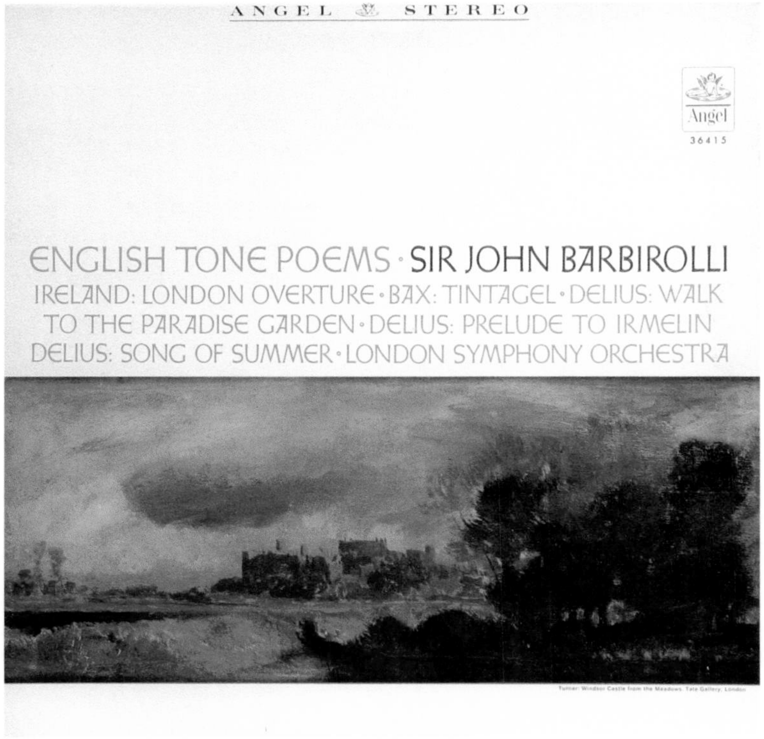

314

315

315 UNICORN. DKP9008, GB 1981, CD: Arvan Studios, Lancaster; CA: John Brett
"Britannia's Realm" (reproduced by courtesy of The Tate Gallery, London)
316 EMI. EMX412090, GB 1986, CA: William Langley *"Over the Dunes"* (courtesy of the Fine Art Photographic Library, Ltd)
317 DECCA. SXL6320, GB 1967, CA: Hendrick Dubbels
"A Dutch Yacht and other vessels becalmed near the shore" (National Gallery, London)
318 EMI. ASD3190, GB 1976, CA: Winslow Homer *"Breezing up"* (National Gallery of Art)

316

317

318

319

320

321

322

319 EMI. C06916288, F 1978,
CA: Jean-Francois Raffaelli
"Le Pavillion de Hanovre et le Boulevard des Italiens"
(Musée des Beaux-Arts, Lyon);
Ph: Lauros-Giraudon

320 EMI. C065-11259, F 1973, CA: Monticelli
"Les Saltimbanques"
(Musée Grobet-Labadié, Marseille);
Ph: Giraudon, Paris [Design as EMI ASD2306]

321 EMI. C06916301, F 1979

322 EMI. EAC80569, J 1979

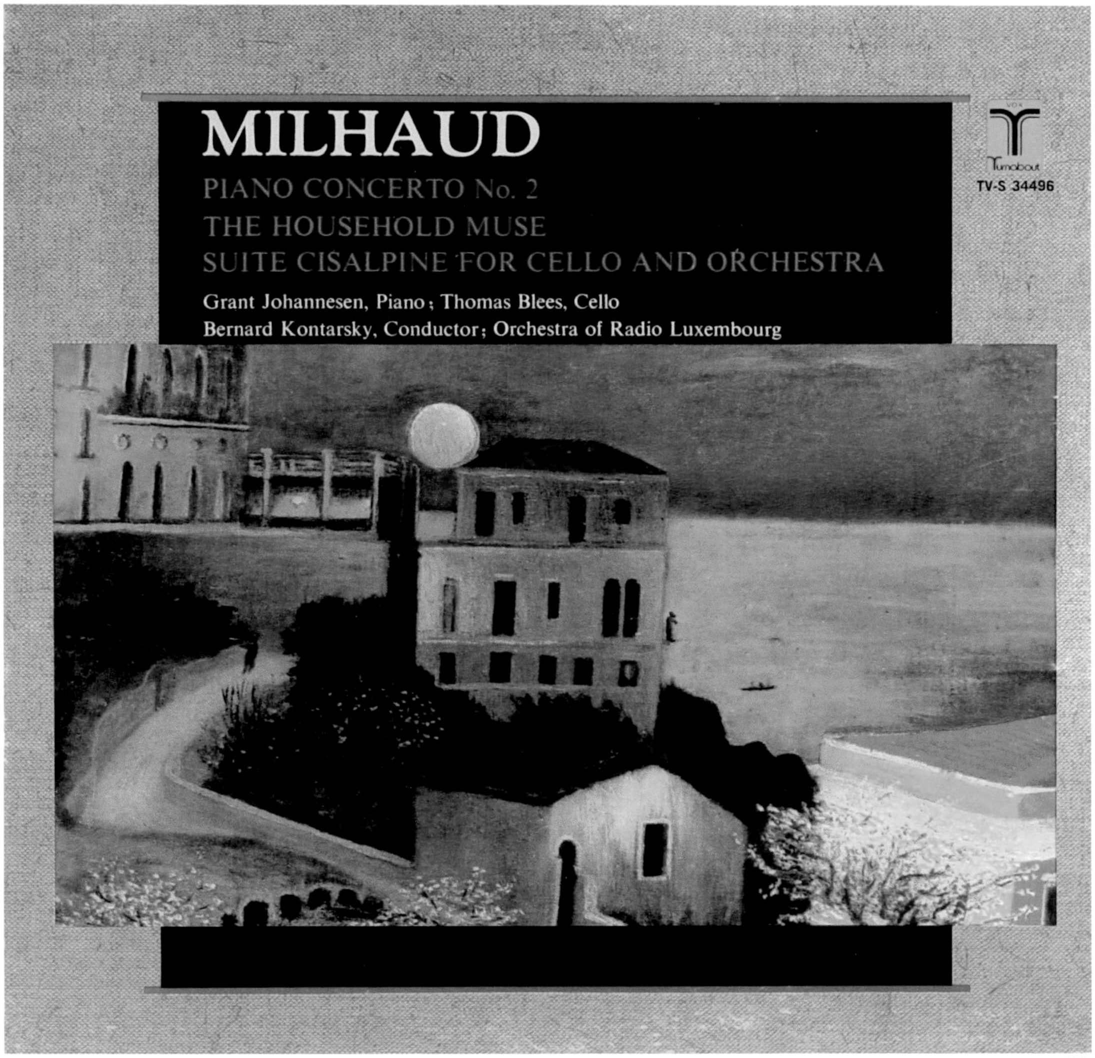
MILHAUD
PIANO CONCERTO No. 2
THE HOUSEHOLD MUSE
SUITE CISALPINE FOR CELLO AND ORCHESTRA
Grant Johannesen, Piano; Thomas Blees, Cello
Bernard Kontarsky, Conductor; Orchestra of Radio Luxembourg
Turnabout
TV-S 34496

323

324

323 TURNABOUT. TV34496, USA 1974
324 EMI. 270334, F 1986, CA: Henri-Edmond Cross *"L'air du soir"*; Ph: Jean Pierre Zenobel
325 ANGEL. S37065, USA 1974, CD: Marvin Schwartz; CA: Seurat *"Sunday Afternoon on the Island of La Grande Jatte"*, Detail (courtesy of the Art Institute of Chicago)
326 ANGEL. S37064, USA 1974, CD: Marvin Schwartz; CA: Seurat *"Sunday Afternoon on the Island of La Grande Jatte"*, Detail (courtesy of the Art Institute of Chicago)

325

Angel
The Orchestral
Music of Debussy
Album 1
The Children's Corner · Petite Suite
La Plus que lente · Danse (Tarantelle styrienne) Berceuse héroïque
JEAN MARTINON The French National Radio Orchestra

326

327 PHILIPS. 9500347, EU 1977, CA: Henri-Edmond Cross *"Les Cypres à Cagnes"* (Musée national d'art moderne, Paris); Ph: Lauros-Giraudon, Paris

328 RCA. VICS1358, GFR, CA: van Gogh *"L'Arlésienne"*

329 EMI. ASD2397, GB 1968, CA: Jelka Delius (Delius' house in Grez-sur-Loing, courtesy of Eric Fenby)

330 EMI. C063-14168, GFR 1974, CA: van Gogh *"Sternenlicht über der Rhone"* (Archiv für Kunst und Geschichte, Berlin)

328

327

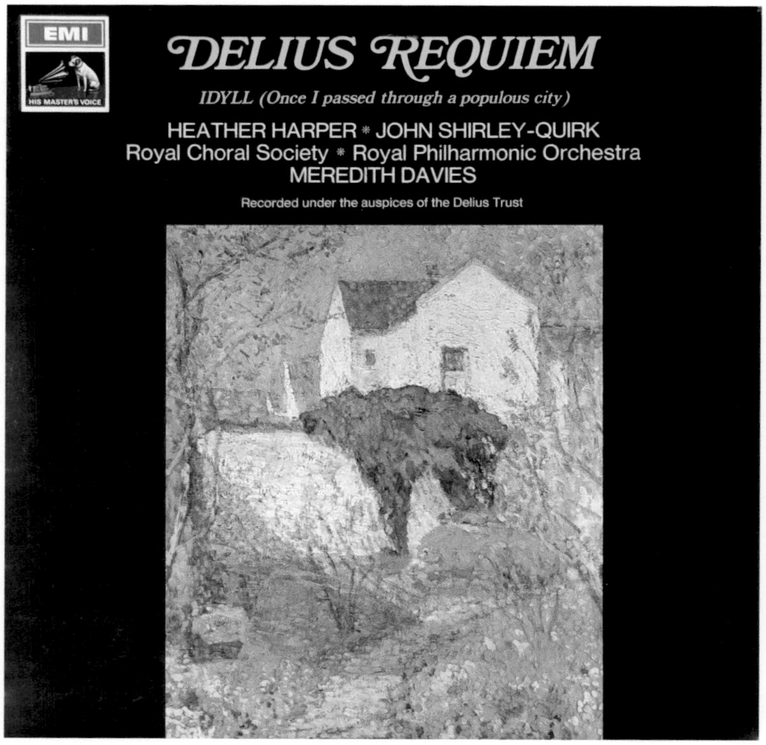

329

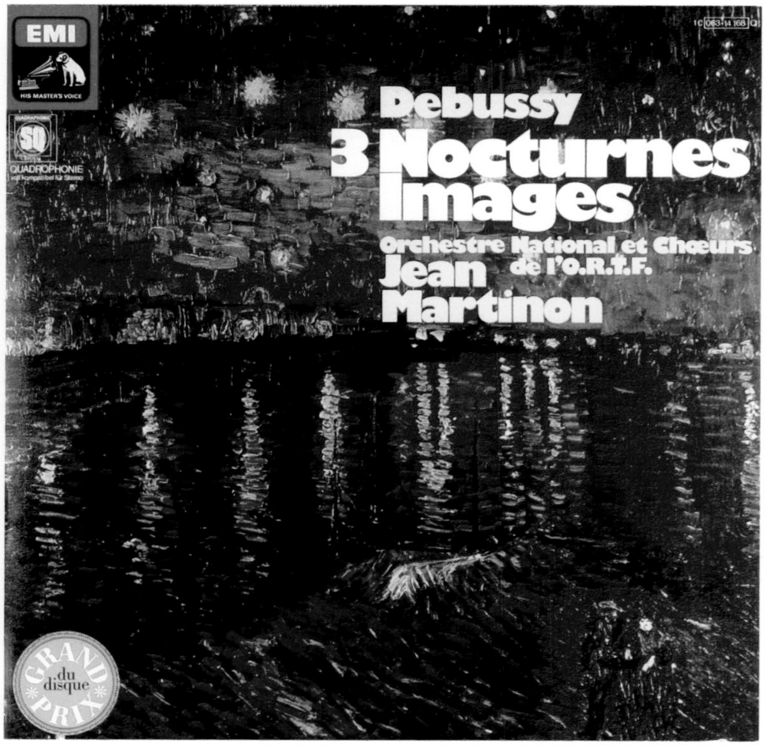

330

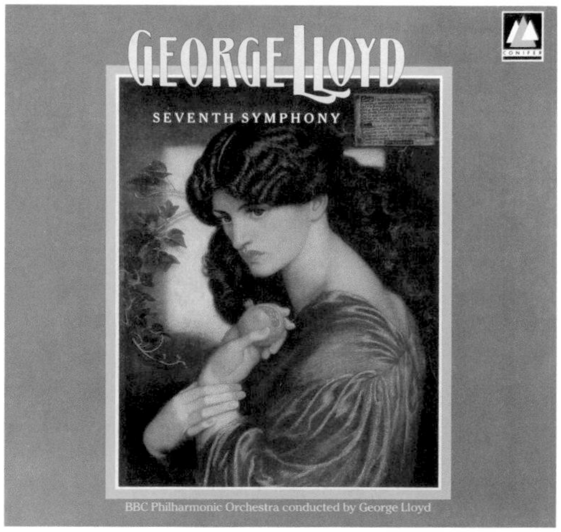

331

332

333

331 CONIFER. CFC143, GB 1986, CA: Dante Gabriel Rossetti *"Proserpine"*, Detail 1874 (reproduced by courtesy of the Trustees of the Tate Gallery, London)
332 EMI. C069-73100, F 1981, CA: Alphonse Osbert *"La Source"* (Fresque, Station Thermal, Vichy); Ph: Pix/Revault; copyright by A.D.A.G.P., Paris, 1982
333 EMI. ASD2673, GB 1971, CA: William Blake *"When the morning stars sang together"* (from illustrations to the Book of Job; by kind permission of Ursula Vaughan Williams)
334 MELODIYA. C15855, SU 1981

334

335

336

6.4 The Twentieth Century (337 - 355)

This category contains both illustrations that have been specially created for the cover and paintings from galleries. As a rule, if a picture title is supplied, the work of art is a gallery painting. The cover from United Artists shows the successfully embedded Picasso painting amidst a grid of colourful rectangles (344). The Melodiya record is, by Russian standards, surprisingly opulent (353). There are only three thematic references to music in this group:

— Cover 338 shows *A Haunted Landscape* by George Crumb.

— The painting on cover 345 is titled with a phrase from *Decsényi's Csontváry Pictures.*

— *"Living Icons"* has been titled with a composition of the same name by the Bulgarian composer Kazandjiev (346).

338

337

335 EMI. C063-01899, GFR 1968, CA: Gustav Klimt *"Der Kuss"* (Österreichische Gallerie, Wien)
336 EMI. ASD3455, GB 1978, CA: Alfonse Mucha *"La Plume et Primevère"* 1899
337 PORTUGAL. Som 860005, Port ca 1968, CA: Mollo Falcao Trigoso *"Dimensao 6"*
338 NEW WORLD. NW326, USA 1985, CD: Bob Defrin; CA: Marshall Arisman

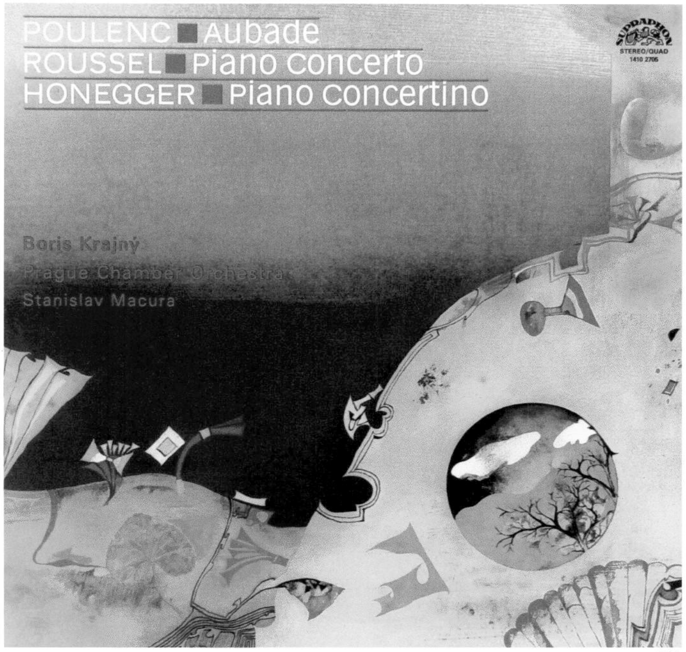

339

340

341

342

343

339 SUPRAPHON. 14102705, CS 1980,
CA: Denisa Wagnerová
340 DECCA. SXL6570, GB 1972
341 SUPRAPHON. 11102280, CS 1979,
CD: Miloslav Žacek; CA: Stanislav Vajce
342 SUPRAPHON. 4102198, CS 1977,
CD: Milan Jaroš; Ph: Václav Ostádal
343 ELECTRECORD. ECE01805, Rum 1977,
CA: Costa Constantin

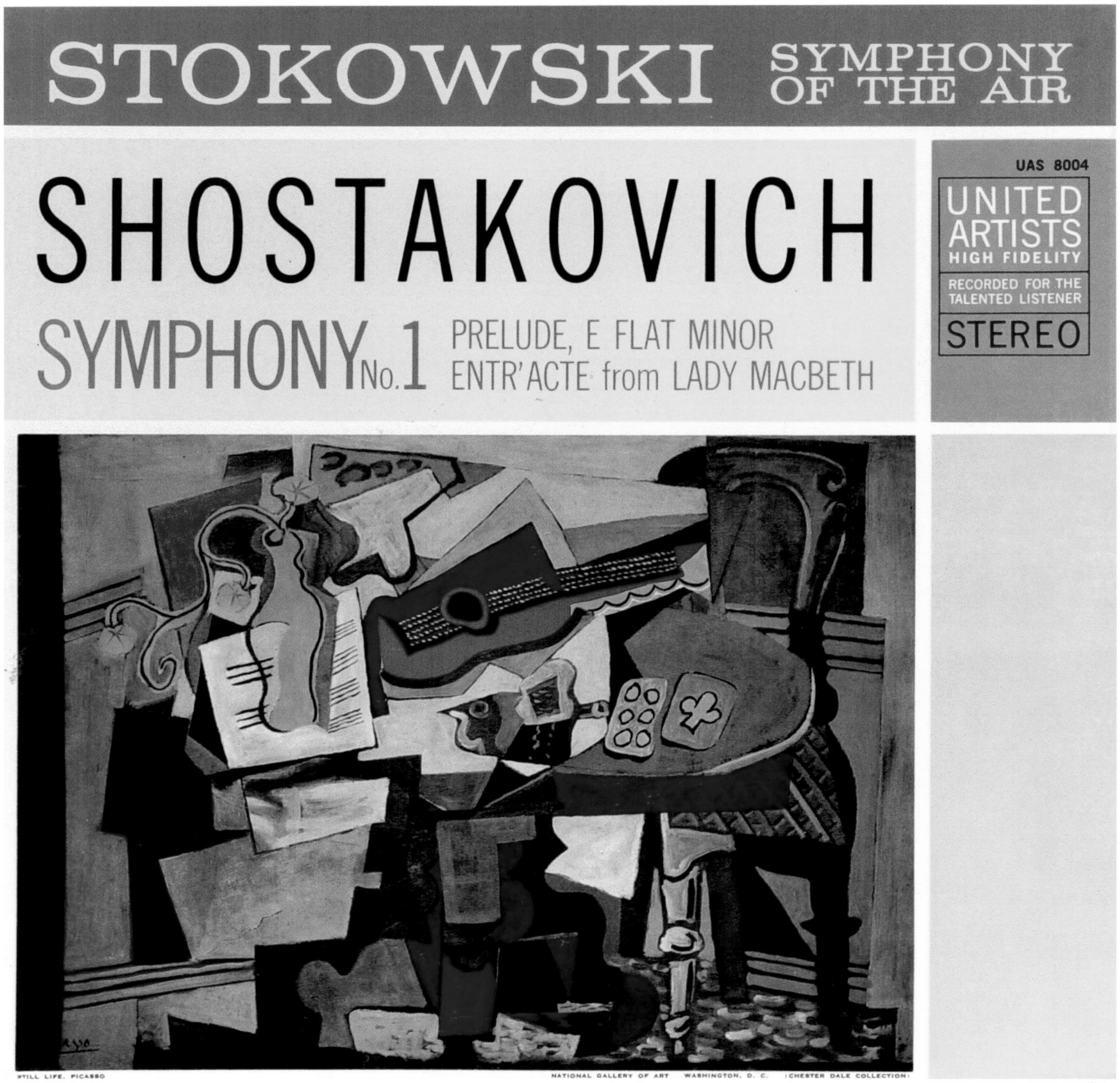

STOKOWSKI
SYMPHONY OF THE AIR
SHOSTAKOVICH
SYMPHONY No. 1
PRELUDE, E FLAT MINOR
ENTR'ACTE from LADY MACBETH
UAS 8004
UNITED ARTISTS
HIGH FIDELITY
RECORDED FOR THE TALENTED LISTENER
STEREO
STILL LIFE, PICASSO
NATIONAL GALLERY OF ART WASHINGTON, D. C. (CHESTER DALE COLLECTION)

344

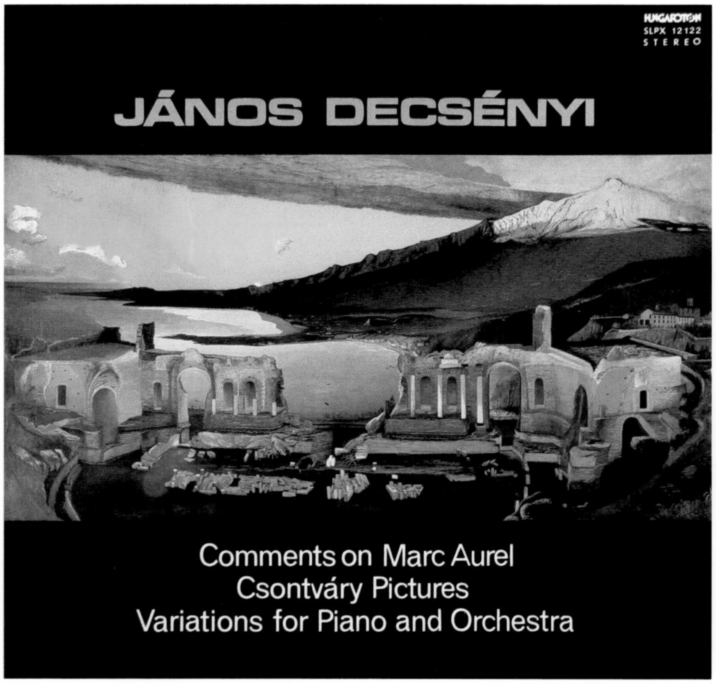

345

344 UNITED ARTISTS. UAS8004, USA 1959, CA: Picasso *"Still Life"* (National Gallery of Art, Washington D.C.; Chester Dale Collection)
345 HUNGAROTON. SLPX12122, Hu 1980, CD: Szilárd Molnár; CA: Csontvary *"The Ruins of the Ancient Greek Theatre in Taormina"*
346 BALKANTON. BCA1424, Bulg

BCA 1424
ВАСИЛ КАЗАНДЖИЕВ
ЖИВИТЕ ИКОНИ
КАРТИНИ ОТ БЪЛГАРИЯ
Камерен ансамбъл „СОФИЙСКИ СОЛИСТИ" · Диригент-Васил Казанджиев
VASSIL KAZANDJIEV
THE LIVING ICONS * PICTURES FROM BULGARIA

346

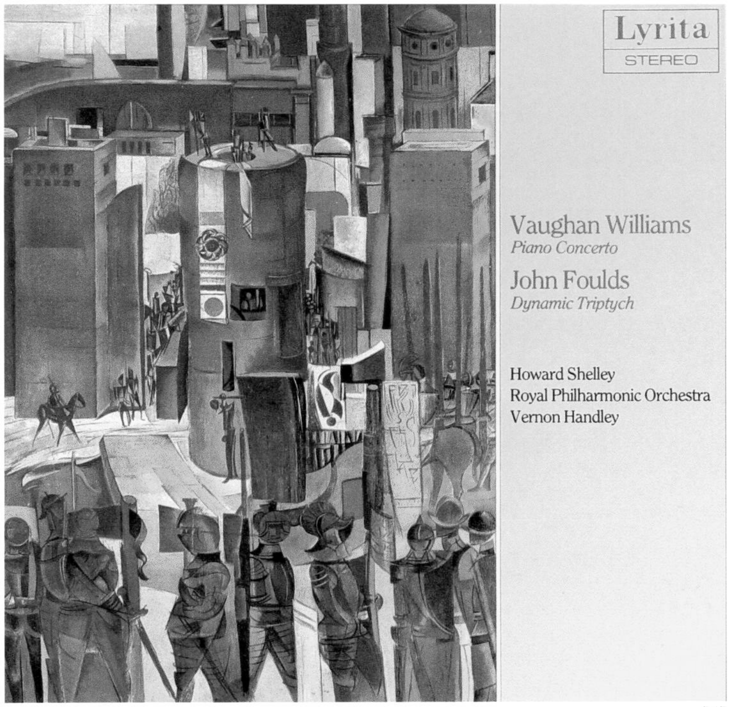

347

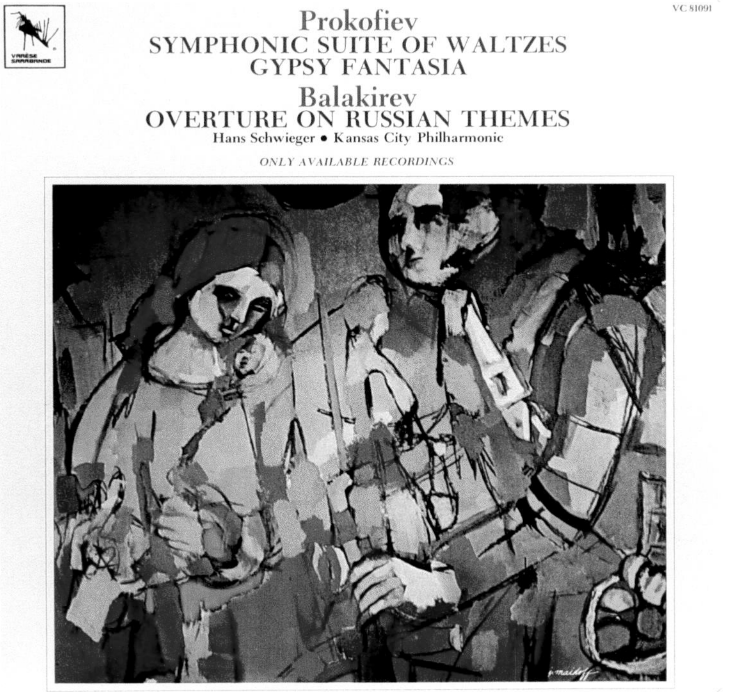

Prokofiev
SYMPHONIC SUITE OF WALTZES
GYPSY FANTASIA
Balakirev
OVERTURE ON RUSSIAN THEMES
Hans Schwieger • Kansas City Philharmonic
ONLY AVAILABLE RECORDINGS

348

349

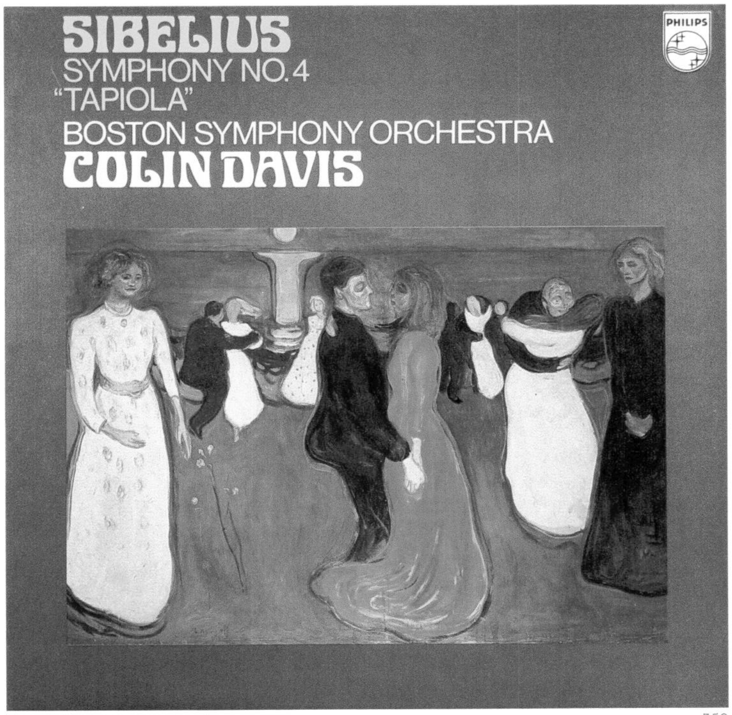

350

347 LYRITA. SRCS130, GB 1984, CA: Percy Wyndham Lewis
"The surrender of Barcelona" (reproduced by kind permission of The Tate Gallery, London)
348 VARESE. VC81091, USA 1979, CA: Jules Maidoff
349 HUNGAROTON. SLPX12018, Hu 1979, CA: István Rész
350 PHILIPS. 9500143, EU 1977, CA: Edvard Munch *"Livets dans"* 1899 (Munch Museum, Oslo)
351 SUPRAPHON. SUAST 50386, CS, CA: Josef Capek *"Promenade"* 1934

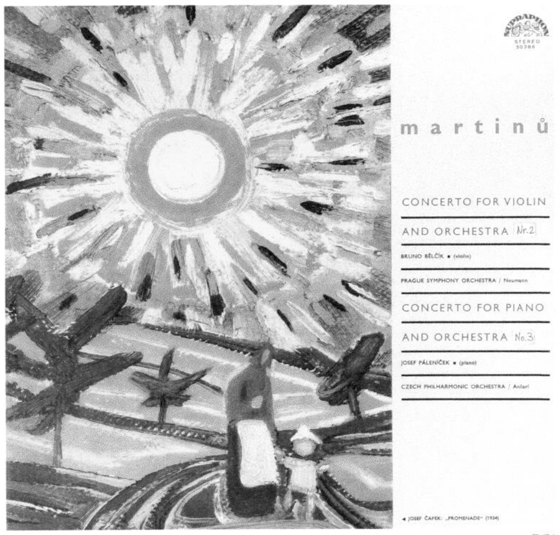

351

352

353

354

355

352 ELECTRECORD. ST-ECE0414, Rum 1966, CA: N. Tonitza *"Iarna in Bucaresti"*
353 MELODIYA. C04195, SU
354 FINLANDIA. FA307, Fin 1979, CA: Alvar Cawén *"Interior of a Studio"* 1922 (Collection of the Ateneum, Helsinki)
355 FINLANDIA. FAD349, Fin 1987, CD: Eero Syvänoja; CA: Ilmari Aalto *"Composition"* 1927 (Private Collection)

6.5 Psychedelia, Surrealism and the Supernatural (356 - 366)

This category is particularly interesting. It includes four covers from the French EMI with spiritual motifs (357, 358, 363, 364). The cover for Stravinsky's *Sacre du Printemps* (362) is rather remarkable: in the centre of the picture is an elephant-like head with a "fertilisation-trunk" seen in profile along with the front view of a human-like face of a mythical creature. The following covers refer specifically to the musical content:

— The illustration reminiscent of Magritte on the Satie record shows the composer (360). The same is true for cover 364.

— Covers 361 and 365 reflect the spiritual content of the compositions.

— The "Toteninsel", by artist Arnold Böcklin served as an inspiration to Rachmaninov's composition *The Isle of the Dead* (366).

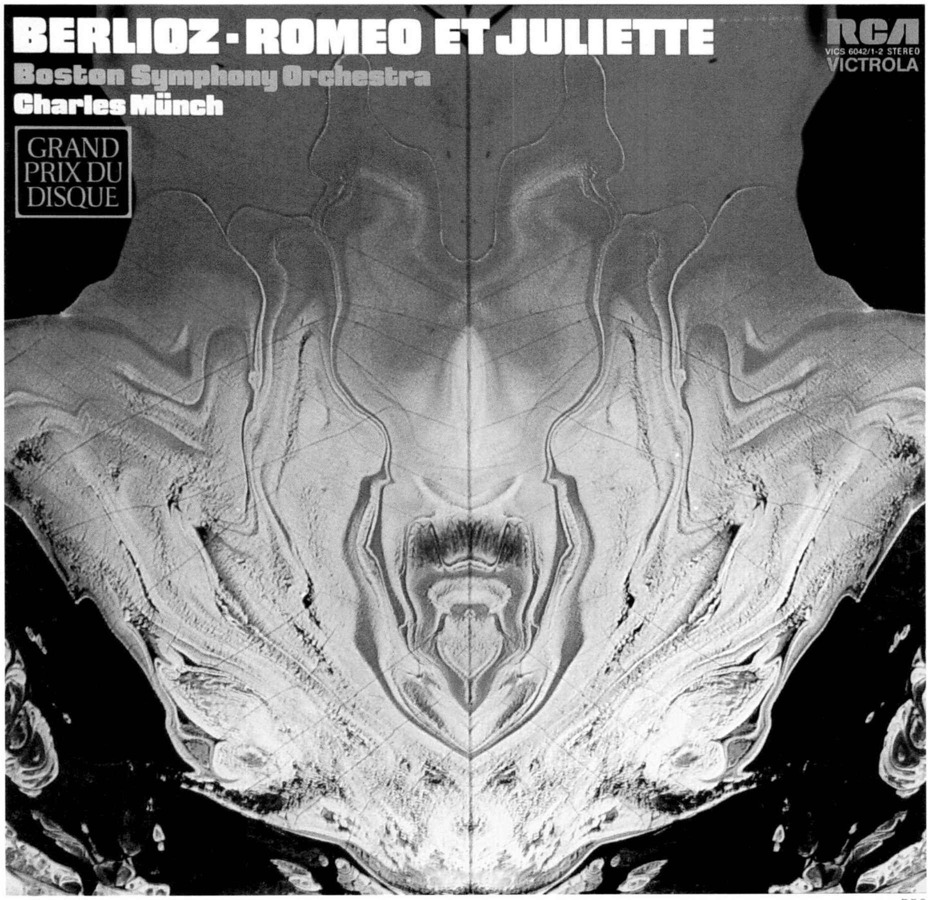

356

357

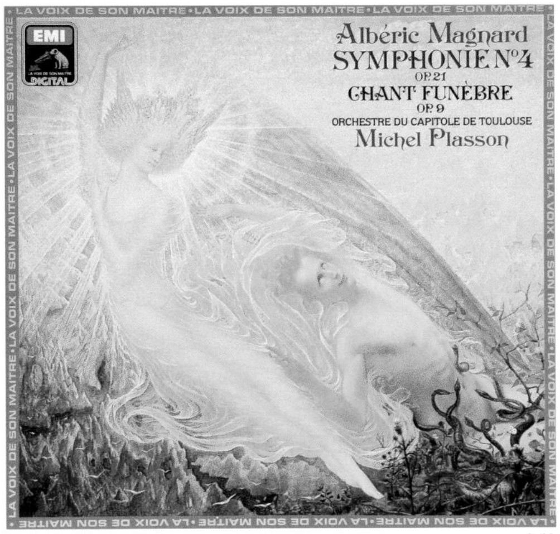

358

356 RCA. VICS6042, D ca 1975, CA: Mim & Paul Maler
357 EMI. 749080, F 1987, CA: Louis Janmot *"L'envol de l'ame"* (Musée des Beaux Arts, Lyon); Ph: Hubert Josse
358 EMI. 173184, F 1983, CA: Jean Delville *"L'Ange des Splendeurs"* 1894 (Collection Gillion-Crowet,

359

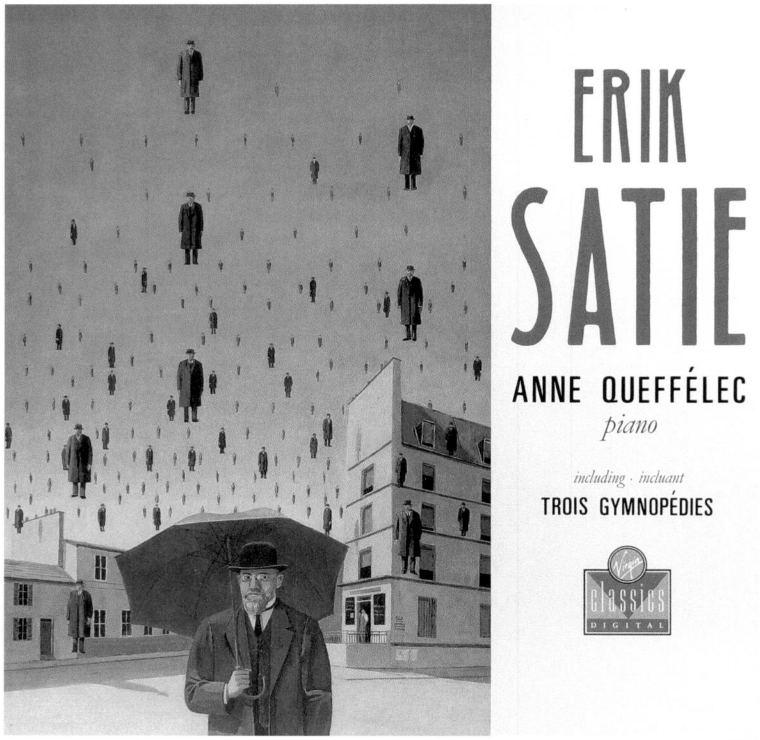

360

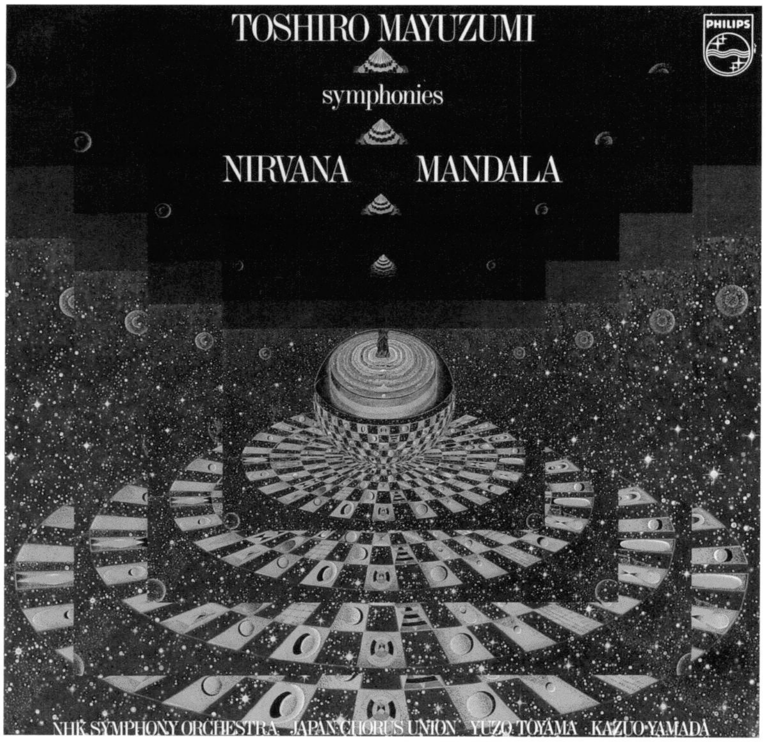

TOSHIRO MAYUZUMI
symphonies
NIRVANA MANDALA
PHILIPS
NHK SYMPHONY ORCHESTRA JAPAN CHORUS UNION YUZO TOYAMA KAZUO YAMADA

361

359 UNICORN. UNS208, GB 1970, CA: Heinrich Fuseli *"Albtraum"* (Frankfurter Goethemuseum)
360 VIRGIN. VC790754, EU 1988, CD: Mantis Studio, London; CA: Paul Gildea
361 PHILIPS. 9500762, EU 1978, CD: Josaku Maeda
362 DGG. 435222, GFR, CD: Gerd Haase & Wolfgang Behrend

362

363

364

365

363 EMI. 270348, F 1985, CA: Auguste Heiligenstein *"Verre émaillé"* (Connaissance des Arts); Ph: J. Guillot/Edimédia
364 EMI. C063-73096, F 1981, CA: Odilon Redon *"Evocation de Roussel"* (National Gallery, Washington, Chester Dale Collection); Ph: Shark International
365 ERATO. STE50200, F 1964, CA: Jacques Vatoux
366 EMI. ASD3259, GB 1976, CA: Arnold Böcklin *"Die Toteninsel"* (courtesy Archiv für Kunst und Geschichte, Berlin)

366

367

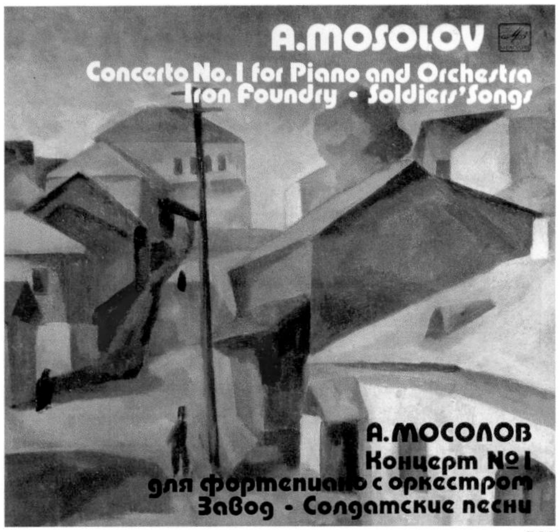

368

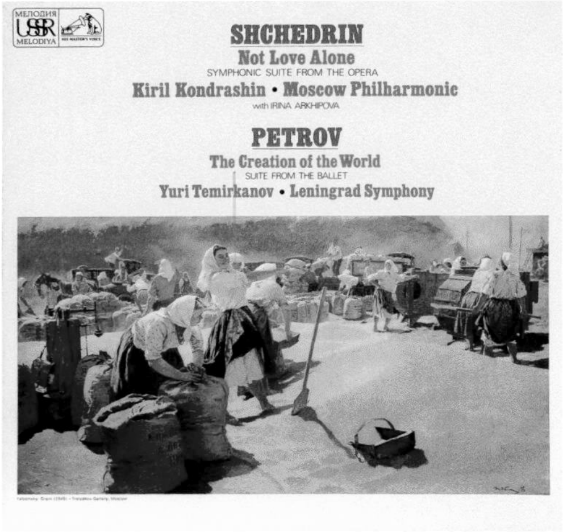

369

6.6 Pictures from Russia and the Soviet Union (367 - 396)

Russian and Soviet composers are a key focus in my record collection. The majority of these records are original Melodiya albums. The cover art on many of the other originals often doesn't satisfy Western demands, which has led to the fact that some of the covers shown are Melodiya license editions or decorate Western recordings, where the aim is to illustrate the Russian origin of the music. Soviet records destined for export with bilingual or tri-lingual texts were often decorated with pictures from the Tretyakov Gallery in Moscow or the Hermitage in Leningrad: forest and winter scenes, landscapes, village settings or scenes taken from Russian history are shown on cover 389, for example. Editions designated for the domestic market were less elaborately designed, with coarse paper, no lamination and a standard cover. The titles of the paintings are referenced in the legend, providing that they are indicated on the record. Precise references to musical content can only be seen on cover 382 *(Song of the Forests)* and 392 *(The Fair at Sorochinsk)*. The other covers only indicate the geographic reference.

— Picture 369 is my favourite among the Russian covers, even if it is deceptive: the painting from 1949 had a propagandistic purpose: it was meant to give evidence of the excess generated by the Soviet Kolchoz system. It is a typical example of the Soviet Realism of this period.

— Please also note the three pictures by Armenian artists with landscapes of their homeland (367, 379, 393).

367 MELODIYA. C25195, SU 1987, CA: Burzyantsev
"Mountain in Spring"
368 MELODIYA. C17429, SU 1984, CA: Falk
369 EMI. ASD3447, GB 1978, CA: Yablonskaya
"Grain" (Tretyakov Gallery, Moscow)

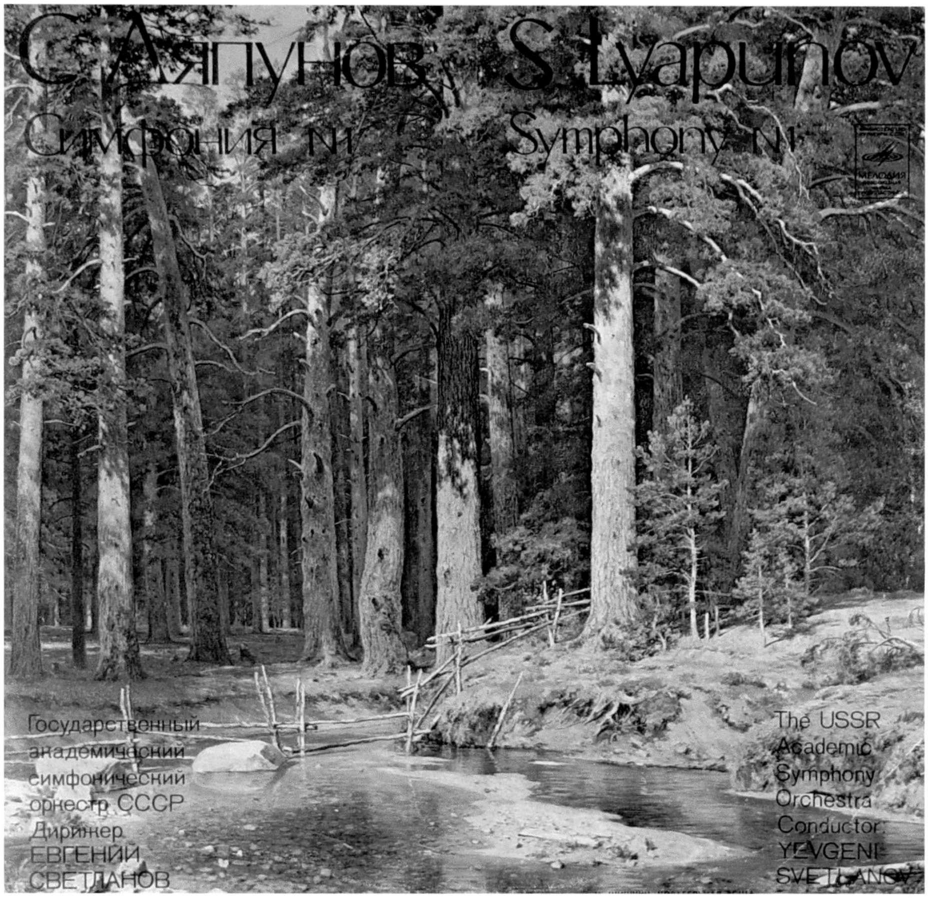

370

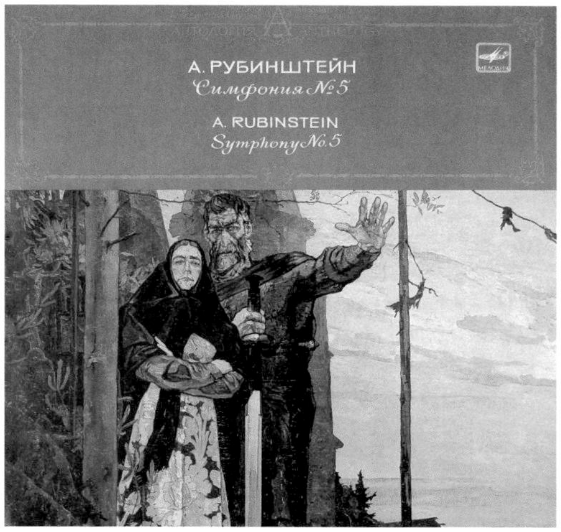

371

372

373

370 MELODIYA. C14385, SU ca 1980, CA: Shishkin
371 MELODIYA. C28977, SU 1989, CA: Korin
"Northern Ballad"
372 EMI. ASD3106, GB 1975, CA: Kandinsky
"Russian Beauty in Landscape" (State Gallery, Monaco)
373 MELODIYA. C11403, SU 1980, CA: V. Maltine

374

375

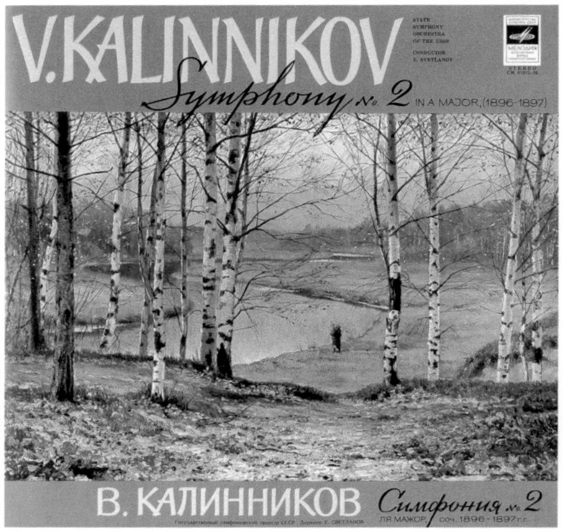

376

377

378

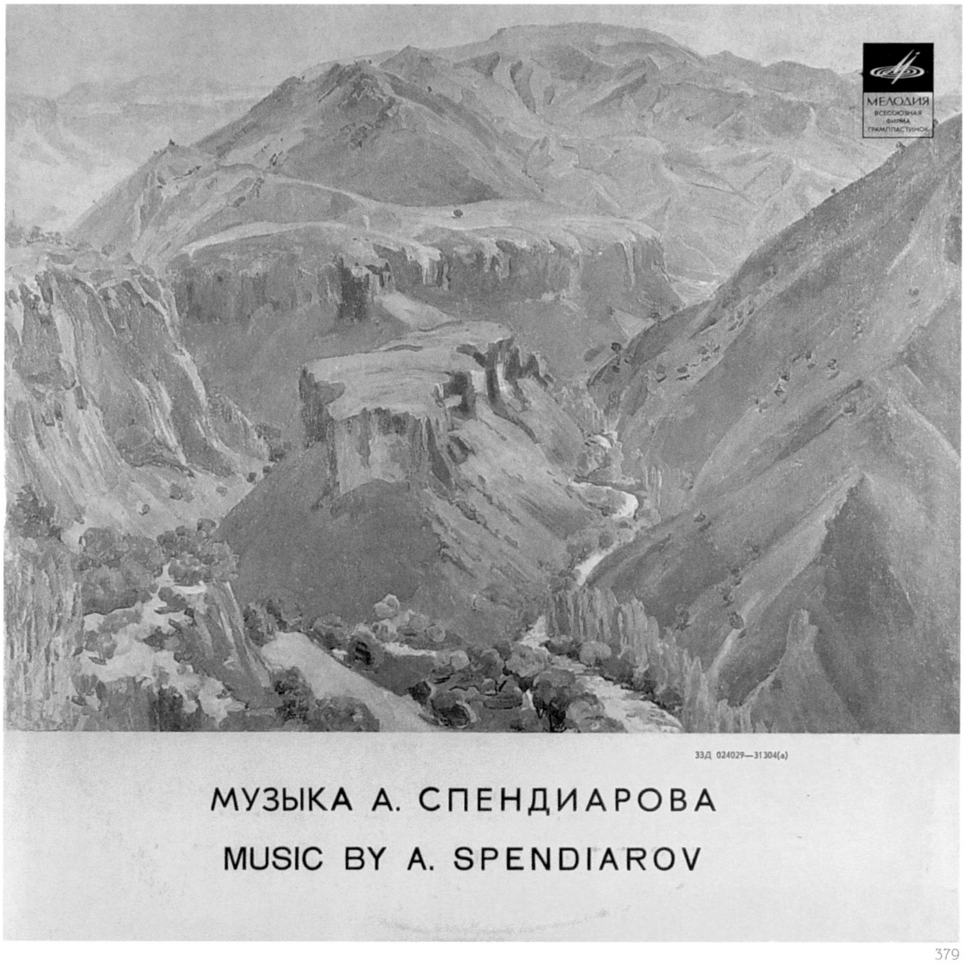

379

374 MELODIYA. C19855, SU 1983
375 MELODIYA. C16211, SU 1981
376 MELODIYA. C01915, SU 1970, CA: Bolkov (Tretyakov Gallery, Moscow)
377 MELODIYA. C01677, SU 1968, CA: K. Yoon (Tretyakov Gallery, Moscow)
378 MELODIYA. C22845, SU 1985, CD: Sveshnikova; CA: Polyushchenko *"Spring Evening"*
379 MELODIYA. D024029, SU

380

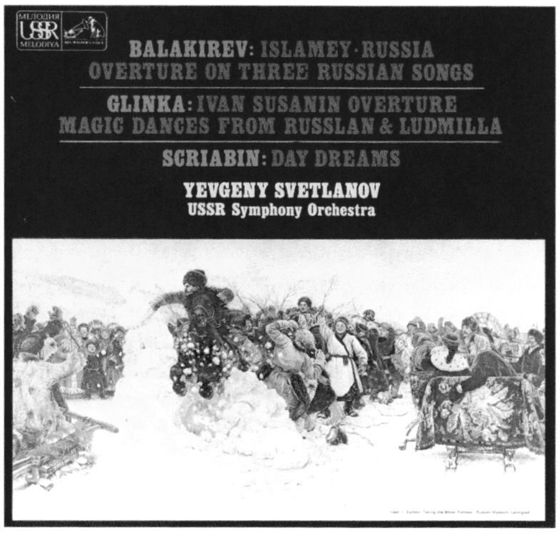

381

380 MELODIYA. C22419, SU 1985, CA: Kustodiev *"Shrovetide"*
381 EMI. ASD3709, GB 1979, CA: Surikov *"Taking the Snow-Fortress"* (Russian Museum, Leningrad)
382 EMI. ASD2875, GB 1973, CA: Shiskin *"Mordvinov's Wood"* (Tretyakov Gallery, Moscow)
383 MELODIYA. C27611, SU 1988, CA: Polenov *"Old Pond"*
384 EMI. ASD3504, GB 1978, CA: Levergne *"Troitsky Gate"*

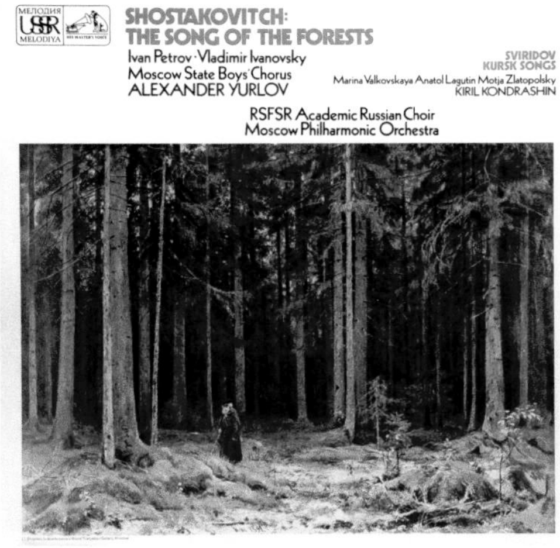

МЕЛОДИЯ
USSR
MELODIYA
SHOSTAKOVITCH:
THE SONG OF THE FORESTS
Ivan Petrov · Vladimir Ivanovsky
Moscow State Boys' Chorus
ALEXANDER YURLOV
SVIRIDOV
KURSK SONGS
Marina Valkovskaya Anatol Lagutin Motja Zlatopolsky
KIRIL KONDRASHIN
RSFSR Academic Russian Choir
Moscow Philharmonic Orchestra

382

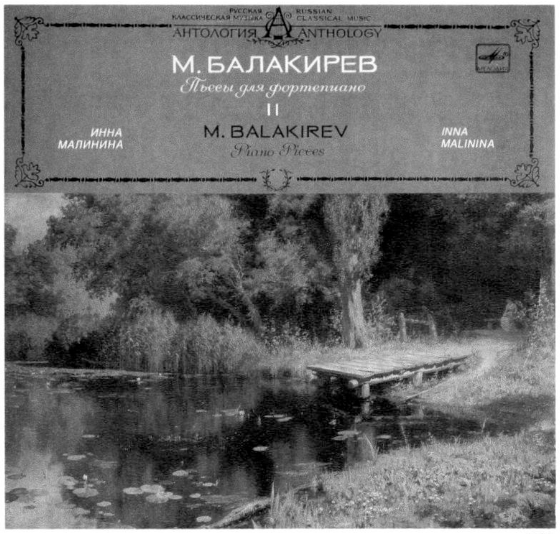

383

384

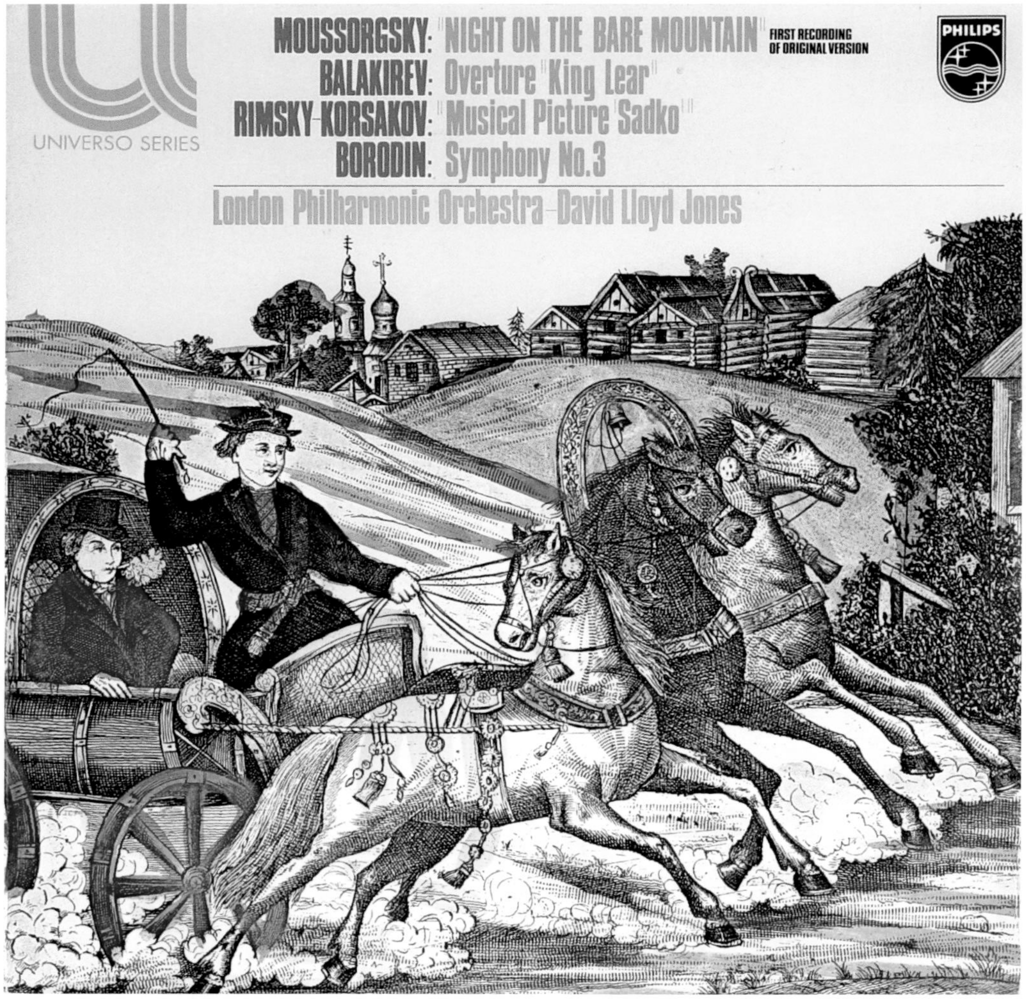
UNIVERSO SERIES
MOUSSORGSKY: "NIGHT ON THE BARE MOUNTAIN"
FIRST RECORDING OF ORIGINAL VERSION
BALAKIREV: Overture "King Lear"
RIMSKY-KORSAKOV: "Musical Picture 'Sadko'"
BORODIN: Symphony No.3
London Philharmonic Orchestra–David Lloyd Jones
PHILIPS

385

M·BALAKIREV
RUSSIA • CONCERTO FOR PIANO AND ORCHESTRA • IN CZECHIA • ISLAMEI

386

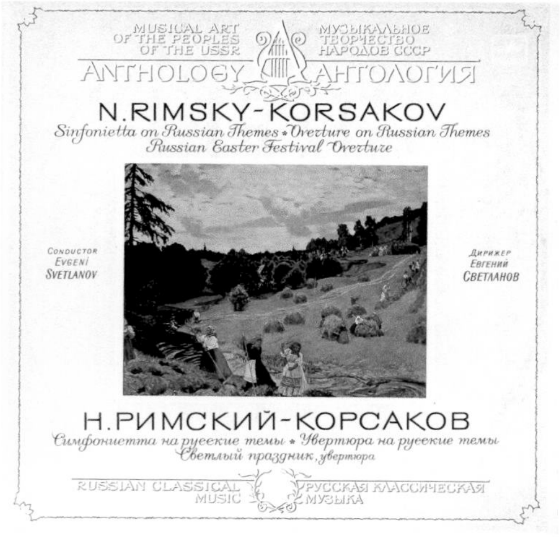
MUSICAL ART OF THE PEOPLES OF THE USSR
МУЗЫКАЛЬНОЕ ТВОРЧЕСТВО НАРОДОВ СССР
ANTHOLOGY
АНТОЛОГИЯ
N. RIMSKY-KORSAKOV
Sinfonietta on Russian Themes • Overture on Russian Themes
Russian Easter Festival Overture
CONDUCTOR
EVGENI
SVETLANOV
ДИРИЖЕР
ЕВГЕНИЙ
СВЕТЛАНОВ
Н. РИМСКИЙ-КОРСАКОВ
Симфониетта на русские темы • Увертюра на русские темы
Светлый праздник, увертюра
RUSSIAN CLASSICAL MUSIC
РУССКАЯ КЛАССИЧЕСКАЯ МУЗЫКА

387

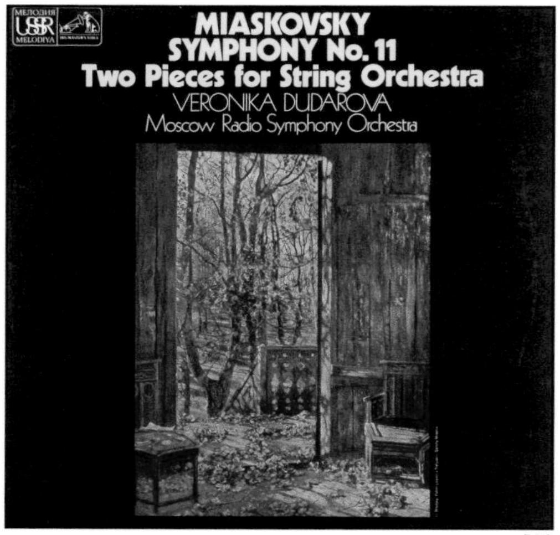
MIASKOVSKY
SYMPHONY No. 11
Two Pieces for String Orchestra
VERONIKA DUDAROVA
Moscow Radio Symphony Orchestra

388

385 PHILIPS. 6580053, GB ca 1971
386 MELODIYA. C03557, SU ca 1975, CA: Basnetov *"Bayan"* (Russian Museum, Leningrad)
387 MELODIYA. C23327, SU 1985, CD: B. Belov; CA: Kustodiev *"Haymaking"*
388 EMI. ASD3879, GB 1980, CA: Brodsky *"Fallen Leaves"* (Tretyakov Gallery, Moscow)

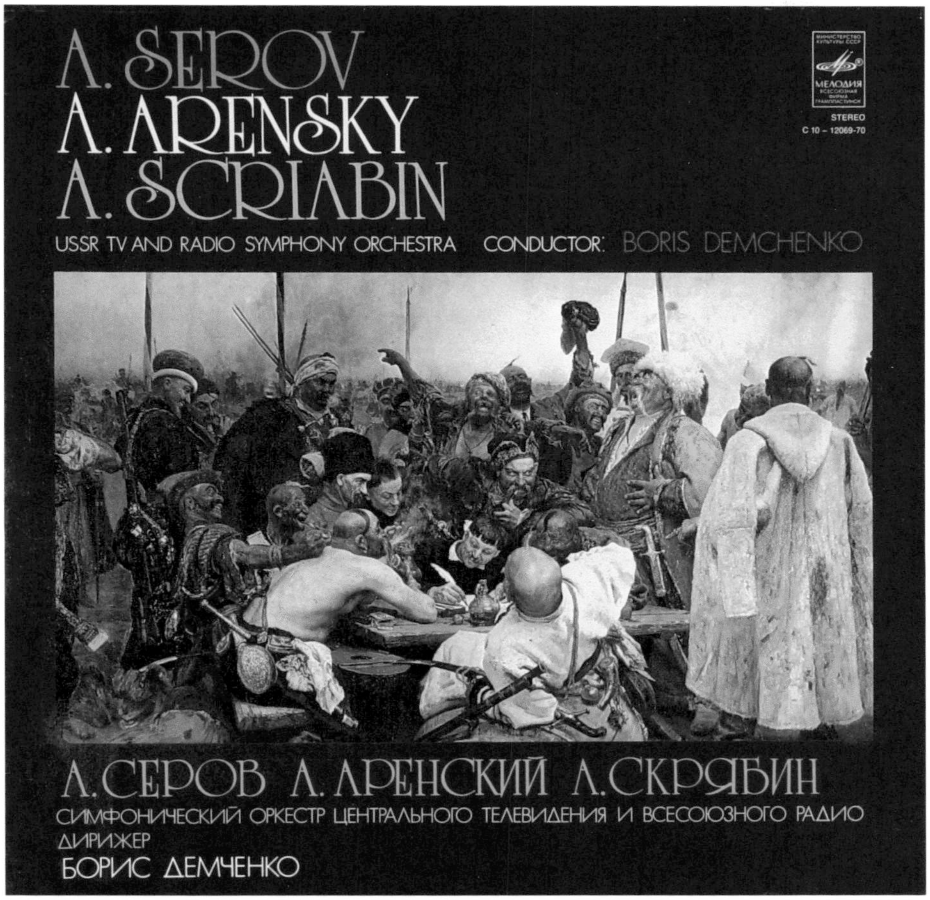

389

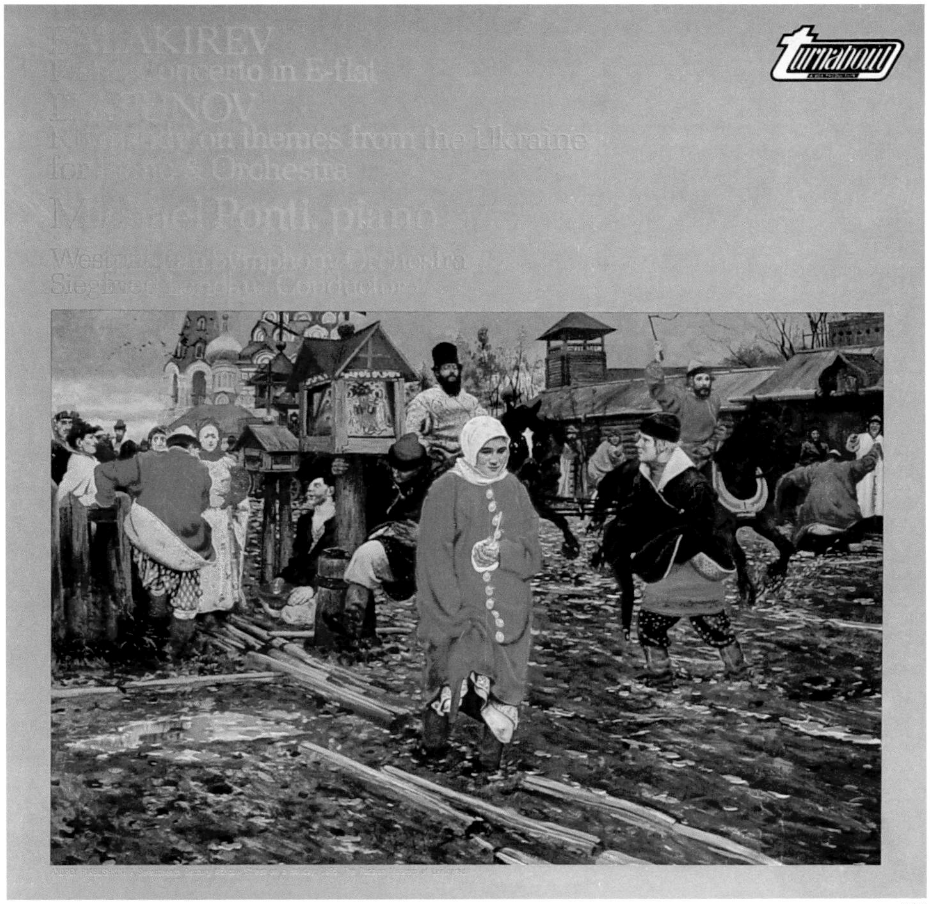

390

391

389 MELODIYA. C12069, SU 1979, CA: Repin *"Zaporozhye Cossacks Reply to the Sultan of Turkey"*
390 TURNABOUT. TV34645, USA 1976, CA: Riabushkin *"Seventeenth Century Moscow Street on a Holiday"* (Russian Museum, Leningrad)
391 EMI. ASD3383, GB 1977, CA: Polenev *"Moscow Courtyard"*

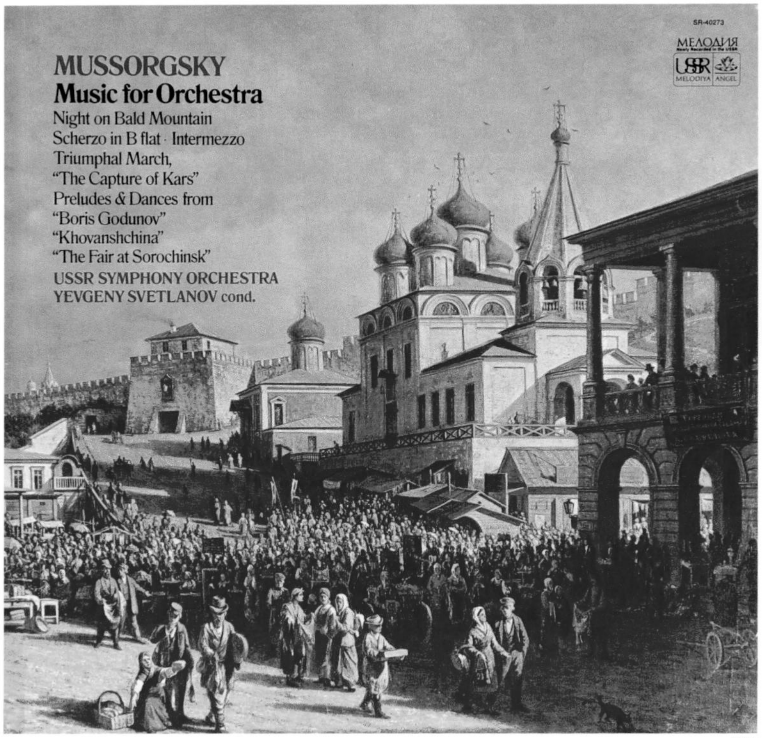

392

Государственный симфонический оркестр Министерства культуры СССР
The USSR Ministry of Culture Orchestra
Геннадий Рождественский
Gennadi Rozhdestvensky
A.TERTERYAN
SYMPHONIES Nos.4 and 5
А.ТЕРТЕРЯН
СИМФОНИИ N. 4 и 5

393

392 ANGEL. SR40273, USA 1975, CD: Marvin Schwartz
393 MELODIYA. C19949, SU 1983, CA: M. Saryan *"Armenia"*
394 RCA. RL30372, GFR 1979, CA: Nesterov *"In the Mountains"* 1896
(Copyright Archiv für Kunst und Geschichte, Berlin)
395 DECCA. SXL6583, GB 1973, CA: Levitan *"Eternal Peace"*, Detail
(Tretyakov Gallery, Moscow; courtesy Novosti Press)
396 DGG. 2530616, GFR 1975, CD: Werner Koberstein; CA: M. Abegyan; Ph: A. Sverdlov

» *[opposite page]*
397 ELECTRECORD. ECE0444, Rum 1971, CD: Ion Mitrici
398 PANTON. 81100352, CS 1984, CD: Vladimír Rocman
399 TURNABOUT. TV34733, USA 1976. CD: The Moss Group
400 ANGEL. S36295, USA 1965

RCA
THE UNKNOWN RUSSIA · UNBEKANNTES RUSSLAND · LA RUSSIE INSOLITE
SERGE
TANEJEW

394

395

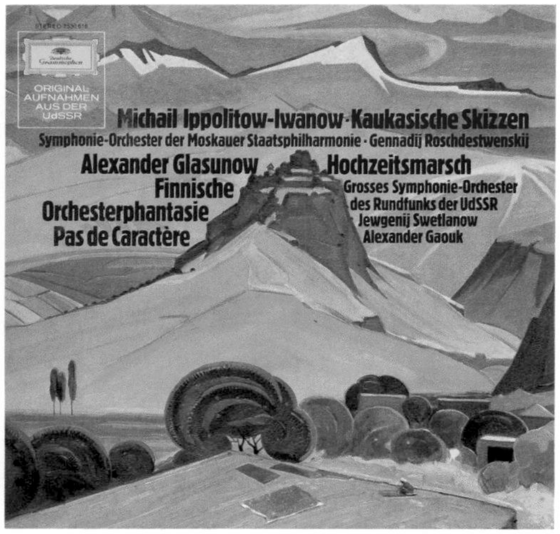

ORIGINAL-AUFNAHMEN AUS DER UdSSR
Michail Ippolitow-Iwanow · Kaukasische Skizzen
Symphonie-Orchester der Moskauer Staatsphilharmonie · Gennadij Roschdestwenskij
Alexander Glasunow
Finnische Orchesterphantasie
Pas de Caractère
Hochzeitsmarsch
Grosses Symphonie-Orchester des Rundfunks der UdSSR
Jewgenij Swetlanow
Alexander Gaouk

396

7.0 Cover Design with Abstract Art (397 – 420)

An abstract work of art on the album cover signalises "modern" or contemporary music to the buyer. The covers shown here have however been selected according to aesthetic aspects. Commentary is superfluous, as is the search for a reference to musical content. The finished work of art was not always created specifically for the cover. Among the covers selected are those from modern painters who can also be found in a gallery.

— Cover 404 is an example of a design for "Modern Music series" from Philips.

— Covers of records with popular classical music are not usually designed with abstract images, such as the one in picture 406. Maybe the subject is bon bons, as the title suggests.

— Supraphon has illustrated their series "Musica Nova Bohemica" with interesting abstract covers (409, 410).

— The covers from RCA and Capitol (413, 418), with their scant brush-strokes, are evidence of the humble efforts made by the major record producers in the late 1950s to indicate to the buyer that the music was "modern".

— Cover 414 initially appears to be "abstract" art. At the same time, it creates a tie to the Jewish tradition, thus establishing a reference to the music on the record. This work of art, produced with a collage of book spines from old Jewish books, Hebrew book pages and Jewish ornaments, make this cover one of the most classy in my entire collection.

— Cover 419, from Varese-Sarabande, is illustrated with a painting from the composer Ernst Krenek.

397

398

399

400

397 ELECTRECORD. ECE0444, Rum 1971, CD: Ion Mitrici
398 PANTON. 81100352, CS 1984, CD: Vladimír Rocman
399 TURNABOUT. TV34733, USA 1976. CD: The Moss Group
400 ANGEL. S36295, USA 1965

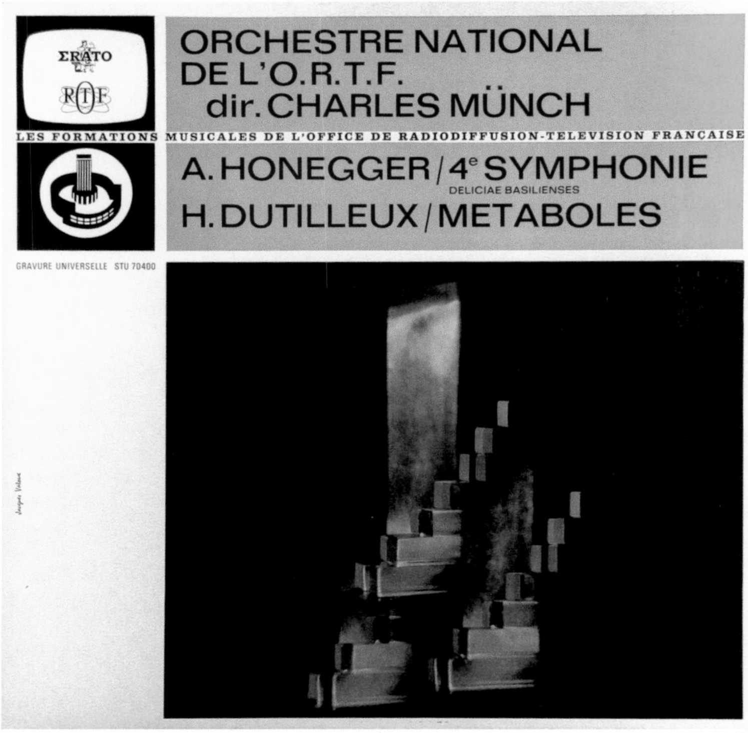

401

402

403

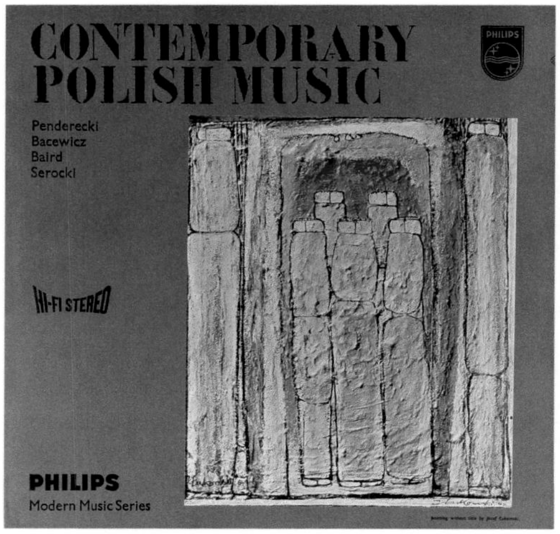

404

405

406

401 ERATO. STU70400, F, CA: Jacques Vatoux
402 ERATO. STU70451, F, CA: Jacques Vatoux
403 ERATO. STU70430, F, CD: Merri
404 PHILIPS. 835261AY, EU ca 1965, CA: Jozef Lukomski
405 BALKANTON. 344, Bulg
406 DECCA. SDD150, GB 1966

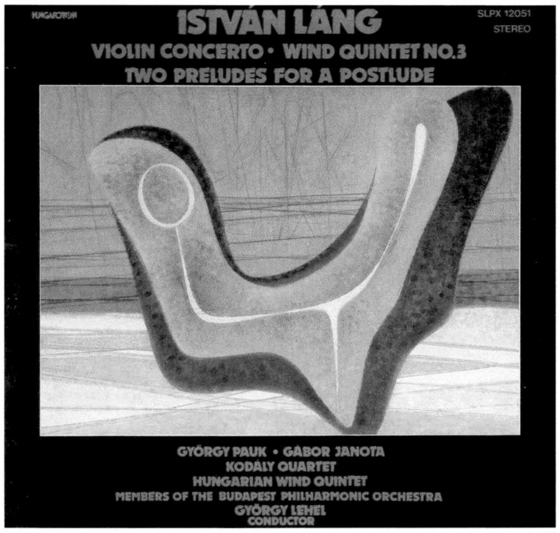

407

410

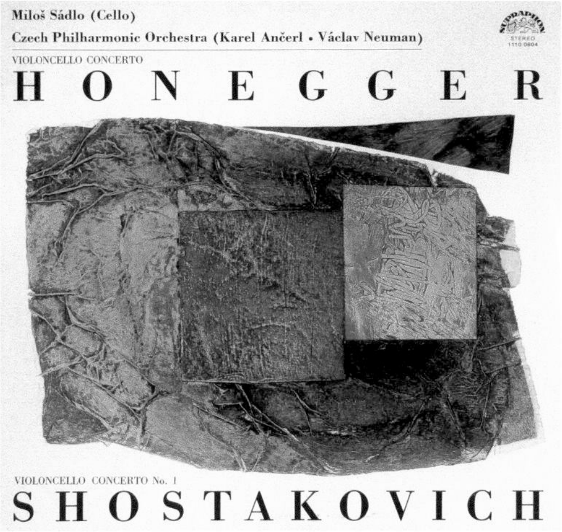

411

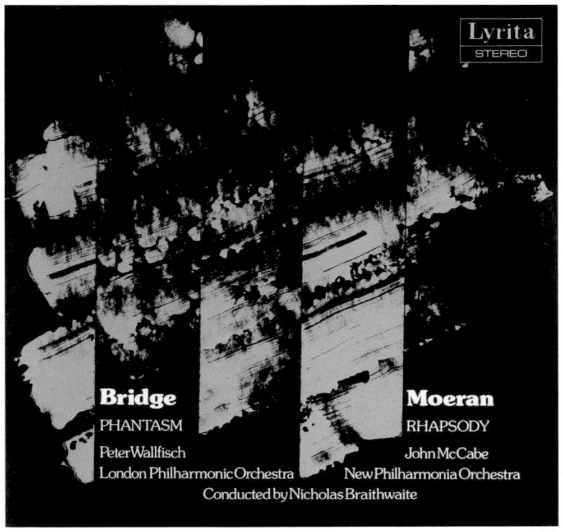

408

409

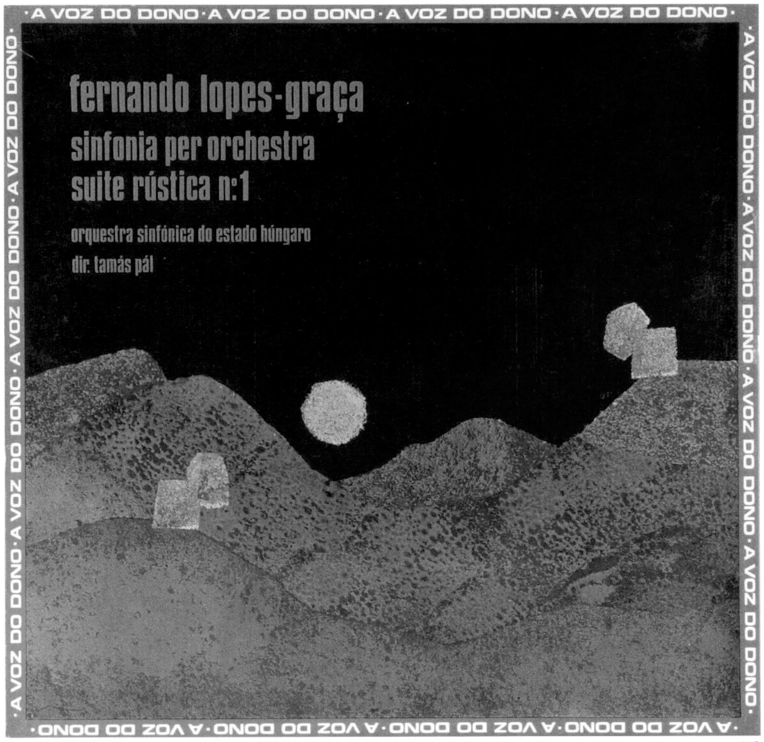

412

407 HUNGAROTON. SLPX12051, Hu 1979, CA: Csontvary *"Blue Swamp"*
408 LYRITA. SRCS091, GB 1977, CD: Keith Hensby
409 SUPRAPHON. 11113377,CS 1986, CA: Vladimir Kintera
410 SUPRAPHON. 1101959, CS 1977, CA: Jan Hamrik
411 SUPRAPHON. 11100604, CS 1969, CA: Miloslav Žácek
412 EMI. E063-40344, Port 1974, CD: Helder Pereira

413

414

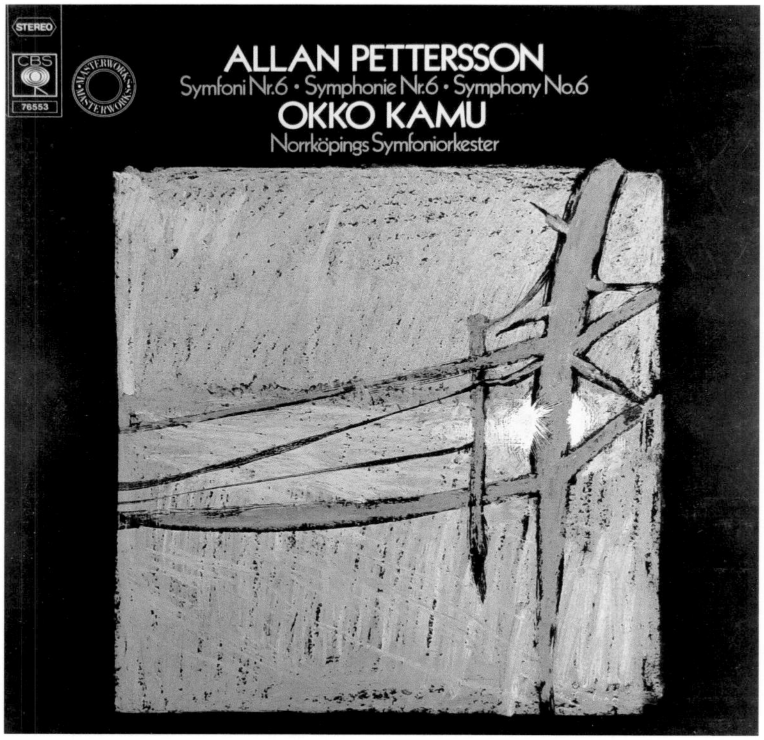

415

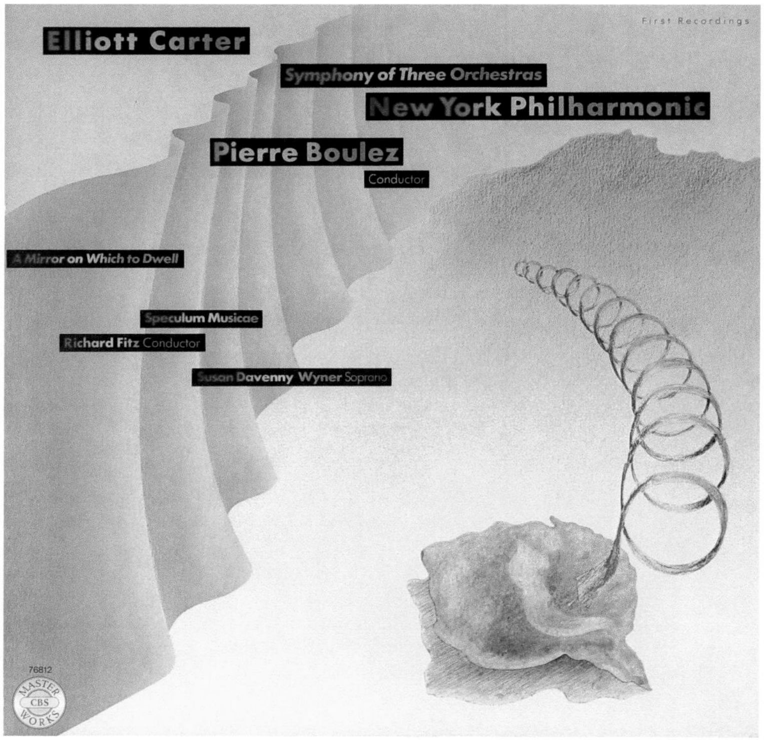

416

413 RCA. LSC1934, USA 1958
414 JERUSALEM. ATD8305, Isr 1984, CD: Michael Horton; CA: Yitzak Greenfield from the *"Jerusalem"* series
415 CBS. 76553, EU 1976, CA: Martin Lamm
416 CBS. 76812, EU 1980, CA: Virginia Team

417

418

419

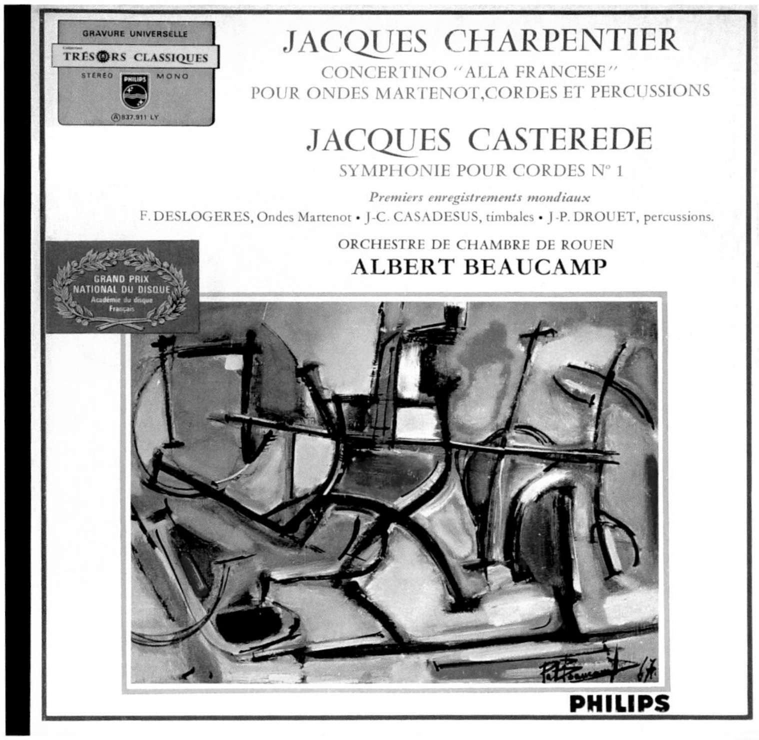

420

417 MERCURY. 130581MLY, F ca 1965, CA: Paul Coupille
418 SUPRAPHON. SUAST50950, CS 1968, CA: Stanislav Vajce
419 VARESE. VR81200, USA 1979, CA: Ernst Krenek *"Abstraction 5"*; Ph: Toni Dolinski
420 PHILIPS. 837911LY, F ca 1970, CA: Patrice Beaucomp *"Instruments de Musique"*

8.0 Composers

Composers are put on the cover particularly when they are less popular or when the record is a complete edition of a genre by the composer. Many of the composers portrayed here are painted. Only the most emphatic photographs have been selected for presentation. As always, the selection has been compiled according to the rule that the covers must be expressive and an artistic accomplishment. Due to my special interest in English, Russian-Soviet and American composers, these nationalities have been accounted for separately.

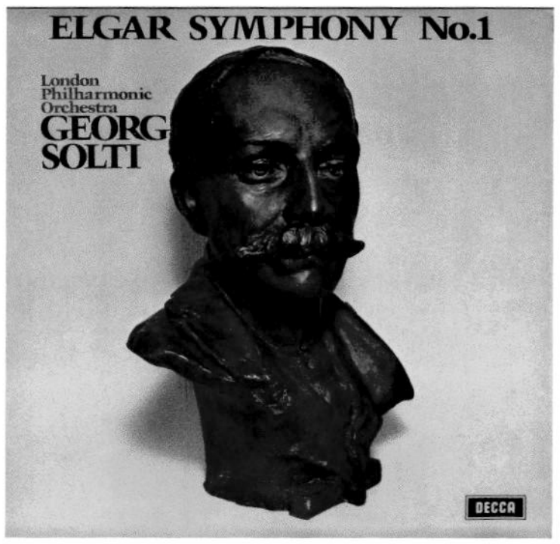

421

8.1 English Composers (421 - 430)

England's contribution to European music of the 20th Century is insufficiently valued in continental Europe. The English composers thereby perpetuated a development that had ended in Central Europe with Hartmann, Hindemith, Honegger or Korngold. Neo-Romanticism and Neo-Classicism were further developed in the works of Sir Arnold Bax, William Alwyn, Edmund Rubbra, Sir Lennox Berkeley and Michael Tippett. There are still many others who are worthy of mention.

— Of all the English composers, I hold Ralph Vaughan Williams in the highest esteem (428).

— I am especially fond of picture 429. Who wouldn't have wanted this friendly old gentleman to be their grandfather?

— On cover 430, the photographer has created a successful aesthetic synthesis of old and modern, set in the studio of composer Michael Tippett.

421 DECCA. SXL6569, GB 1972, CA: Wax model of Elgar by Percival Hedley; Ph: John Thomson
422 LYRITA. SRCS094, GB 1978, CD: Keith Hensby; CA: Derek Hill (by kind permission of the artist and the owner)
423 LYRITA. SRCS128, GB 1982. CD: Keith Hensby; CA: Millicent Woodfore (courtesy of National Portrait Gallery, London)
424 DECCA. SXL6006, GB 1962. CA: from an original photography by M. Stern

422

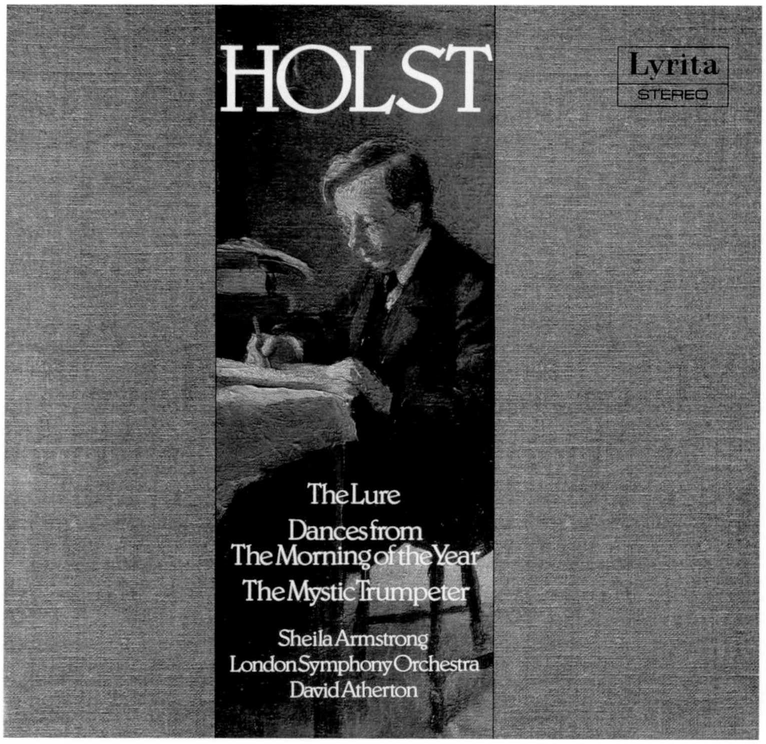

423

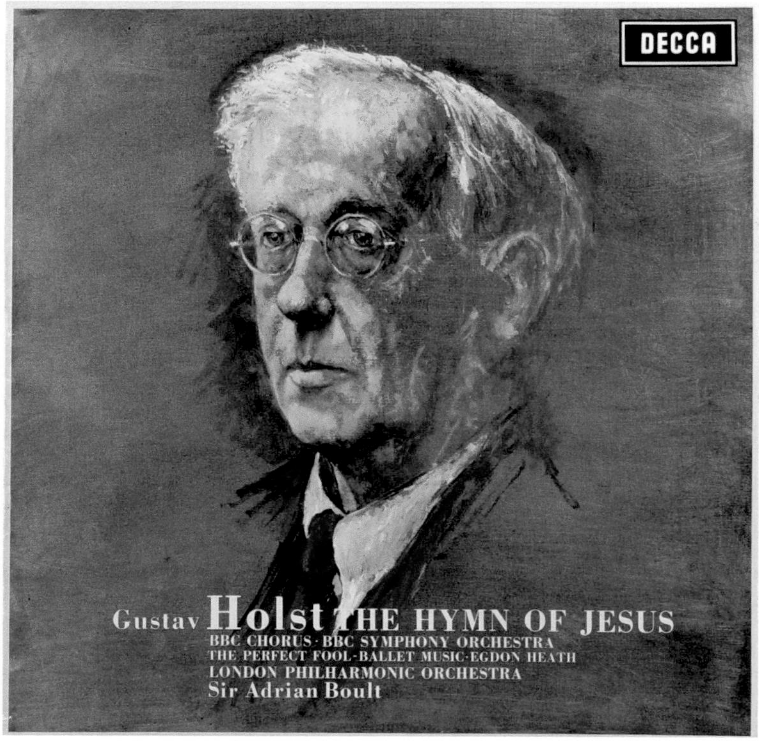

424

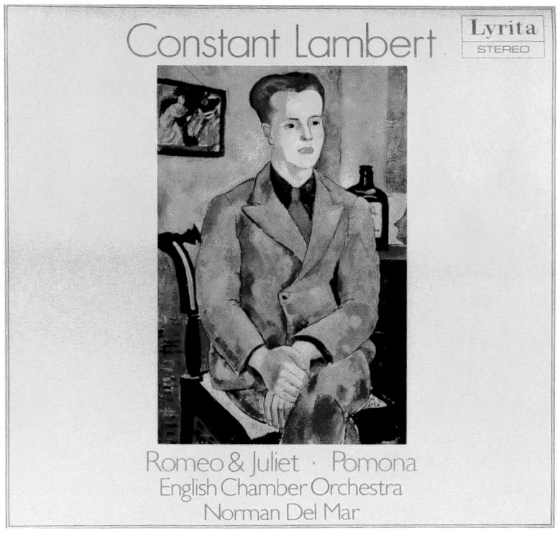

425

425 LYRITA. SRCS110, GB 1979, CA: Christopher Wood
(reproduced by kind permission of the National Portrait Gallery, London)
426 EMI. ESD7057, GB 1978
427 SERAPHIM. S60147, USA before 1976
428 EMI. ASD2847, GB 1970, CA: Sir Gerald Kelly
(by courtesy of the Principal of the Royal College of Music)
429 RCA. RL25027, GB 1977. Ph: Roy Round
430 ARGO. ZRG535, GB 1968, Ph: Axel Poignant

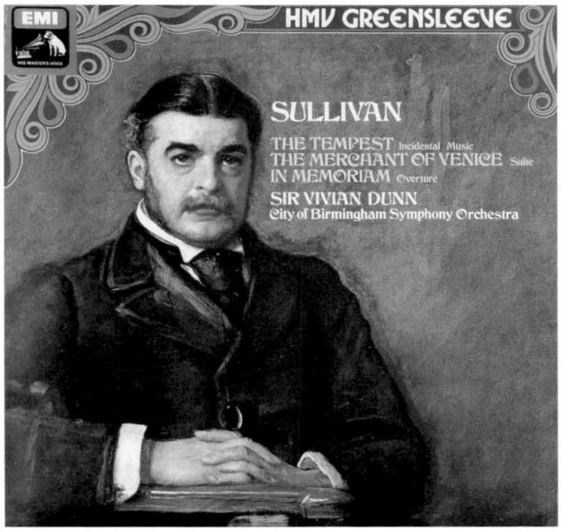

426

427

428

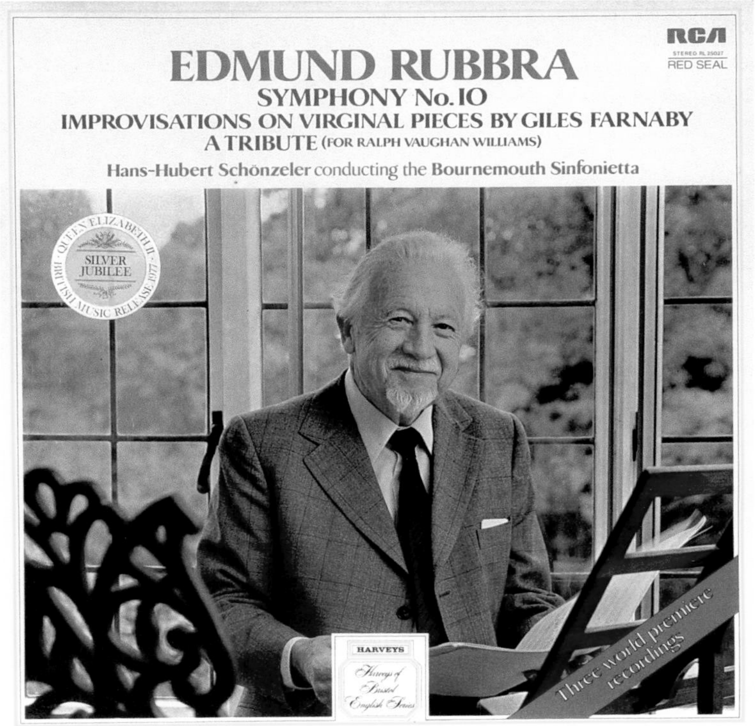

429

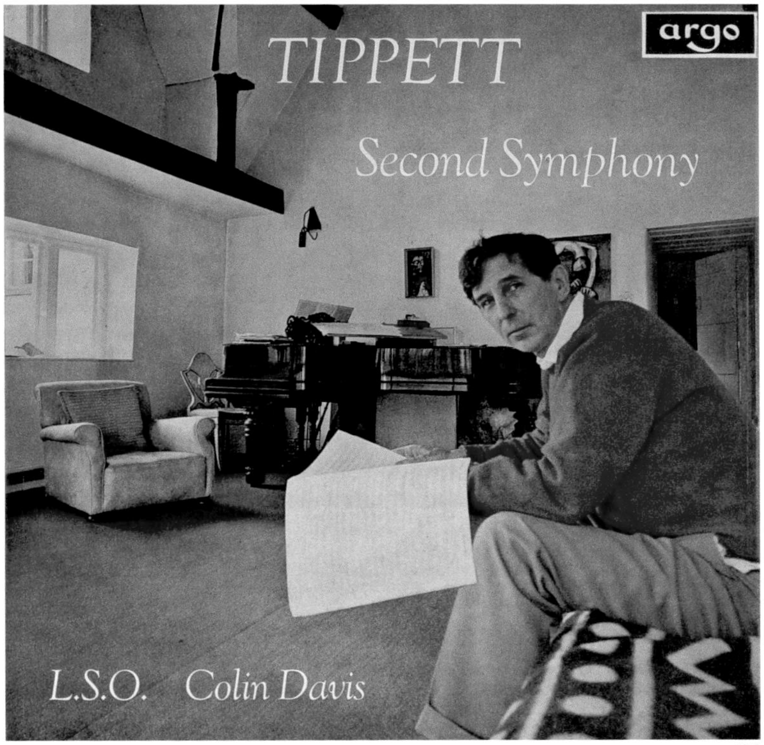

430

8.2 Russian and Soviet Composers (431 - 446)

431

With the exception of Glinka and Rachmaninov, all of the composers presented here are "Soviet" composers – as proclaimed by the Ministry of Culture. Among them, there were some who suffered severely under the restrictions of the Composers' Association of the USSR, such as Dimitri Shostakovitch (434, 437, 441). Others secured their patronage with "favourable" works, such as the multiple honour recipient Vyacheslav Ovchinnikov, with his ballad of the workers on the Baikal-Amur main railway line (436). But he also composed a marvellous *Ave Maria.* It is unusual to see a Soviet composer in such a pompous pose. The picture is painted. The composers from the Soviet Union offer a colourful oeuvre, in part with elements of folk music, which is not surprising, given the variety of races belonging to the former Soviet Union.

— Picture 432: Fikret Amirov from Azerbaijan.
— Picture 433: Aleksey Machavariani from Georgia. Note the Georgian script in the upper part and the Cyrillic script below.
— Picture 435: Andrey Eshpay from The Republic of Mari.
— Pictures 438 and 442: Aram Khatchaturian from Georgia.
— Picture 439: Kara Karayev from Azerbaijan.

432

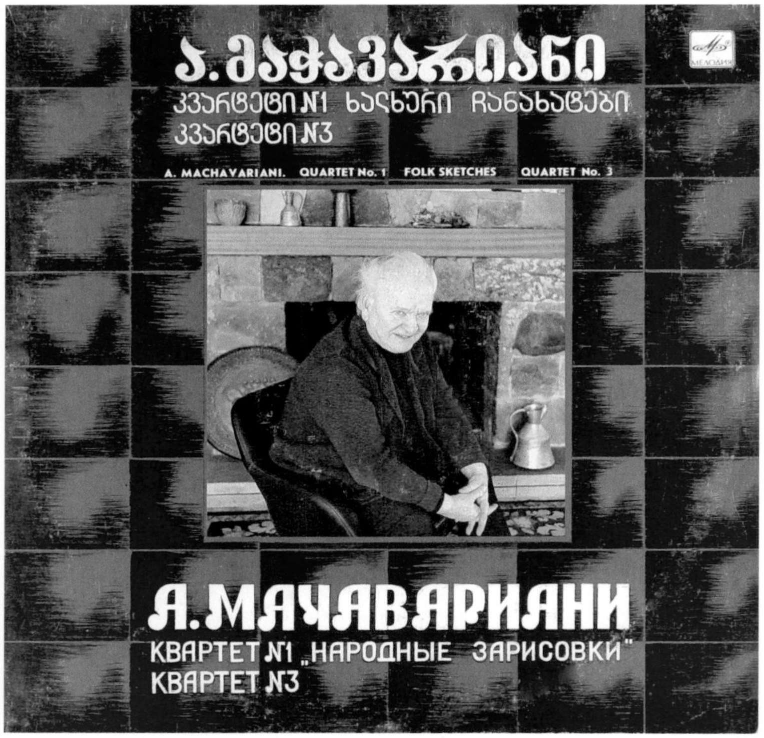

433

434

435

436

SHOSTAKOVITCH
BALLET SUITES, 1, 2 and 3
Overture on Russian and Kirghiz Songs
Bolshoi Theatre Orchestra
MAXIM
SHOSTAKOVITCH
МЕЛОДИЯ
USSR
MELODIYA

437

438

439

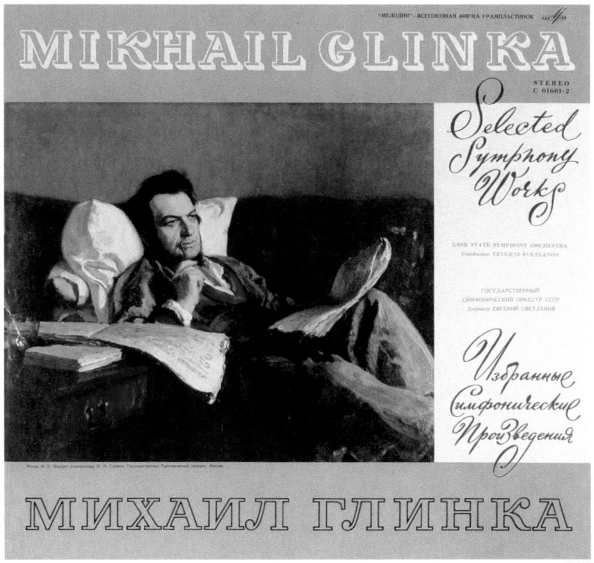

440

441

442

431 MELODIYA. C08031, SU
432 MELODIYA. C08711, SU
433 MELODIYA. C28859, SU 1989
434 EMI. ASD2917, GB 1973, Ph: Reg Wilson
435 MELODIYA. C16731, SU 1983
436 MELODIYA. C25599, SU 1987, CA: A. Shilov

« (opposite page)

437 EMI. ASD2781, GB 1972, CA: Frank Page
438 MELODIYA. C06957, SU 1980
439 MELODIYA. C01701, SU 1969
440 MELODIYA. C01681, SU 1968. CA: Repin (Tretyakov Gallery, Moscow)
441 MELODIYA. C01693, SU 1986. CA: D. Borovsky
442 MELODIYA. C11983, SU 1984. CA: M. Saryan

443

444

445

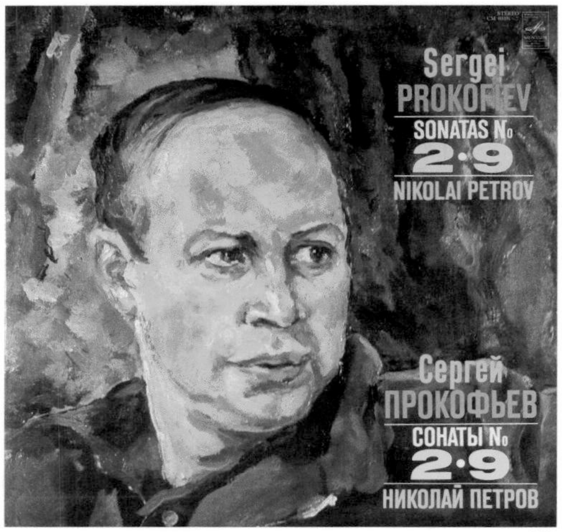

446

443 EMI .ASD4005, GB 1981. CD: Pando
444 EMI. C063-02861, GFR 1977, CD: Oden (Design as original ASD3369)
445 EMI. ASD3556, GB 1978, CA: G. Glodowska
446 MELODIYA. C03491, SU c. 1980

8.3 European Composers (447 - 458)

— Cover 447 shows a self-portrait of the composer Arnold Schönberg.
— The cover of the Vanguard record album portrays Johannes Brahms (455). In its striking simplicity, it is one of the most artistically interesting.

8.4 Composers from the "New World" (459 - 462)

— Charles Ives wrote several "patriotic" works. The album cover presented here houses one of them (460).
— Carlos Chavez is the most popular Mexican composer (462).

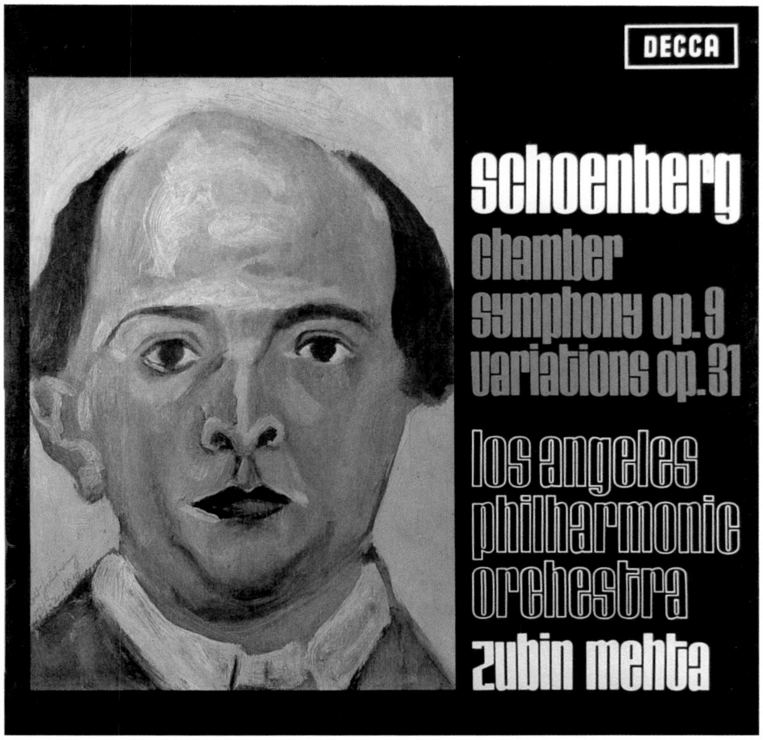

447

448

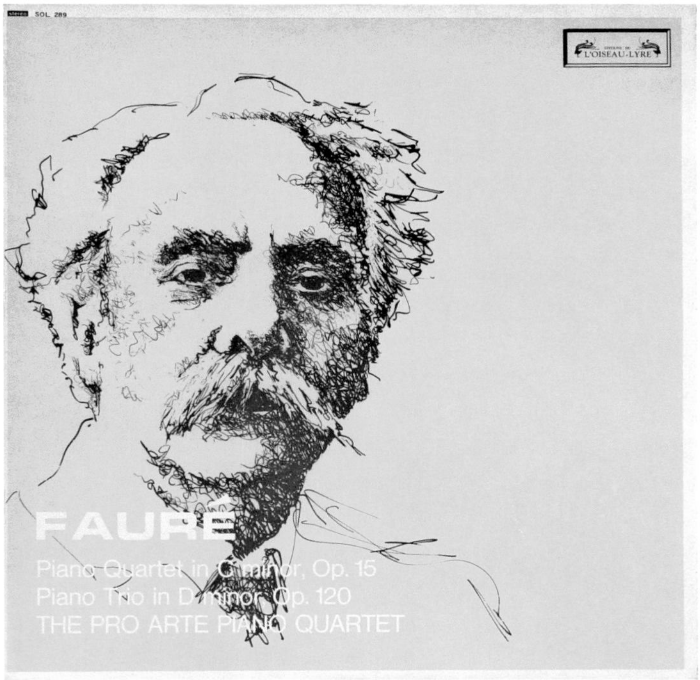

449

450

451

447 DECCA. SXL6390, GB 1969, CA: Schoenberg (Self-portrait of the composer, courtesy Lawrence Schoenberg)
448 DECCA. SXL6544, GB 1972, CA: "Franz Schmidt als Cellist", Detail (Historisches Museum der Stadt Wien)
449 OISEAU-LYRE. SOL289, GB 1966, CD: DPAD
450 DECCA. SXLM6665, GB 1974, CA: Caesar Kunold
451 EMI. SXLP30420, GB 1980

452

453

454

455

456

457

458

459

460

461

462

452 EMI. C063-12563, GFR 1971, Drawing by P. Renossard
453 DECCA. SXL6167, GB 1965
454 DECCA. SXL6395, GB 1969, Ph: Roger-Viollet, Paris (the Photo shows Magnard)
455 VANGUARD. SRV221SD, USA 1967
456 CBS. 61130, GB 1976, CD: Ed Lee/Andy Engel; CA: Philip Hays
457 DGG. 2531135, GFR 1979, CA: Anne Marie Telmányi, daughter of Carl Nielsen (National Historical Museum Frederiksborg)
« (opposite page)

458 ANGEL. S35548, USA 1962, Ph: Mercure Ed. Paris
459 COLUMBIA. MS6168, USA 1960, CA: Edward Casper; Ph: Robert Cato
460 RCA. SB6687, GB 1966
461 COLUMBIA. MG32793, USA 1974, CA: Roger Hane
462 RCA. ARL1-3341, USA 1979, CA: Wendell Minor

9.0 The Diversity of Themes

463

464

465

467

9.1 Magnificent Operas (463 - 478)

No other genre is better suited for embellishment with the most magnificent covers than the opera. Here, the reference of the picture to the work is never in doubt.

9.2 Immortal Ballet (479 - 496)

9.3 Knights and Folk Heroes (497 - 503)

Two famous folk heroes should be mentioned in particular: Ilya Murometz from Ukraine (497, 498) and Alexander Nevsky, after whom the main thoroughfare in St. Petersburg, Nevsky Prospect, has been named (499, 500).

466

463 MELODIYA. C06847, SU c. 1980
464 SUPRAPHON. SUAST50440, CS 1963, CA: Ludmilla Jirincová
465 ANGEL. S3639C/L, USA 1963, CA: Moroni
466 DECCA. SET609, GB 1976
467 DECCA. SET399, GB 1969

468

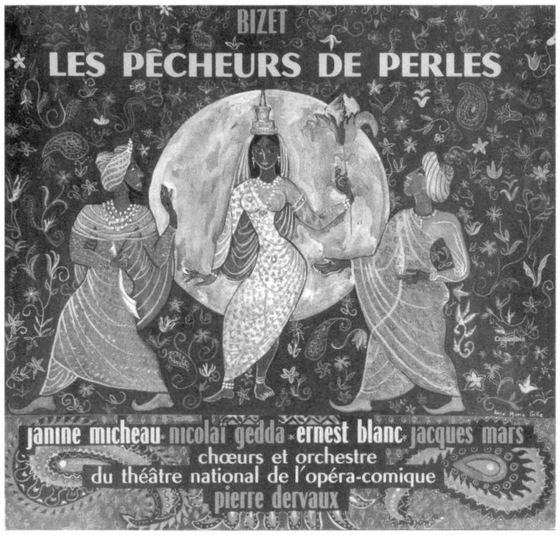

469

470

468 EMI. ASDF876, F
469 EMI. C165-12082, F 1974, CD: Anne-Marie Gille
470 DGG. 2720079, GFR 1964, CD: Horst Breitkreuz

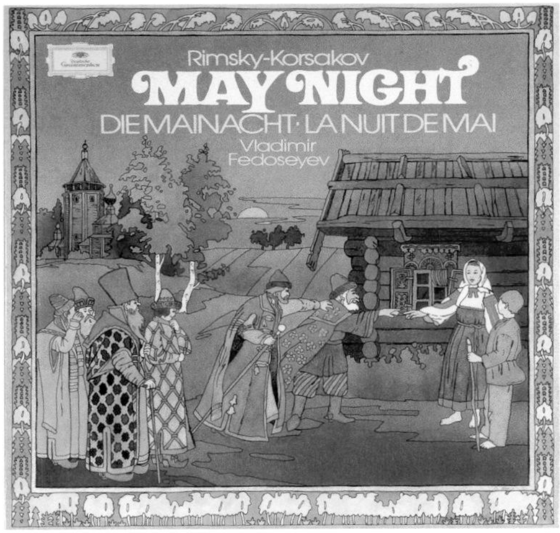

471

472

473

471 DGG. 2709063, GFR 1976, CD: Gerd Haase
472 EMI. SLS962, GB 1972
473 EMI. SLS852, GB 1973

474

475

476

474 DECCA. SKL4708-9, GB 1965
475 MELODIYA. D02252, SU
476 MELODIYA. C00377, SU 1985, CA: N. Parilov

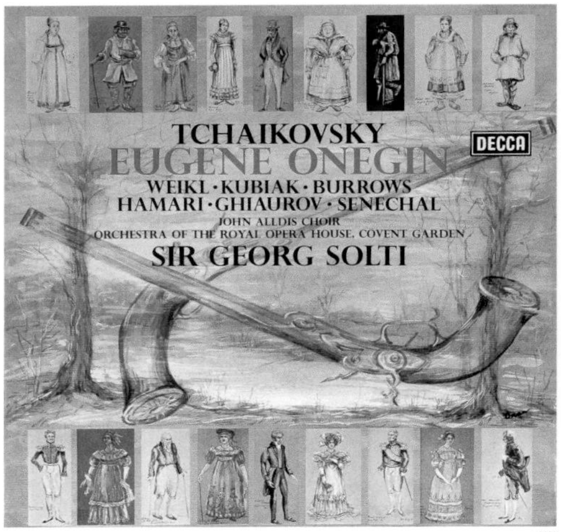

477

478

477 DECCA. SET596, GB 1975, CA: Joman
478 MELODIYA. C29809, SU 1990, CD: V. Baikov
479 CBS. 77247, D c. 1975
480 ANGEL. S35529, USA 1958

» (opposite page)
481 ANGEL. S35588, USA 1959
482 ANGEL. SR40103, USA 1970
483 EMI. CSD1286, GB 1959, Ph: Houston Rogers
484 CAPITOL. SG7245, USA 1961, CD: Boyle
485 CAPITOL. SG7188, USA 1958, CD: Boyle

479

480

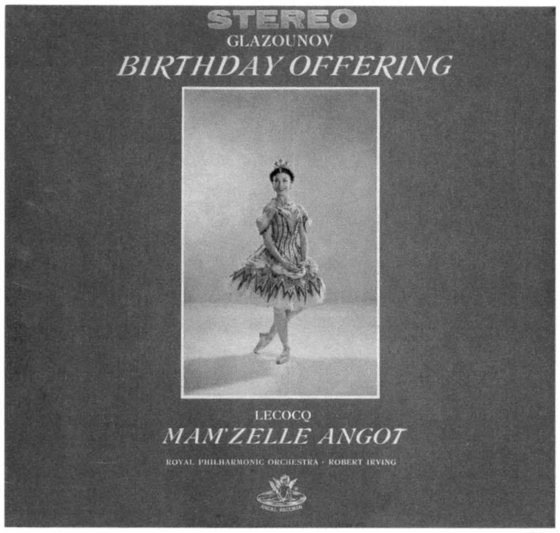

481

482

483

484

485

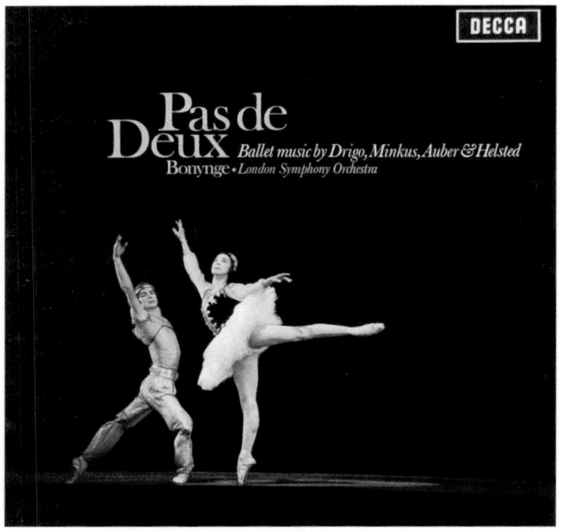

486

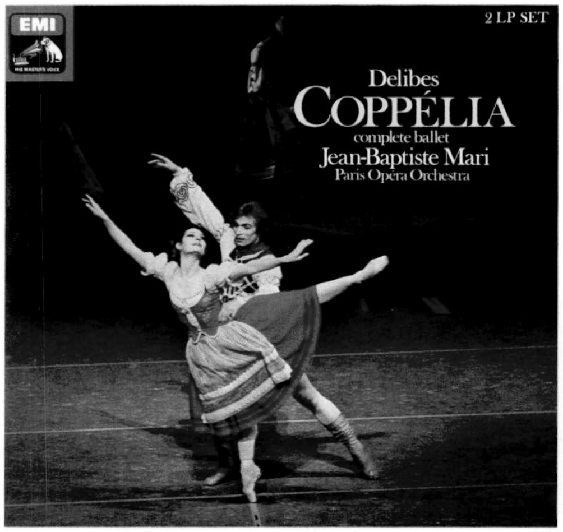

487

489

488

490

486 DECCA. SXL6137, GB 1964, Ph: Reg Wilson (Margot Fonteyn and Rudolf Nureyev)
487 EMI. SLS5091, GB 1977, Ph: MIRA (Veronica Tennant and Rudolf Nureyev)
488 MELODIYA. C17683, SU 1982, CD: V. Dudakov (Ballet The Sea Gull, based on Tchechov)
489 EMI-COLUMBIA. SAX2285, GB 1959, Ph: Houston Rogers (Beryl Grey as Odette)
490 LONDON. CSA2232, USA 1972, CD: Alan Davis; Ph: Opera News (Anna Pavlova)

491

492

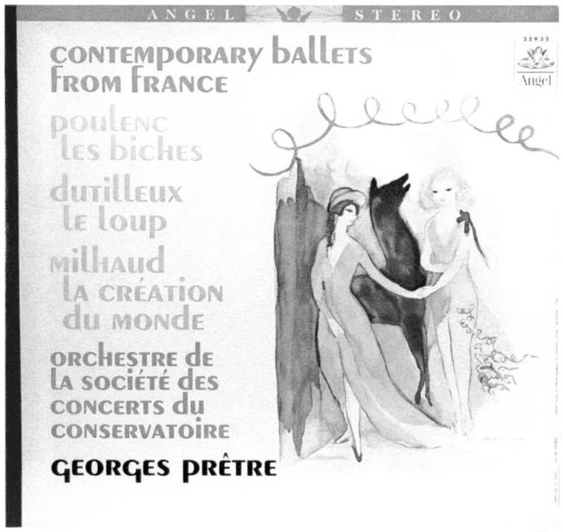

493

494

495

496

491 DESTO. DC6432, USA c. 1970
492 DECCA. SXL6188, GB 1965,
CA: Illustration by kind permission of The Harvard Theatre Collection, Cambridge, Mass.
493 ANGEL. S35932, USA 1962, CA: Maurine Laurencin for the ballett Les Biches
(Mercure Ed. Paris, Atelier Joubert) [Design as EMI ASD496]
494 EMI. SHZE362, GFR 1972, CA: Dick Elescas
495 EMI. ASD0371, GB 1960, Ph: Houston Rogers
496 EMI. ASD2448, GB 1968, The photo shows Maya Plisetskaya as Carmen in the ballet by Alberto Alonso

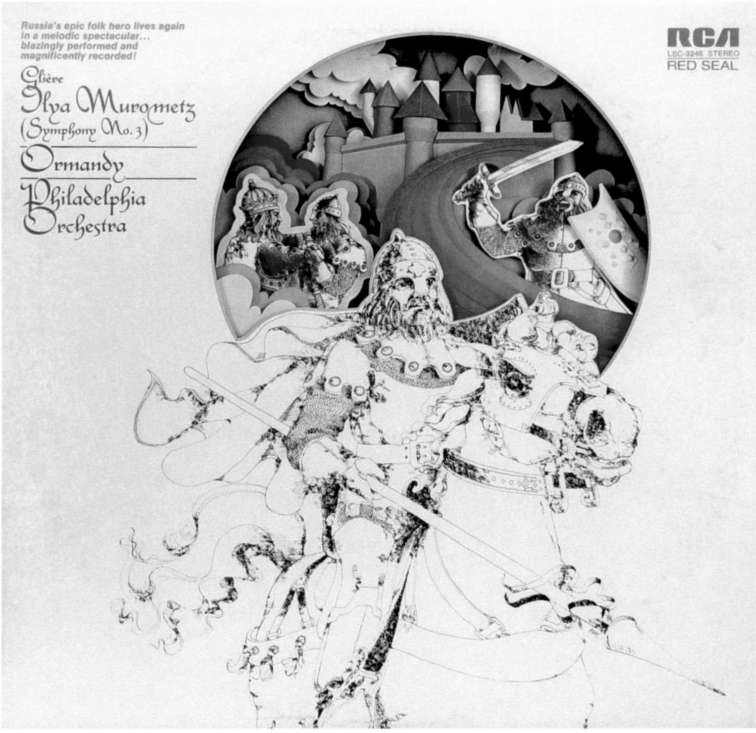

497

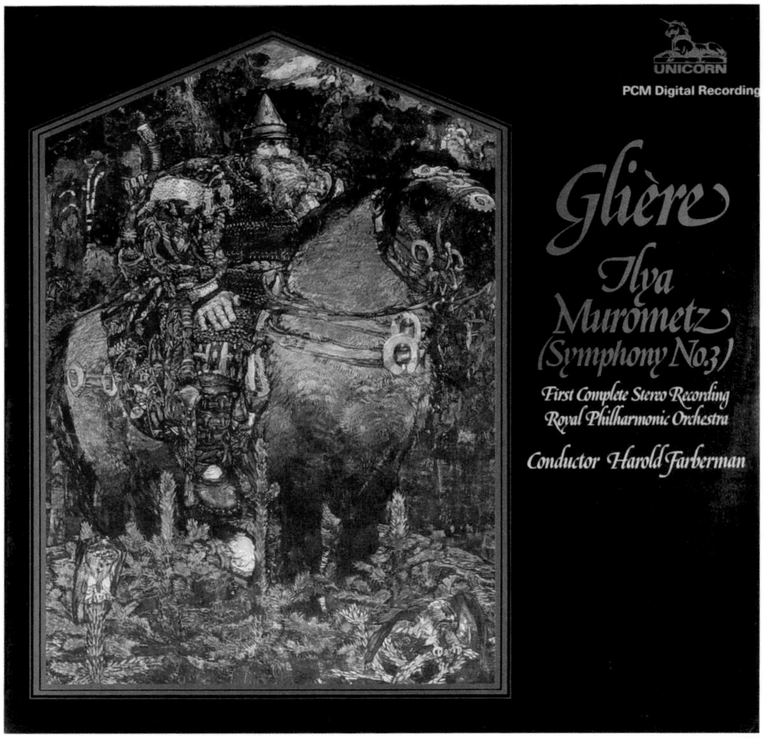

498

499

500

501

497 RCA. LSC3246, USA 1972, CA: Oni
498 UNICORN. PCM500, GB 1978, CD: Leslie Marshall & Eric Tranter; CA: Mikhail Vrubel *"Bogatyr"* 1898 (Russian Museum, Leningrad)
499 RCA. VICS1652, GB 1972, CA: Ley, Dover & Associates
500 CHANDOS. ABRD1275, GB 1987, CD: Jane Embley; CA: Nick Theato
501 MUZA. SXL0968, PL, CD: K. Kartowska-Gruszecka

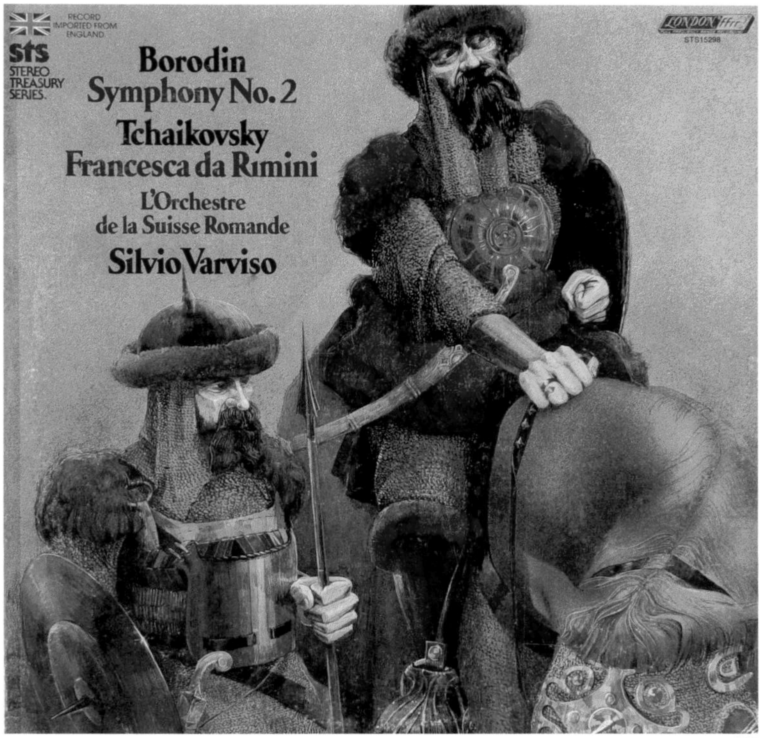

502

9.4 Proud America (504 - 511)

Covers 506, 507, 510 and 511 are on record albums with patriotic works by American composers.

9.5 American Idyll (512 - 520)

It goes without saying that only composers from the USA have been placed in this category.

9.6 English Countryside (521 - 536)

The music on all of the records in this category comes from England or Wales.

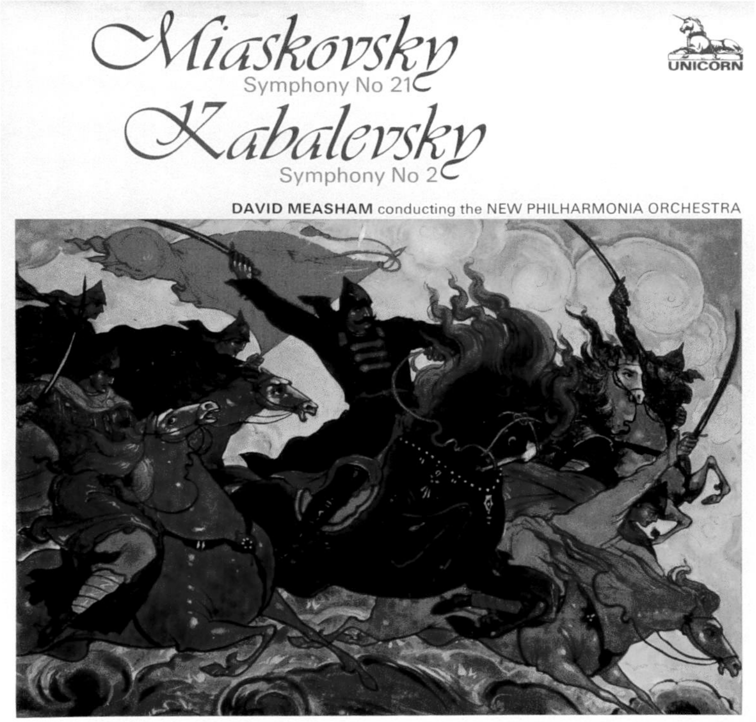

503

502 LONDON. STS15298, USA 1976
503 UNICORN. RHS346, GB 1973, CA: K.S. Semaikin *"Red Cavalrymen"* (reproduced by kind permission of Novosti Press Agency, London)
504 COLUMBIA. M32792, USA 1974, CD: John Berg
505 LONDON. CS6943, USA 1975
506 ANGEL. S37315, USA 1978, CD: Jim Endicott

504

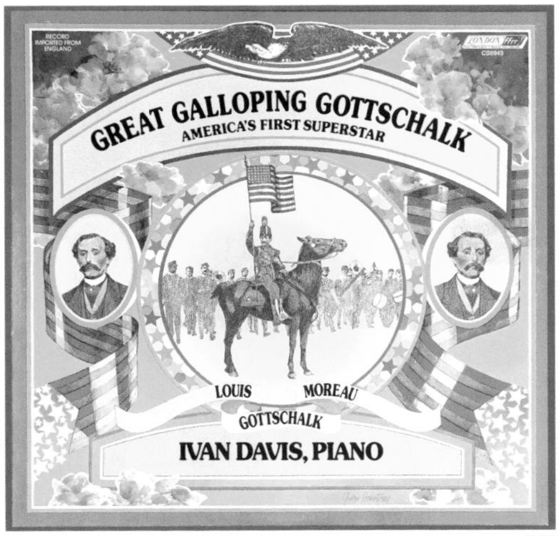

505

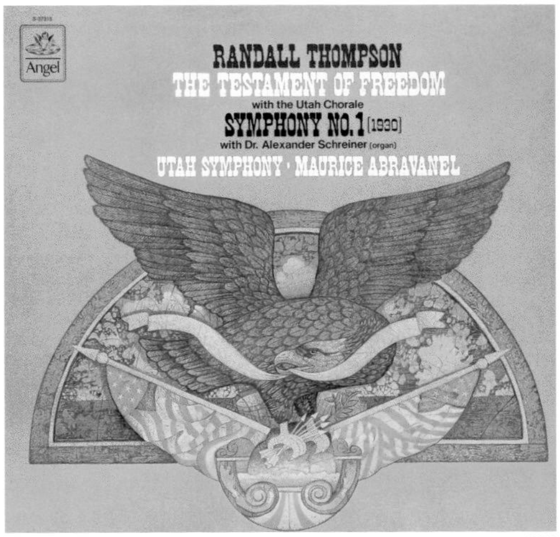

506

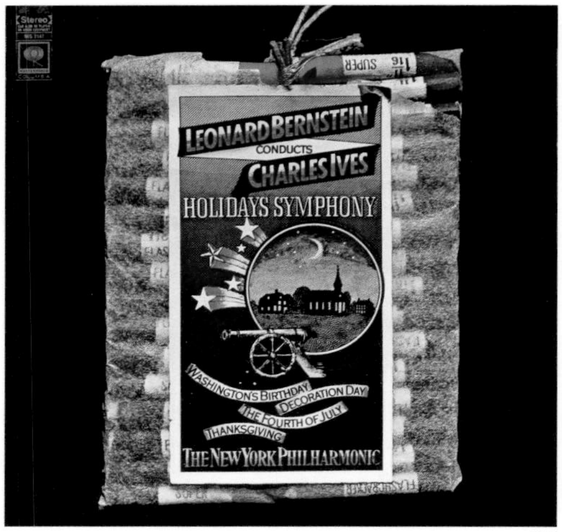

507

508

509

510

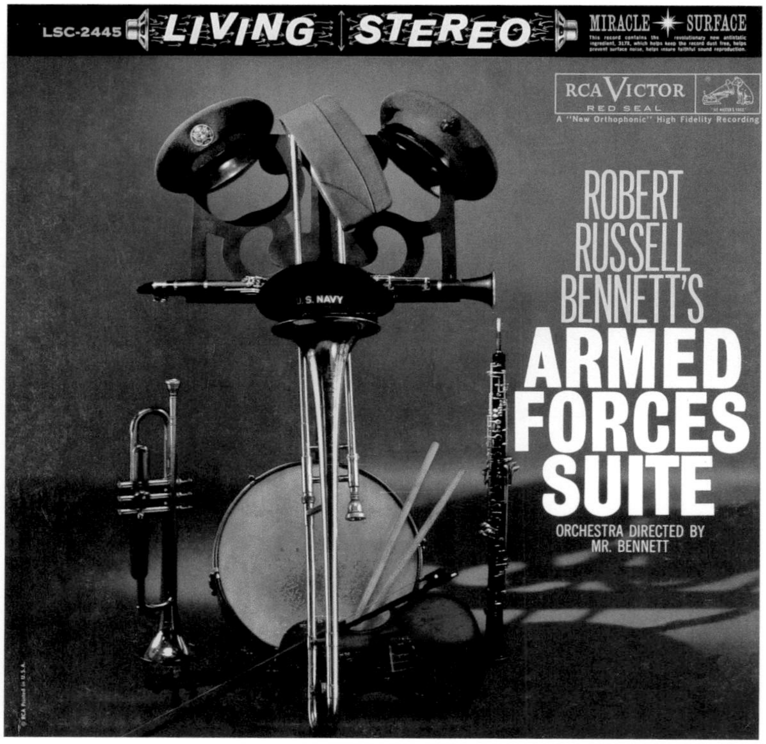

511

512

507 COLUMBIA. MS7147, USA 1968, CD: Bob Cato; CA: John Crocker
508 RCA. SB6719, GB 1967
509 ANGEL. S36091, USA 1975, CA: Mizuo Hamilton
510 CAPITOL. SP8523, USA 1960
511 RCA. LSC2445, USA 1960

« [opposite page]

512 MERCURY. SR175020, EU
513 COLUMBIA. MQ32736, USA 1974, CD: Ed Lee; CA: Robert Giusti
514 EVEREST. SDBR 3002, USA 1958
515 TURNABOUT. TV34459, USA 1972, CA: Herbert Norton Rogoff

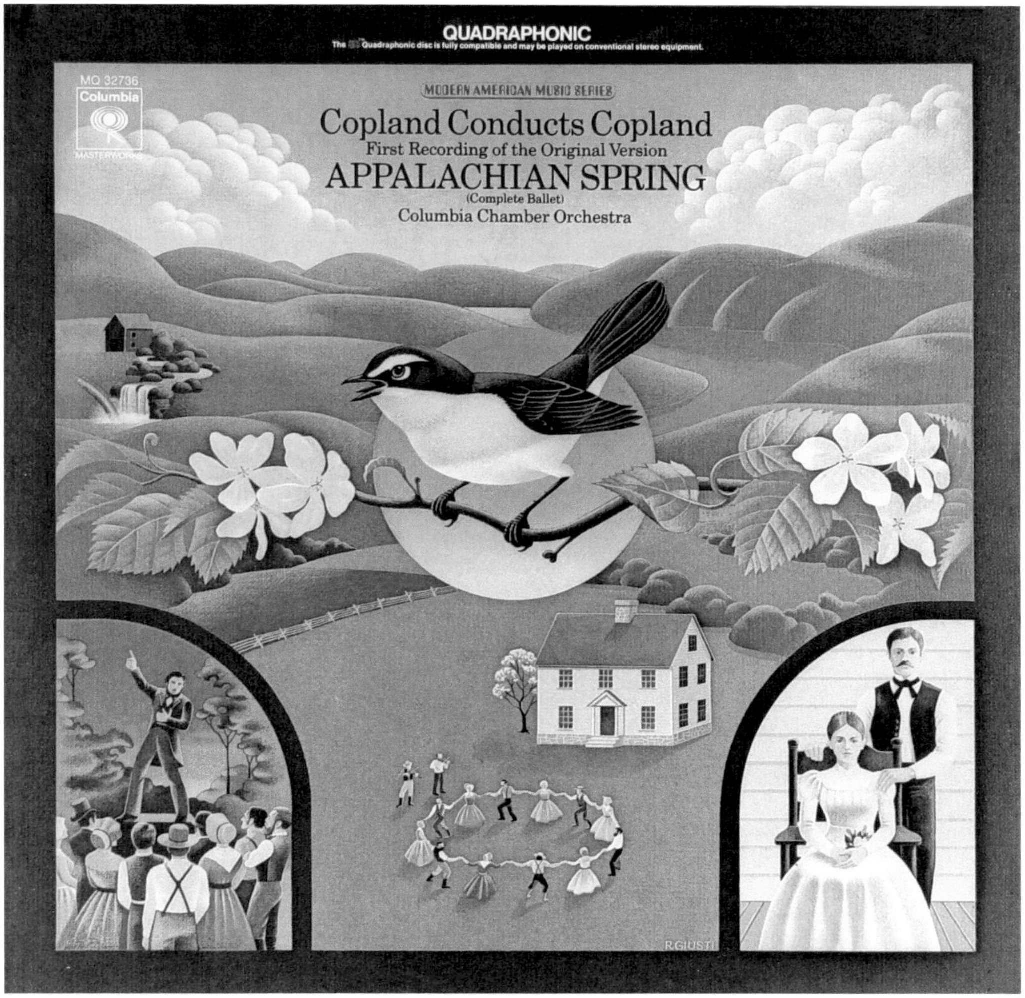

513

514

515

516

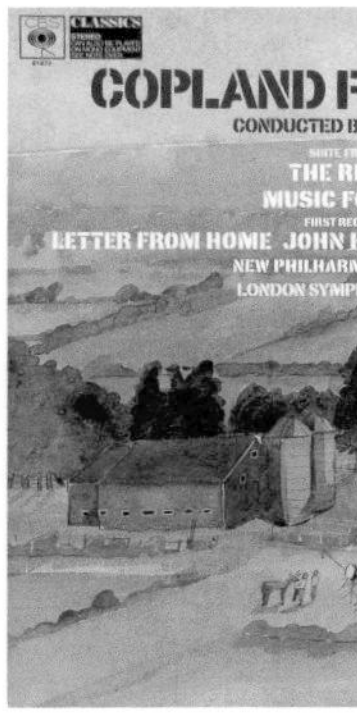

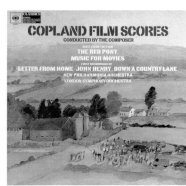

517

516 CBS. 61728, GB 1969, CD: Tony Lane; CA: Grant Wood *"Stone City"* (Joslin Art Museum, Omaha, Nebraska)
517 CBS. 61672, GB 1975, CD: John Berg; CA: Robert A. Parker
518 CBS. 77406, D c. 1975
519 EMI. ASD3294, GB 1976, CA: John Steuart Curry *"The Homestead"* (courtesy U.S. Department of the Interior)
520 DGG. 2535339, GB 1970. Ph: Three Lions, N.Y.

518

519

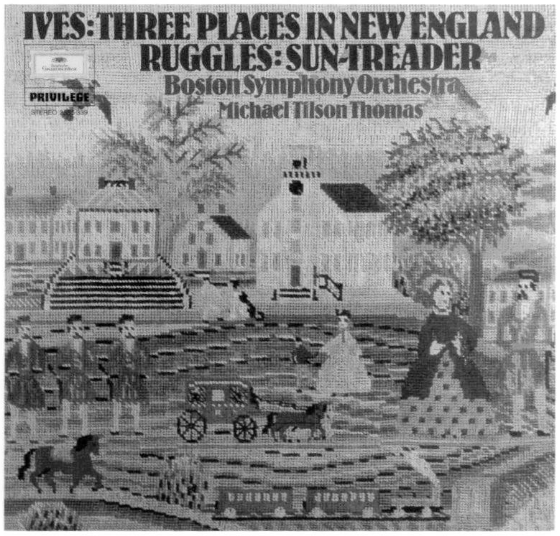

520

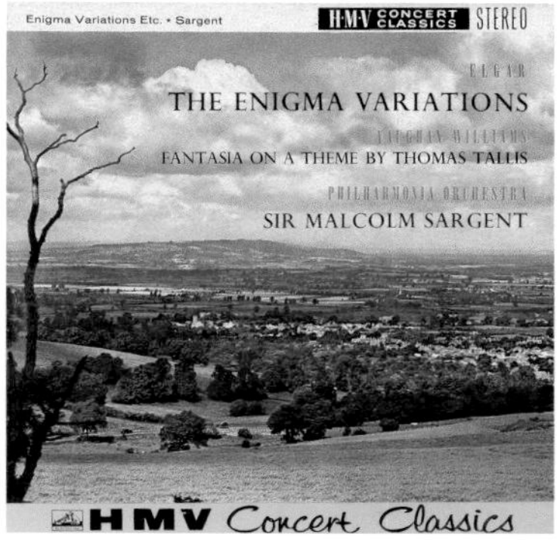

521

522

523

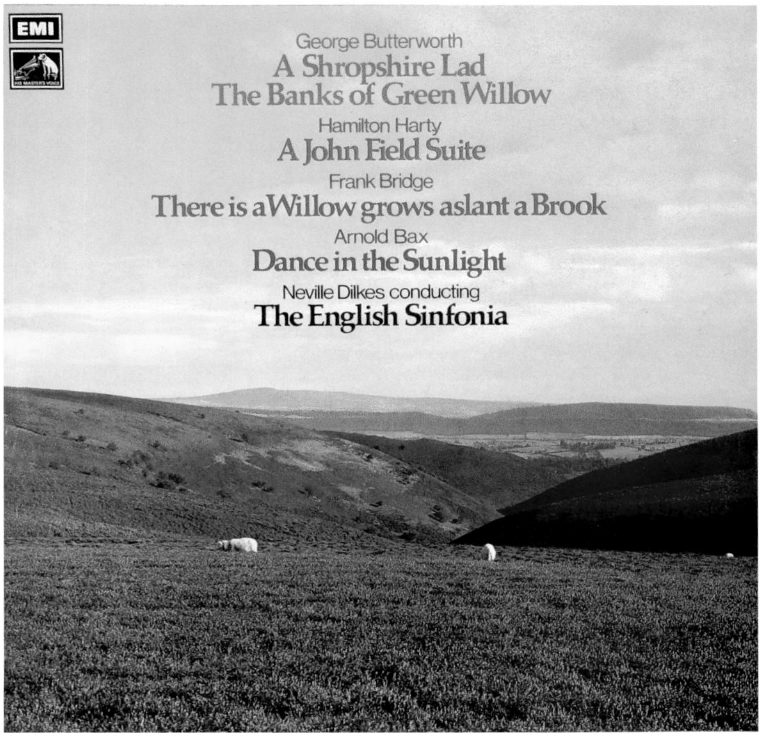

524

525

526

521 EMI. SXLP20007, GB 1963, Ph: A C K Ware
522 EMI. SAN393, GB 1976, Ph: Colour Library International (Monsal Dale, Derbishire)
523 EMI. ASD2913, GB 1975, Ph: Peter Baker (Coast of Derrinane, Ring of Kerry)
524 EMI. CSD3696, GB 1971, Ph: A.F. Kersting (The Long Minn, Shropshire)
525 ORIEL. ORM1004, GB 1981, Ph: British Tourist Authority (Menai Bridge, Gwynedd)
526 EMI-COLUMBIA. TWO226, GB 1968, Ph: Iris Hardwick (River Arrow, Eardis Land, Herefordshire)

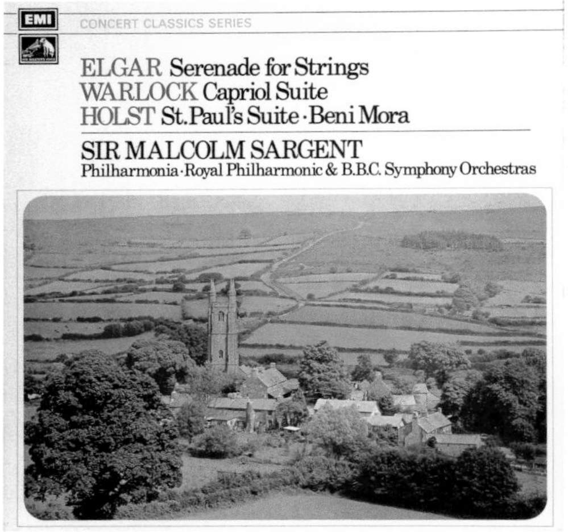
EMI
CONCERT CLASSICS SERIES
ELGAR Serenade for Strings
WARLOCK Capriol Suite
HOLST St.Paul's Suite · Beni Mora
SIR MALCOLM SARGENT
Philharmonia · Royal Philharmonic & B.B.C. Symphony Orchestras
527

EMI
HMV Concert Classics
BRITISH CONCERT 'POPS'
VAUGHAN WILLIAMS Greensleeves Fantasia
ELGAR Chanson de Matin DELIUS La Calinda
COLERIDGE TAYLOR Petite Suite de Concert
music by Grainger, Harty, Coates and Arnold
GEORGE WELDON/Philharmonia Orchestra
528

WELSH CONCERTOS
DECCA
CLARINET CONCERTO OP.3 ~ HARP CONCERTO OP.11: ALUN HODDINOTT
PIANO CONCERTO NO.3 OP.40: WILLIAM MATHIAS
LONDON SYMPHONY ORCHESTRA / DAVID ATHERTON
WITH
GERVASE DE PEYER: CLARINET
OSIAN ELLIS: HARP
PETER KATIN: PIANO
529

Welsh Music for Strings
DECCA
English Chamber Orchestra
David Atherton
530

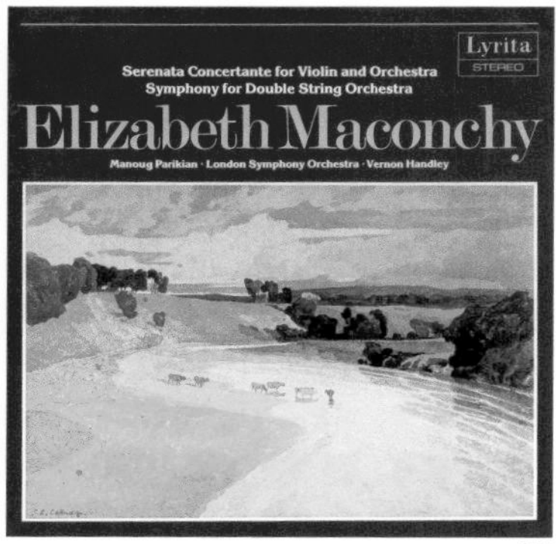
Lyrita
STEREO
Serenata Concertante for Violin and Orchestra
Symphony for Double String Orchestra
Elizabeth Maconchy
Manoug Parikian · London Symphony Orchestra · Vernon Handley
531

527 EMI. SXLP30126, GB 1972
528 EMI. SXLP30243, GB 1978
529 DECCA. SXL6513, GB 1971
530 DECCA. SXL6468, GB 1970
531 LYRITA. SRCS116, GB 1982, CD: Keith Hensby; CA: John Sell Cotman
"Landscape with river and cattle"
(reproduced by courtesy of E.T. Archive of Victoria and Albert Museum)

532

533

534

532 EMI. ASD3139, GB 1975, Ph: Colour Library International (Kettlewell, Yorkshire)
533 LYRITA. SRCS107, GB 1979, CA: John Constable *"Harnham Ridge"* (reproduced by kind permission of The Tate Gallery, London)
534 EMI. ASD2502, GB 1970
535 EMI. ASD3301, GB 1976, CA: Graham Clarke *"Sunflowers"* [reproduced by kind permission of the artist]
536 VARESE. VC81081, USA 1978, CA: John Constable "Weymouth Bay" (Museum of Fine Arts, Boston)

536

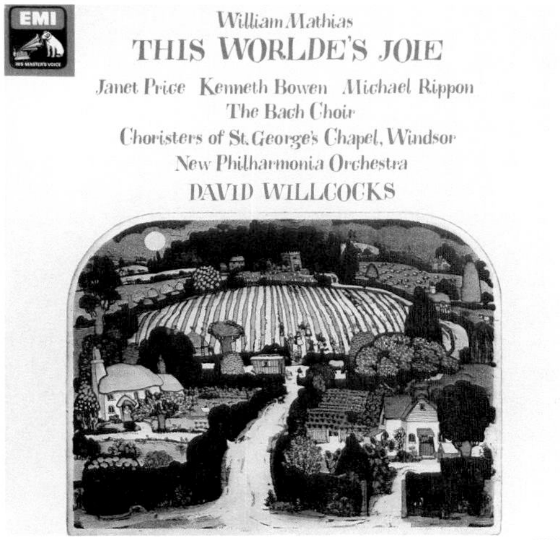

535

9.7 Variations on a Theme (537 - 553)

Just as for opera and ballet, an elaborately illustrated cover that refers to the storyline is also appropriate for programme music. Interesting here is the comparison of the different results for the very same work. The reference to the musical programme is indisputable.

— The musical fairy tale *Peter and the Wolf* by Sergei Prokofiev (537-541), see also picture 20.
— *Scheherazade* by Nikolai Rimsky-Korsakov (542-546).
— The *Golden Cockerell,* another work by Rimsky-Korsakov (547-550).
— The biblical story of *Belshazzar's Feast* set to music by William Walton (551-553); see also cover 745.
— See also covers 497-500 with two additional themes.

537

538

537 PHILIPS. 6599436, GB 1974, CD: Hans Noordhoff
538 EMI. C063-10381, F 1969. CD: Robert L. Haberfield
539 EMI. C063-02558, GFR 1973, CD: Roberto Patelli
540 DECCA. SXL2218, GB 1960
541 EMI. CTRE6173, F ca 1965, CD: Clark-Bresson

539

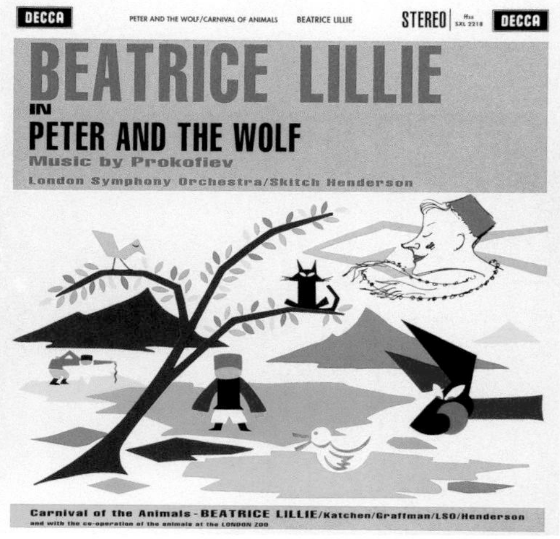

540

541

542

543

544

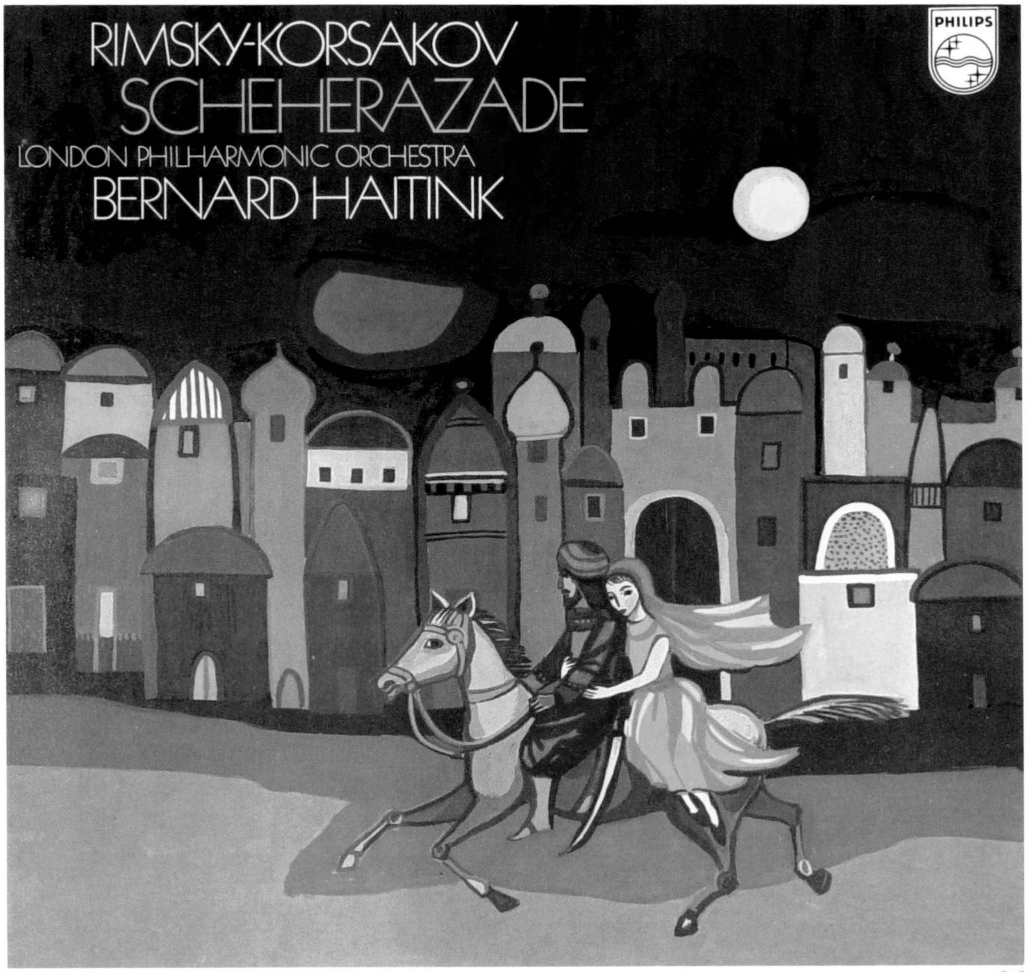

545

546

542 EMI. ASD0251, GB 1957, CA: Bakst
(Original decor of Scheherazade; Musée des Arts decoratifs; copyrights S.P.A.D.E.M., Paris)
543 RCA. LSC2446, USA 1960
544 EMI. CFP40341, GB 1980
545 PHILIPS. 6500410, EU 1972, CD: Elly Griepink-Meijer
546 COLUMBIA. MS6365, USA 1962, Ph: Tom Palumbo

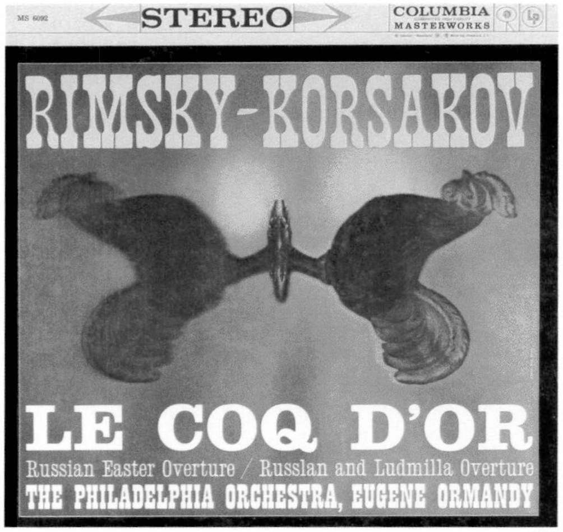

547

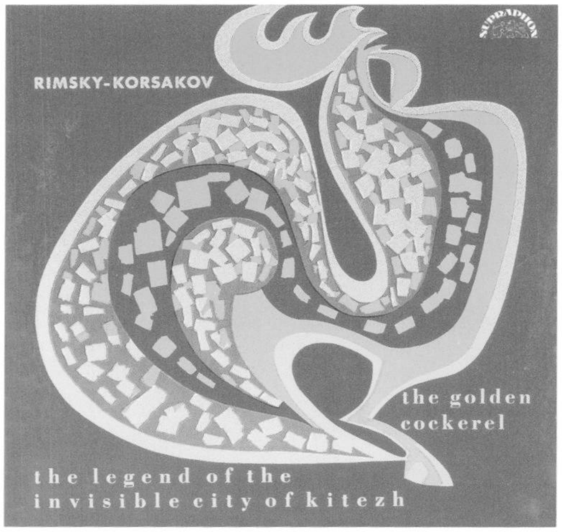

548

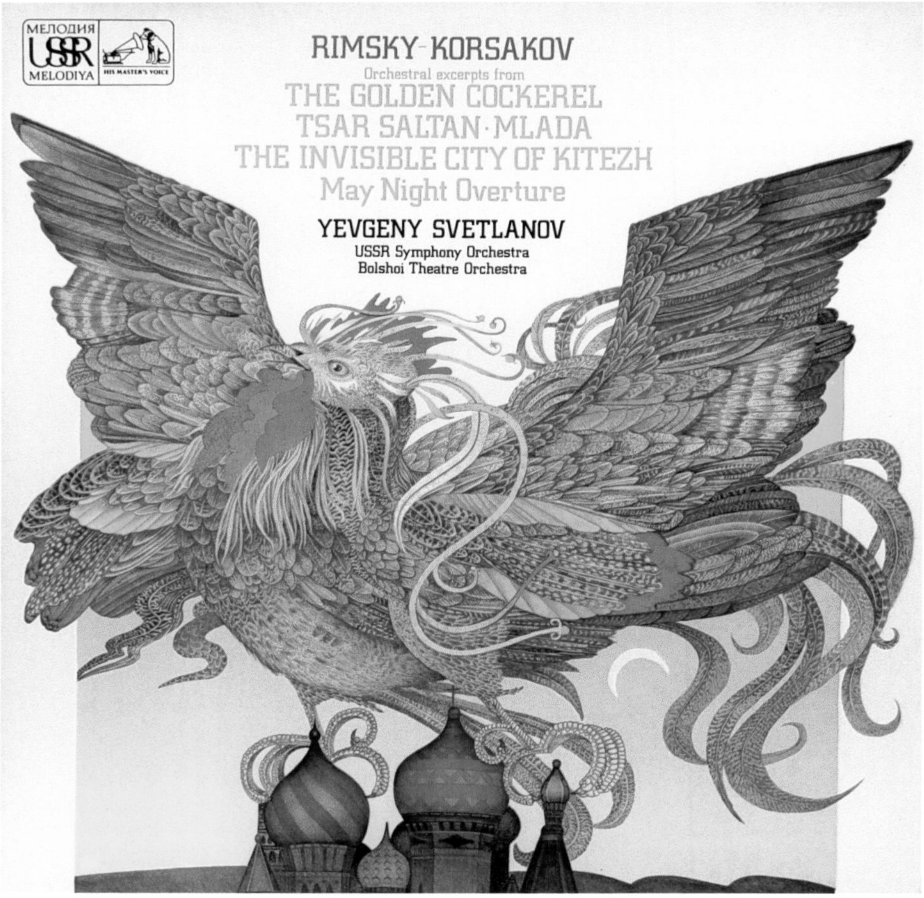

549

550

547 COLUMBIA. MS6092, USA 1959, Ph: Bob Ritta
548 SUPRAPHON. SUAST50099, CS 1963, CD: Artia
549 EMI. ASD3710, GB 1979
550 CAPITOL. SP8445, USA 1958

551

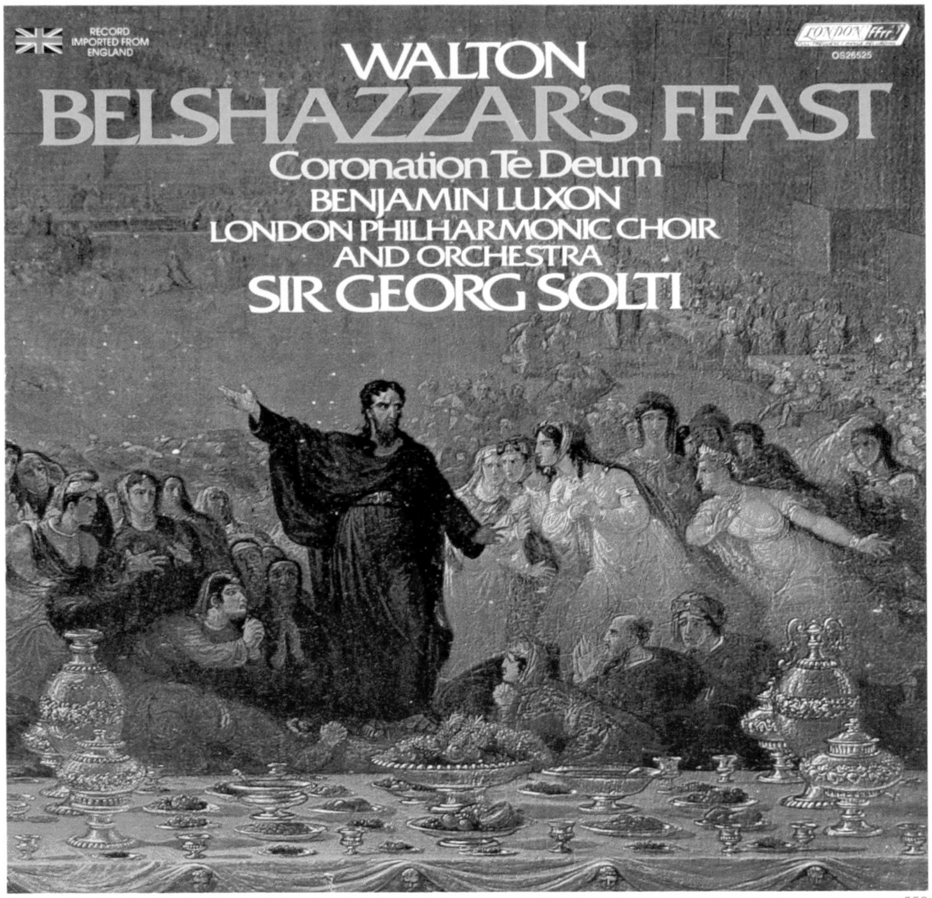

552

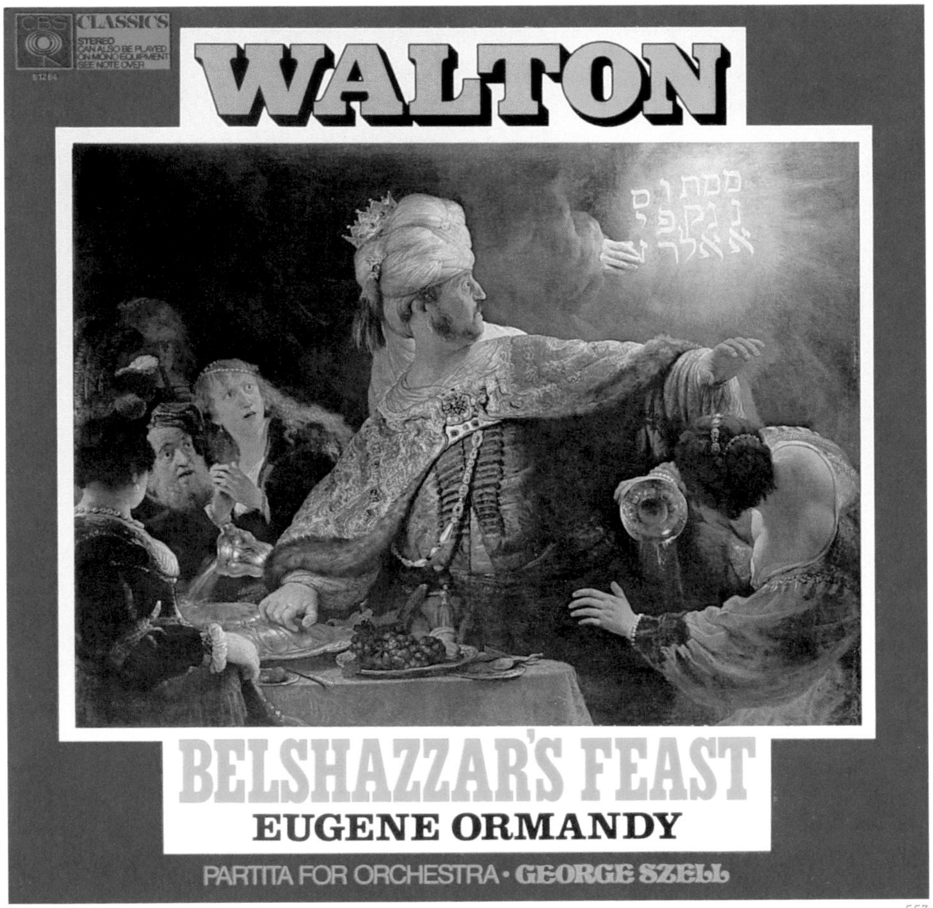

553

551 EMI. SAN324, GB 1972, Ph: Bas-relief of the Istar Gate, Babylon (Holle-Verlag, Baden-Baden)
552 LONDON. OS26525, USA 1977 [Design as original Decca SET618]
553 CBS. 61264, GB, CA: Rembrandt *"Belshazzar's Feast"* (National Gallery, London)

10.0 Without Colour Pencil and Paintbrush – Printing Techniques (554 – 573)

This group consists of covers whose graphic design has been realised with a wide range of different printing techniques – wood and linoleum cuts, engraving, etc. The works of art have not necessarily have been produced especially for the cover. Photographic reproductions of existing works of art are also included here. Cover 554, an atmospheric pen and ink drawing of a dilapidated church in Armenia, moves me time and time again. All of the Poseidon records from the American (Armenian-Scottish) composer Alan Hovhaness were designed in this manner.

554

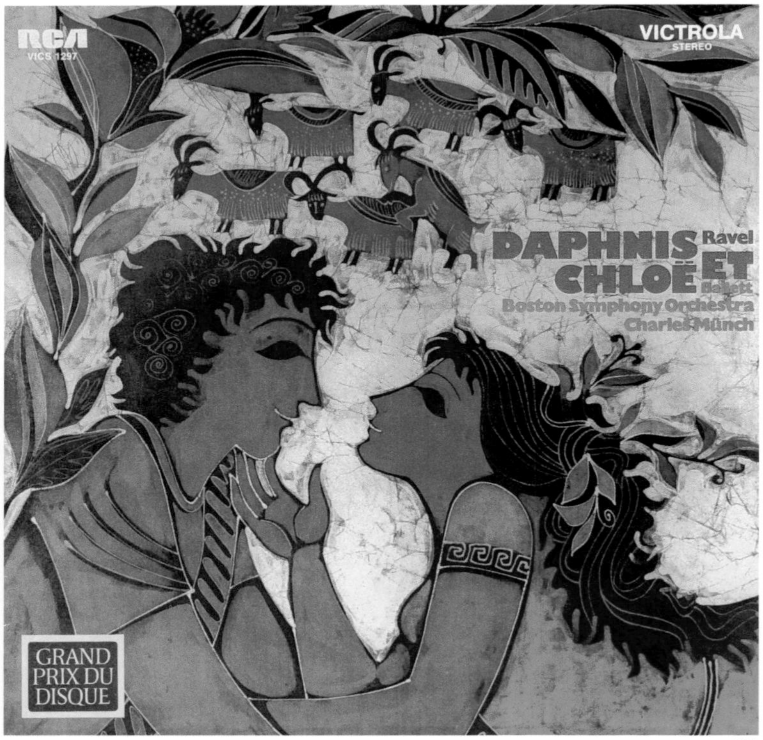

556

555

557

558

559

560

561

562

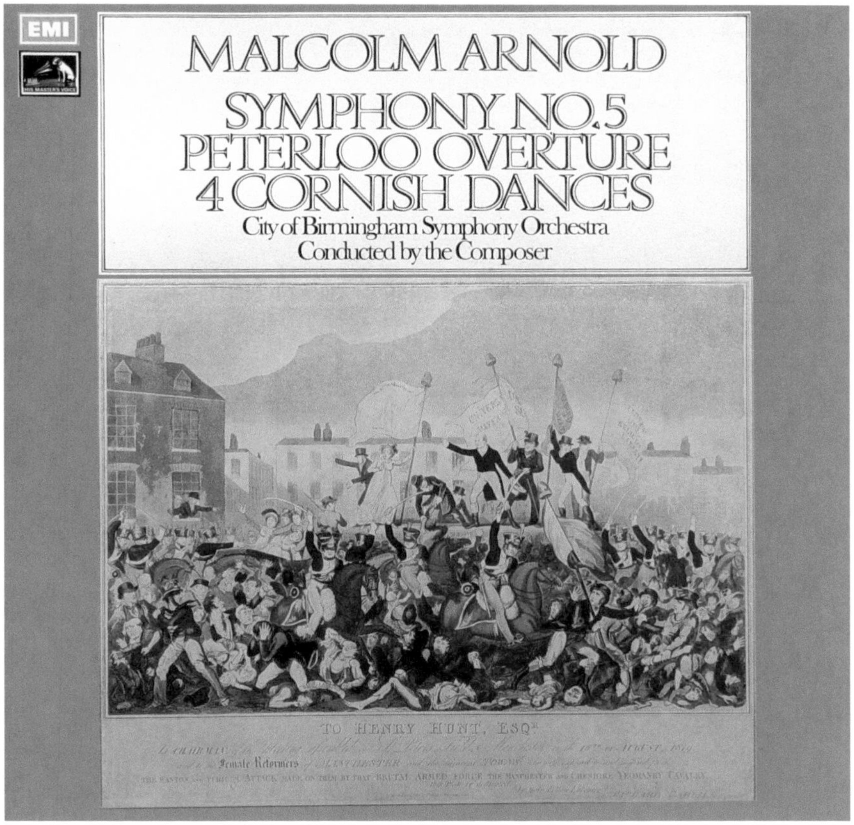

563

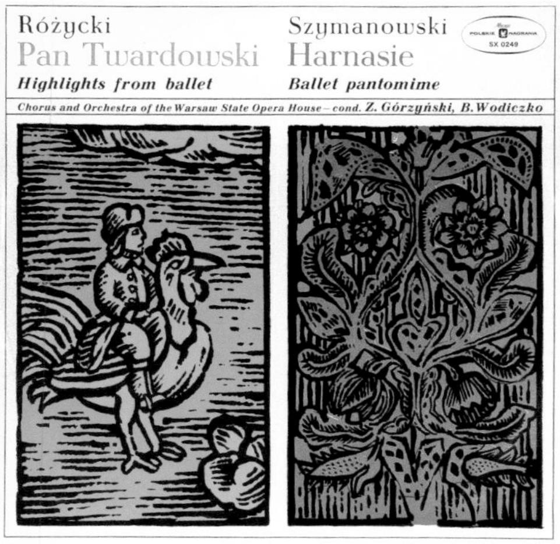

564

565

554 POSEIDON. 1012, USA, CA: Spitakavor Astvatzatzin (Church in the Eghegnadzor Region, Armenia)
555 LYRITA. SRCS033, GB 1966, CD: Keith Hensby, based on an old engraving of seventeenth century Birmingham
556 RCA. VICS1297, D c. 1975, Batik: Jutta Lamprecht
557 MUZA. SX1317, PL, CA: Stefan Bernacinski
558 URANIA. URLP7130, USA 1954, CA: Galster

« (opposite page)

559 MELODIYA. C11339, SU
560 ANGEL. 3CBX413, Brasil 1965
561 EMI-COLUMBIA. SAXF211, F 1961
562 PRIVAT. WRC1-3315, Can 1984, Ph: by permission of the Music Division, National Library, Ottawa
563 EMI. ASD2878, GB 1973, CA: George Cruikshank *"The Peterloo massacre 1819"* (courtesy City of Manchester Art Galleries)
564 MUZA. SX0249, PL 1975
565 EMI. C065-03597, GFR 1979, CA: Woodcut by Ricardo

566

567

568

569

570

566 RCA. LSC3151, F 1969
567 RCA. SB6720, GB 1966, CA: Eric Carie
568 ANGEL. S35427, USA c. 1960
569 MELODIYA. C16189, SU 1981, CD: A. Saltanov
570 MELODIYA. C01643, SU 1968, CD: W. Penzin
571 LONDON. CS6423, USA 1965
572 LONDON. CS6718, USA 1971
573 LYRITA. SRCS32, GB 1966, CD: Keith Hensby

571

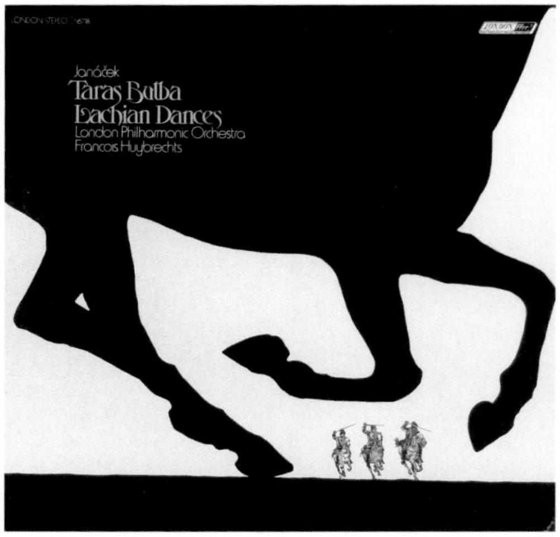

572

573w

11.0 The Best Covers from the Czech Republic

In former Czechoslovakia, there were three record companies: Supraphon, Panton and Opus, with the latter in Slovakia. The covers presented here are a selection of Panton and Supraphon records. Some of them use previously existing works of art (if this is the case, it is noted in the picture title) and a harmoniously designed typography. With the exception of Bohuslav Foerster's *Cyrano de Bergerac* (595) and covers 576, 577 and 585, the musical reference is not clear.

11.1 Panton (574 - 578)

11.2 Supraphon (579 - 596)

574

575

576

577

574 PANTON. 81100022, CS 1979, CD: J.E. Jránec; CA: Franticek Muzika *"Requiem"*
575 PANTON. 81100024, CS 1979, CD: J.E. Jránec; CA: Franticek Tichi *"Paganini"*
576 PANTON. 81100050, CS 1978, CA: Aleš Striegl
577 PANTON. 110667, CS 1977, CD: Helena Constantinová

578

579

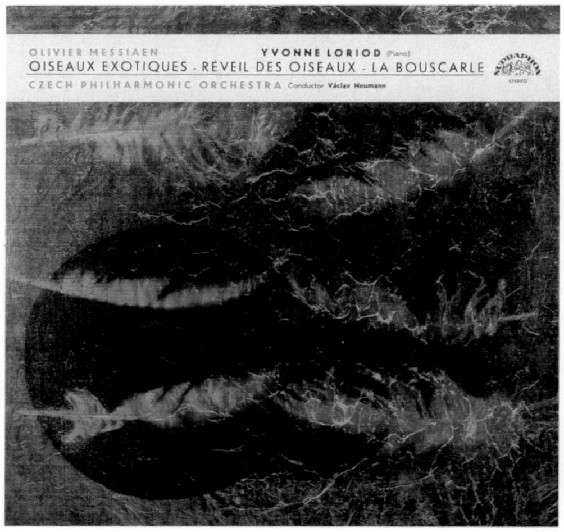

580

582

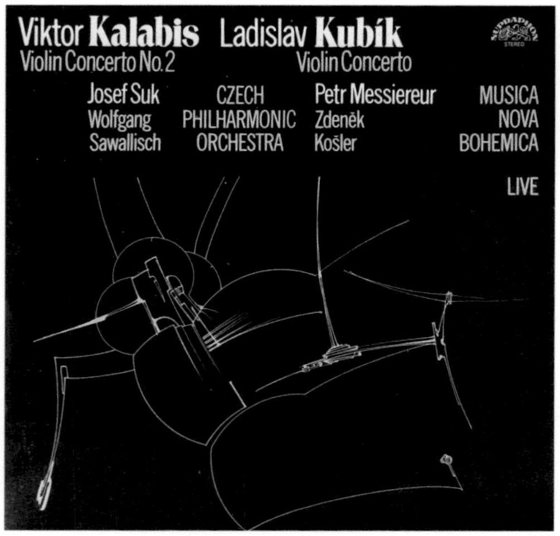

581

578 PANTON. 110127, CS 1968, CD: Hermina Melicharová; CA: Alfons Mucha *"The Sitting Women"* (National Gallery , Prague); Ph: Vladimír Frýman
579 SUPRAPHON. SUAST50874, CS 1968, CA: Jaroslava Kurandová 1968
580 SUPRAPHON. SUAST50749, CS 1967, CD: Zdenék Rypka
581 SUPRAPHON. 11103035, CS 1980, CD: Stanislav Dvorsky (on the basis of Miloš Sikora & Pavel Turnovský's engraving)
582 SUPRAPHON. 1101619, CS 1973, CD: Milan Jarošs; CA: Emil Filla *"The Reader"* 1913

583

584

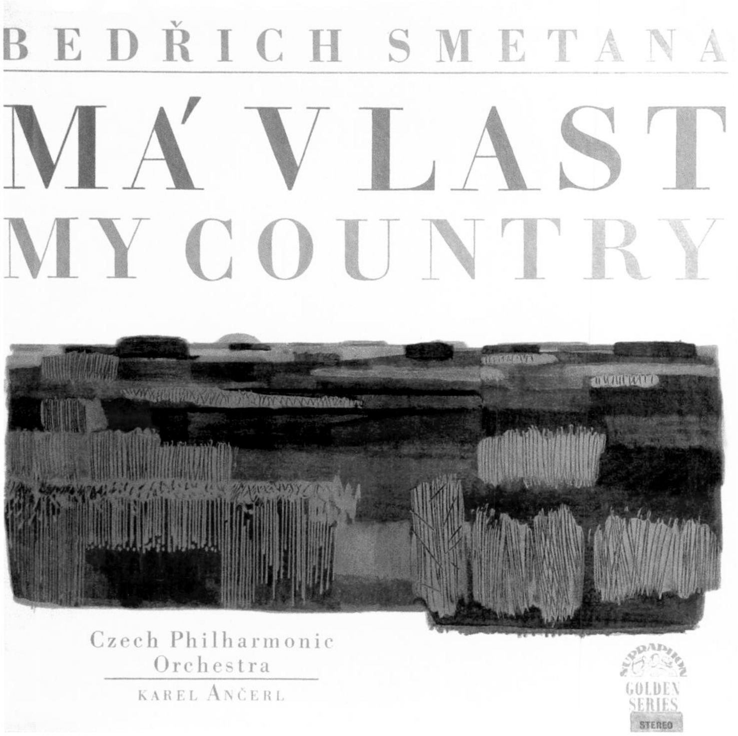

585

586

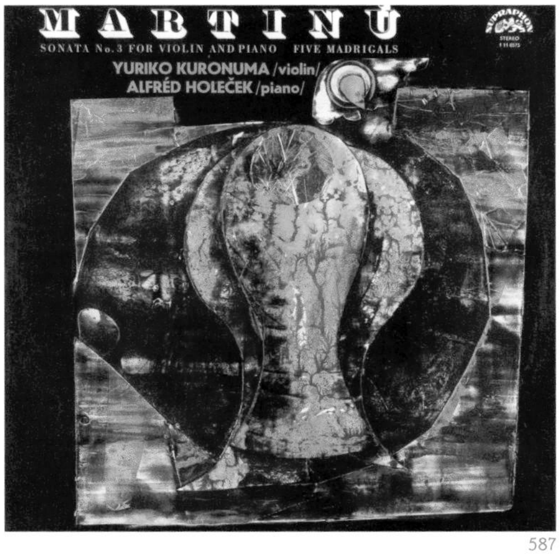

587

583 SUPRAPHON. SUAST50556, CS 1965, CD: Ivo Holý; CA: Josef Sima *"Landscape"* 1927 (National Gallery; Prague)
584 SUPRAPHON. SUAST50824, CS 1967, CD: Ivo Holý; CA: Karel Cerny *"South Bohemian Country"*
585 SUPRAPHON. GSST50521, CS 1963, CA: Jirí Rathouský
586 SUPRAPHON. 1101348, CS 1973, CA: Stanislav Vajce & Milan Jaroš; Typographical arrangement: Miloslav Žácek
587 SUPRAPHON. 1110575, CS 1969, CD: Stanislav Vajce; Typographical arrangement: Miloslav Žácek

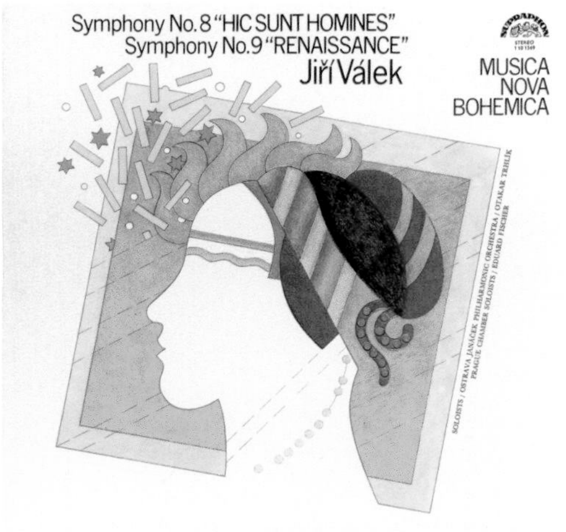

588

589

Martinů
Sinfonia Concertante for Oboe, Bassoon, Violin and Violoncello Soli and Small Orchestra
Rhapsody - Concerto for Viola and Orchestra
Soloists
Czech Philharmonic Orchestra
Zdeněk Košler

590

591

588 SUPRAPHON. 1101569, CS 1973,
CA: Jindrich Cech, Miloslav Žácek, Milan Jaroš
589 SUPRAPHON. 1101784, CS 1975, CA: Ditta Wagnerová
590 SUPRAPHON. 11103378, CS 1979, CD: Ondrej Tuma;
CA: Otakar Coubine
"Spring in Simiane" (National Gallery, Prague)
591 SUPRAPHON. SUAST50689, CS 1966, CD: Jiri Poždena;
CA: Peter Vodkin *"Bathing Women"*

» {opposite page}
592 SUPRAPHON. 11113379, CS 1984,
CD: Liloslav Žácek; CA: Voitech Preissig
"Ostrov"/"The Island" 1905 (National Gallery, Prague)
593 SUPRAPHON. SUAST50740, CS 1965, CD: Josef Kalousek
594 SUPRAPHON. 11102960, CS 1980, CD: Dimitrij Gaydecka;
Ph: Ladislav Neubert (tapestry by R. Schlattauer)
595 SUPRAPHON. 11102456, CS 1978,
CD: Milan Jaroš; CA: Eliška Konopiškā
596 SUPRAPHON. 11102548, CS 1979,
CD: Aleš Najbrt; CA: Eliška Konopiškā

592

BÉLA BARTÓK
GRAND PRIX
ACADEMIE CHARLES CROS
PARIS
STEREO
ANDRÉ GERTLER, Violin
DIANE ANDERSEN, Piano
MILAN ETLÍK, Clarinet
Sonata for Violin and Piano (Unpublished)
"Contrasts" for Violin, Clarinet and Piano

593

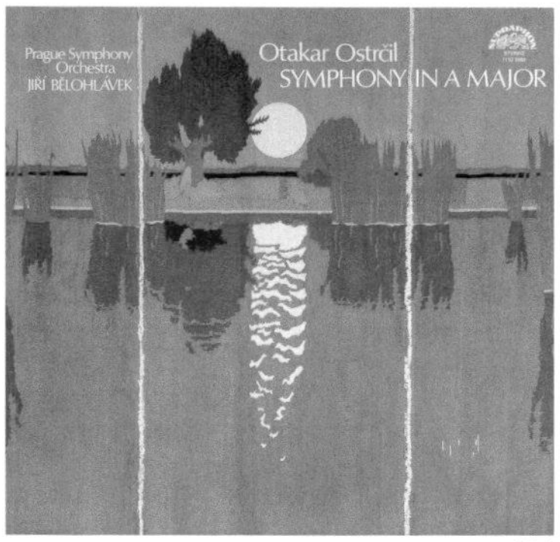

594

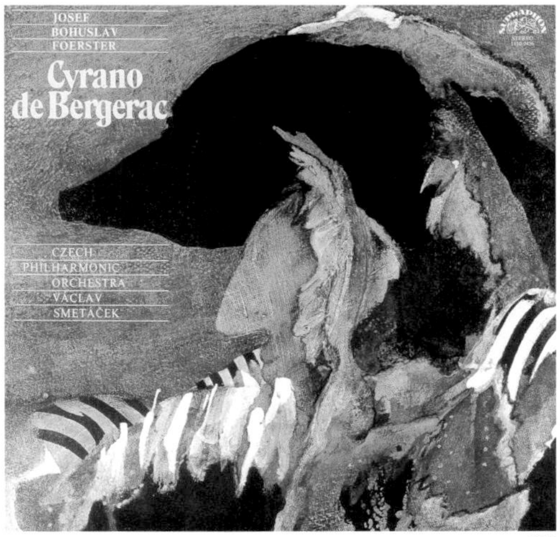

595

596

12.0 Three Decades of Typical Picture Illustration

597

598

599

597 DECCA-USA. DL7101100, USA 1964
598 ANGEL. S35538, USA 1961, CA: Berthe Morisot *"Enfents"* (Private Collection, Paris); Ph: Galerie Charpentier
599 EPIC. BC1023, USA 1959

Of all groups, this one is the largest. The designer of the cover had wide-ranging creative leeway in collaboration with an artist or graphic artist. Illustrations with pictures or graphics usually have a work of art that has been expressly created for the cover. The covers presented here were created from 1959 to 1987. The anthology is designed to depict the developments in style and printing techniques over the course of the decades. Within the five-year time intervals, the pictures are arranged to some extent according to similarity. Some covers do not allow for any recognition of a reference to the musical content (604, 605, 607, 608, 620, 638, 643, 652, 655). Others are self-explanatory. If there are helpful explanations, they can be found in the categories.

12.1 to 1964 (597 - 600)

Most of the covers from Capitol Records and RCA Records belonging to Group II are included in this category. As a result, only four of the covers from this period will be shown here. Only covers 599 and 600 can therefore be referred to specifically as illustrations.

— The Epic record shows a scene from *A Midsummer Night's Dream,* corresponding to Mendelssohn's eponymous stage music (599), although lacking in sophistication.

— The cover in gingerbread style shows a stage set for Carl Maria von Weber's opera *Oberon* (600). Compare this to cover 634.

12.2 1965–1969 (601 – 623)

— The rooster and fox are figures from Stravinsky's opera *Renard* (602).
— Here we see the "Bathing Woman from Trouville" from *Les Mariés de la Tour Eiffel* by Poulenc (610) on an Angel record.
— The Decca Phase 4 record (615) presents the *sorcerer's apprentice* and a Finnish cavalier on horseback, corresponding to the musical poem *Finlandia.*
— The Nonesuch record (617) illustrates the *baroque variations* by Lukas Foss.
— The story from *Ala and Lolly,* originally composed as a ballet by Prokofiev, is set among the Scythians, a tribe of warriors on horseback (619).

600 ANGEL. S36175, USA 1963, CA: Malcles
(Decor for Oberon, Opera Paris; Mercure Ed. Paris - Atelier Joubert)
[Design as original EMI-Columbia. SAX2417]
601 CONCERT HALL. SMS2511, F ca 1966, CA: Pasquirer
602 DECCA. SXL6171, GB 1965
603 ANGEL. S36421, USA 1967

600

601

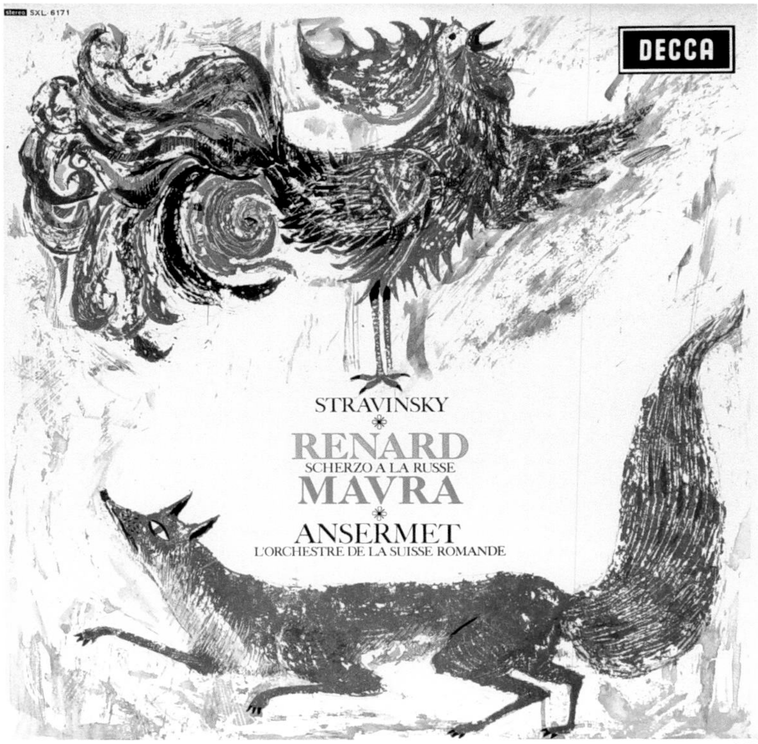

602

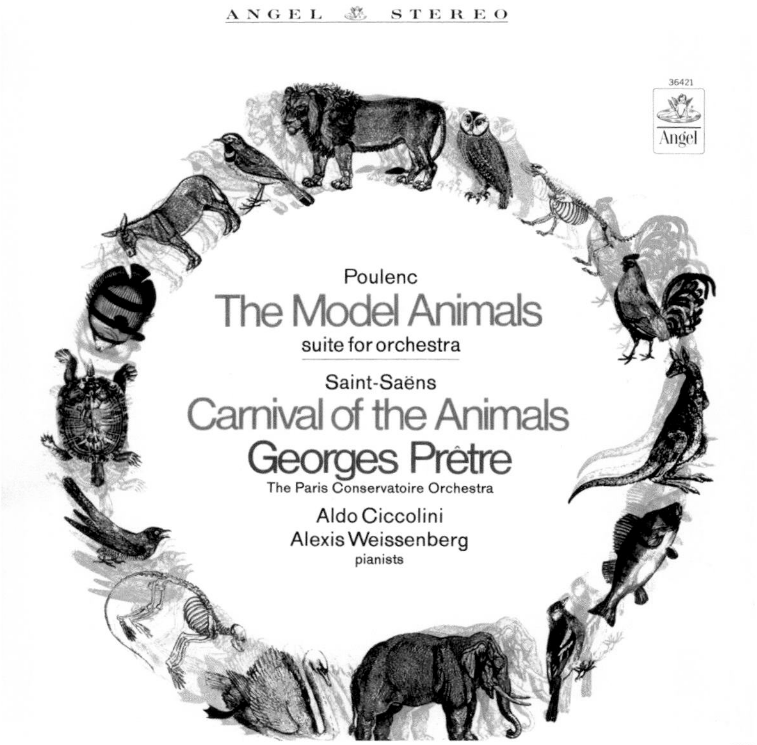

603

604 RCA. LSC2929, USA 1966, CD: Steve Madison
605 RCA. VICS1109, GB 1966
606 PHILIPS. 6580051, GB ca 1965
607 NONESUCH. H71135, USA c. 1966, CD: William S. Harvey; CA: Bob Pepper
608 DGG. 139020, GFR 1967, CA: Goetz Loepelmann
609 DGG. 139304, GFR 1967, CA: Gerhard Noack

605

604

606

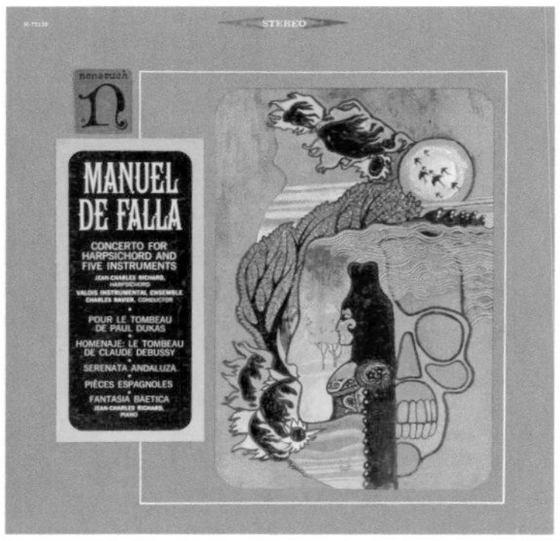

607

608

609

610

611

612

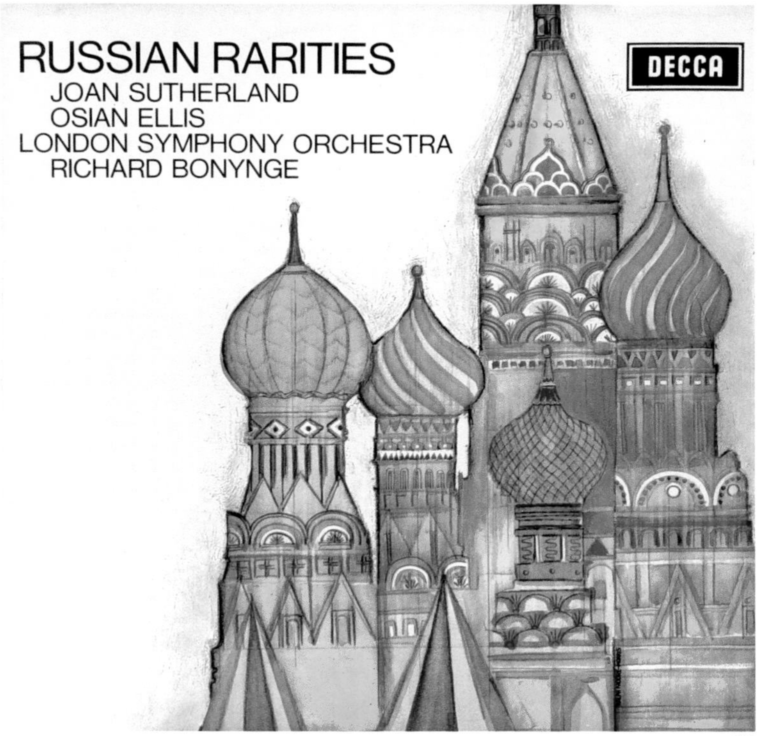

613

614

615

610 ANGEL. S36519, USA 1968, CA: Robert L. Haberfield
611 VANGUARD. SRV275, USA 1968
612 DGG. 138918, GFR 1966
613 DECCA. SXL6406, GB 1969, CA: Ralph Moore-Morris
614 DECCA. GOS558, GB 1968, CA: J. Hughes
615 DECCA. PFS4169, GB 1969, CD: DPAD

617

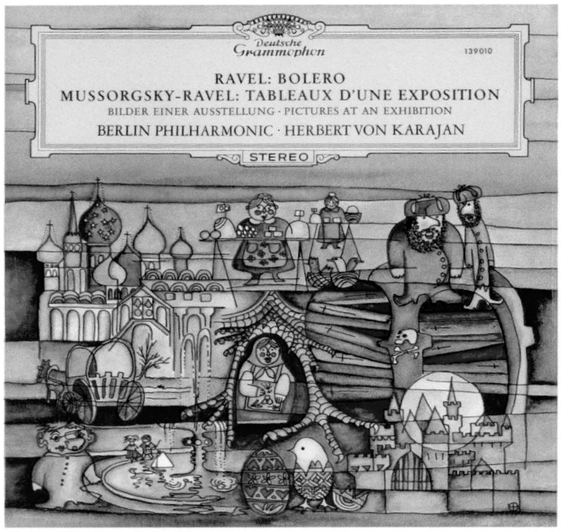

616

618

619

616 DGG. 139010, GFR 1966, CD: Michel Herve
617 NONESUCH. H71202, USA 1968, CA: Gene Szafran
618 DGG. 139032, GFR 1968
619 LONDON. CS6538, USA 1967

620

621

622

623

12.3 1970–1974 (624 - 640)

— *Billy the Kid* and a scene from *Rodeo* are sketched on The Copland Album with the ballet works of the same name (624).
— *Luonnator,* the goddess of wind in Finnish mythology, decorates the record with Sibelius' recording of the same name (625).

620 DGG. 139040, GFR 1969
621 DECCA. SDD216, GB 1969
622 DECCA. SDD192, GB 1969
623 DECCA. SDD223, GB 1969, CD: Heather Payne

— It is most likely *Taras Bulba,* the legendary Cossack hero from Gogol's story set to music by Janáček, who is shown in artistically alienated form on the Janáček record (627).
— A visual synthesis of the composer Delius and his work *Appalachia* is shown on the Angel LP (630): the composer is looking into the window at an American idyll – a very beautiful cover.
— Nielsen's symphony *The Four Temperaments* (632) is represented with three heads – who can find the fourth?
— Maeterlinck's drama *Pelleas et Melisande* in the musical setting by Gabriel Fauré is on the Decca record (639). The scene is set in the castle tower.

624

625

626

627

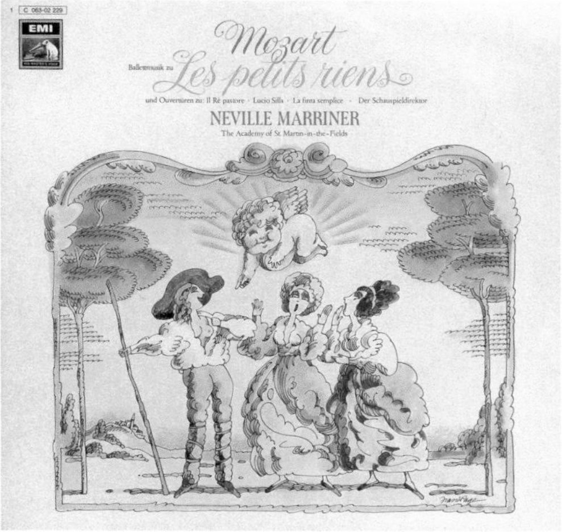

628

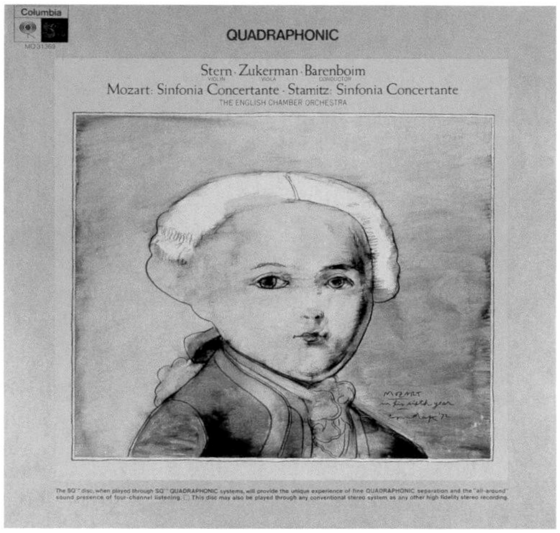

629

630

631

632

624 COLUMBIA. MG30071, USA 1970, CD: John Berg; CA: Thomas B. Allen
625 EMI. ASD2486, GB 1970
626 EMI. C063-02569, GFR 1973, CA: Dick Elescas
627 DGG. 2530075, GFR 1971, CD: John Günther
628 EMI. C063-02229, GFR 1972, CA: Frank Page
« [opposite page]

629 COLUMBIA. MQ31369, USA 1972, CD: Teresa Alfieri & Henriettta Condak; CA: Clifford Condak
630 ANGEL. S36756, USA 1971, CD: as original EMI ASD2635
631 ANGEL. S37001, USA 1974, CA: Frank Page [Design as original EMI ASD2990]
632 COLUMBIA. M32779, USA 1974, CD: John Berg; CA: Milton Glaser

633

634

636

633 EMI. ASD3029, GB 1974. CD: Endicott
634 DGG. 2530315, GFR 1973, CD: John Günther
635 DECCA. SXL6699, GB 1973, CD: Pennie Austee

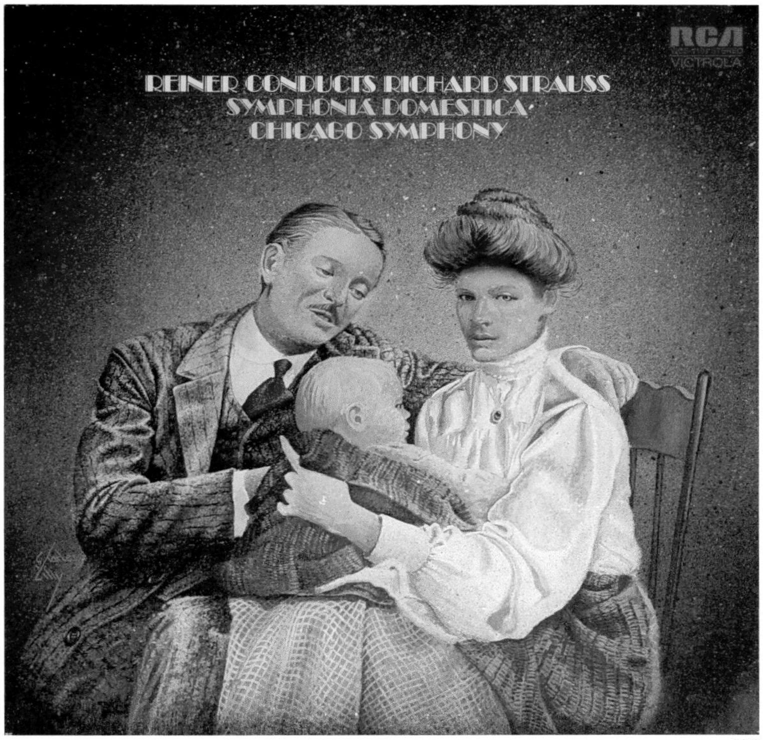

636

637

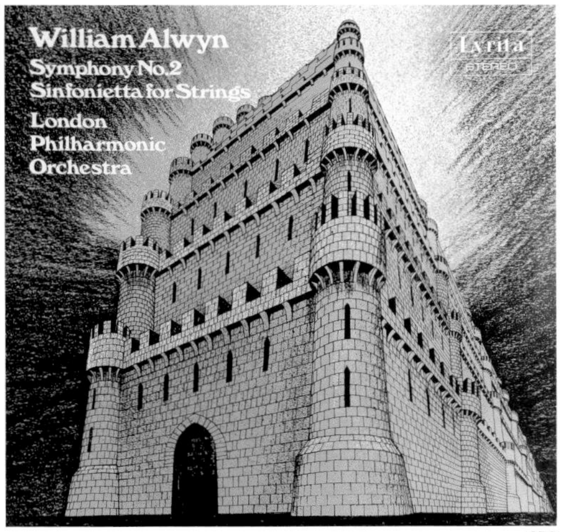

638

— The opera *Oberon* by Carl Maria von Weber is illustrated on the DGG album (634). See also picture 600.

— Britannia's colonial grandeur! Shown here on the Columbia record with works by Edward Elgar, including the *Crown of India Suite* (637).

639

640

636 RCA. VICS1104, USA 1972
637 COLUMBIA. MQ32936, USA 1974,
Collage: Henrietta Condak
638 LYRITA. SRCS085, GB 1975, CD: Keith Hensby
639 DECCA. SDD388, GB 1973, CA: Pam Higgins
640 ODYSSEY. Y32885, USA 1974,
CD: Henrietta Condak; CA: Clifford Condak

12.4 1975–1979 (643 - 657)

— The legendary war hero Lemminkainen, of Finnish mythology, can be seen in all his glory on the EMI record with the *Four Legends* from the Kalevala by Sibelius (646).
— One of the most interesting covers in the collection and a real eye-catcher is the illustration to Roussel's *Le Festin de l'Araignée,* The Spider's Feast (649). When studied carefully, a face hidden in the clouds can be seen. The French graphic artist is popular for his postage stamp designs.
— Siegfried Romberg made the city of Heidelberg world-renowned in the USA with his operetta *The Student Prince,* symbolised here by three beer steins set before an idealised Heidelberg Castle (654).
— The comical illustration on the Mercury record refers to the title *Adventures in a Perambulator* (656).

641 COLUMBIA. M32782, USA 1974, CA: Reynold Ruffins
642 COLUMBIA. M32784, USA 1974, CA: Reynold Ruffins
643 RCA. AGL1-1530, USA 1976, CA: Nancy Munger
644 DECCA. SXL6897, GB 1979, CA: Peter Cross

641

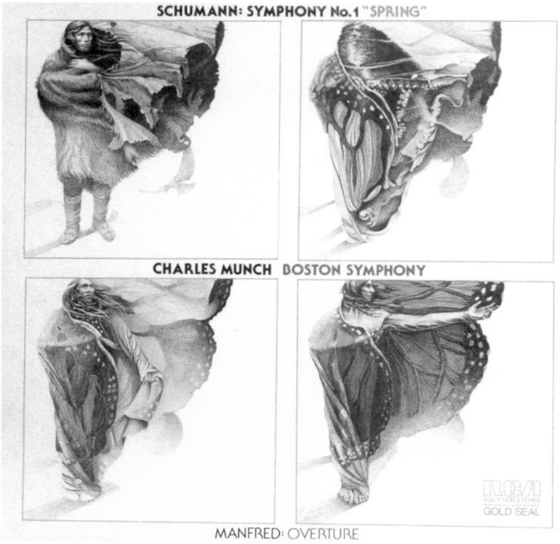

643

644

642

645

645 RCA. RL25035, GB 1977
646 EMI. ASD3092, GB 1975. CD: Dick Elescas
647 RCA. RL25203, USA 1979
648 EMI. ASD3542, GB 1978. CD: Dick Elescas

647

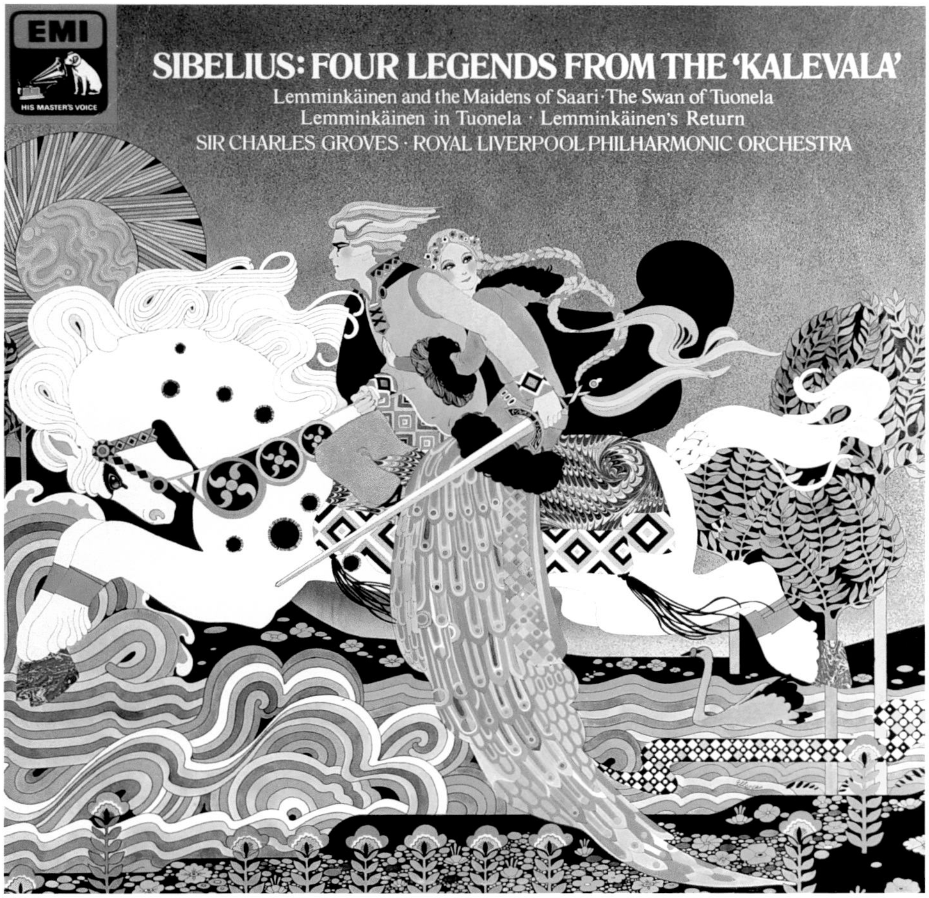

646

648

649

650

649 EMI. C181-52293, F after 1975, CA: Veret-Lemarinier
650 CBS. 61840, GB 1978, CA: Silverman
651 CBS. 61839, GB 1978, CA: Clifford Condak
652 LYRITA. SRCS104, GB 1979, CD: Keith Hensby

652

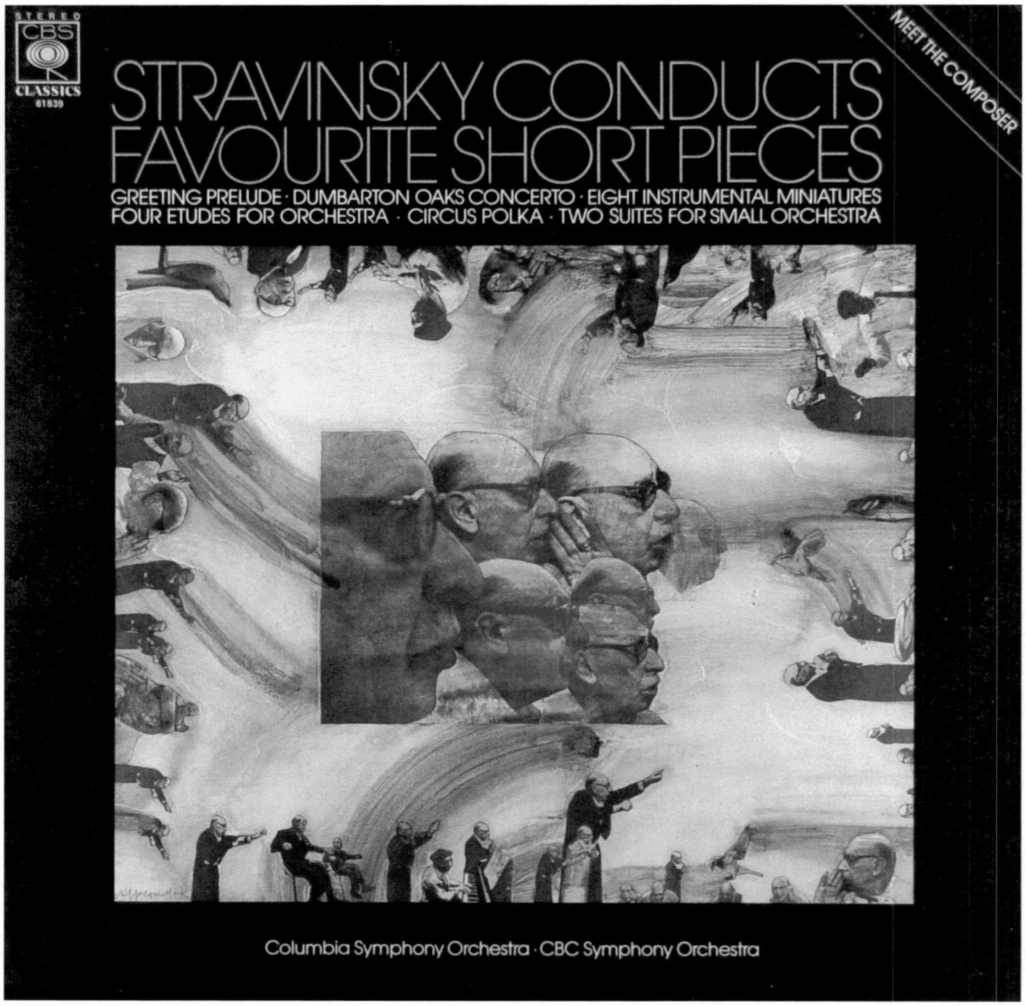

651

653

655

654

656

657

653 EMI. ASD3327, GB 1977, CA: Don Weller
654 ANGEL. S37309, USA 1978, CD: Abe Curvin
655 CRYSTAL. S352, USA 1978, CD: Pat Cieslak
656 MERCURY. SRI75095, EU c. 1978
657 RCA. RL01757, GB 1977, CA: Maurice Sendak *"What the Night Tells Me"* (commissioned by RCA Records) [the composer is sitting in the lodge]

12.5 Beyond 1980 (658 - 664)

The picture fragments from Picasso, Chagall, Kandinsky, Dali and Klee on cover 658 are musically transformed into the *Five Pantomimes* by the composer Tzvi Avni. See also cover 414 from the same series with Israeli composers on the label Jerusalem Records.

— The fabled merman on the Angel album with stage music by Darius Milhaud is Proteus (Protée) from Homer's Odyssey (659).

— Cover 660 is tri-lingual with Georgian, Cyrillic and Latin lettering. The musical reference to the illustration is puzzling.

658 JERUSALEM. ATD8301, Isr 1984, CD: Shy Cohen
659 ANGEL. S37317, USA 1979, CD: Jim Endicott
660 MELODIYA. C14243, SU 1979

658

659

660

661

662

661 BBC. REGL560, GB 1985, CD: Undercover
662 LYRITA. SRCS126, GB 1985, CA: Keith Hensby *"The Stream at Lolham Mill"*
663 CANADIAN MUSIC CENTER. CMC2887, Can 1986, CA: Susan Benson
664 CANADIAN MUSIC CENTER. CMC2987, Can 1987, CA: Susan Benson

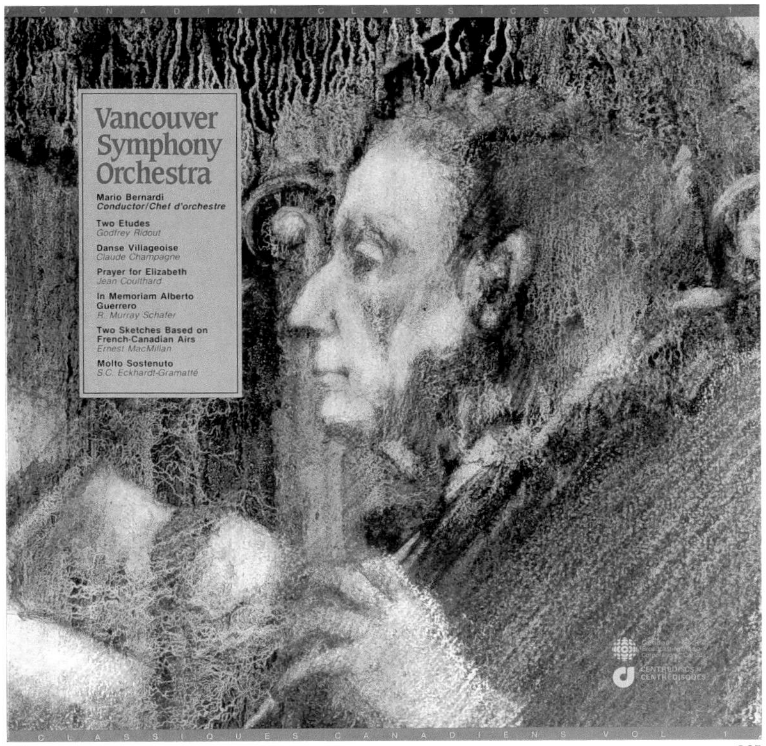

663

664

13.0 The Diversity of Stylistic Devices

While browsing through the most beautiful covers in my collection, nine further categories emerged, that, in a broader sense, belong to the large group of illustrations.

13.1 The World of the Stage (665 - 681)

This category does not only incorporate stage decoration, but also set photos, set design and stage curtains custom-made for a particular production as well as costume design. Many of the pictures shown here are design sketches. All of them are clearly related to the music. Covers 665 to 668 and 670 are from the period to 1965.

665

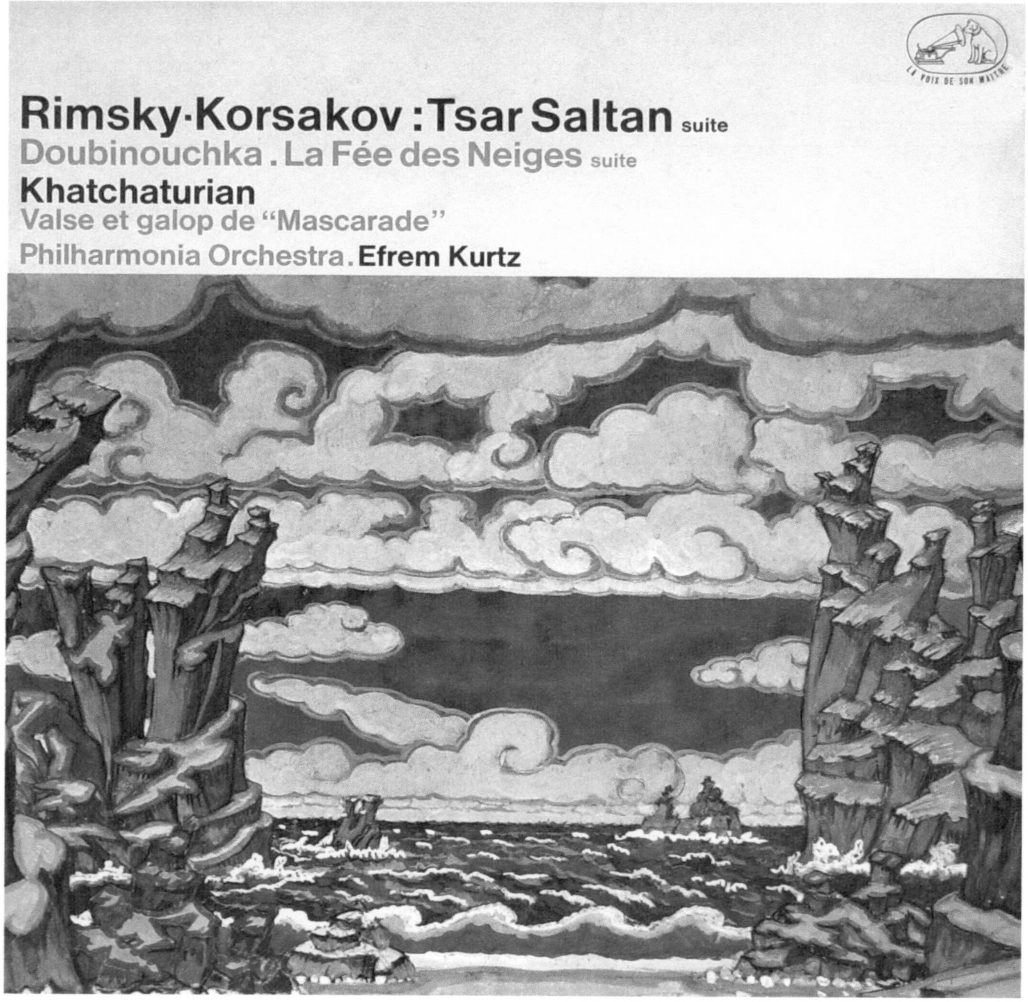

666

667

668

669

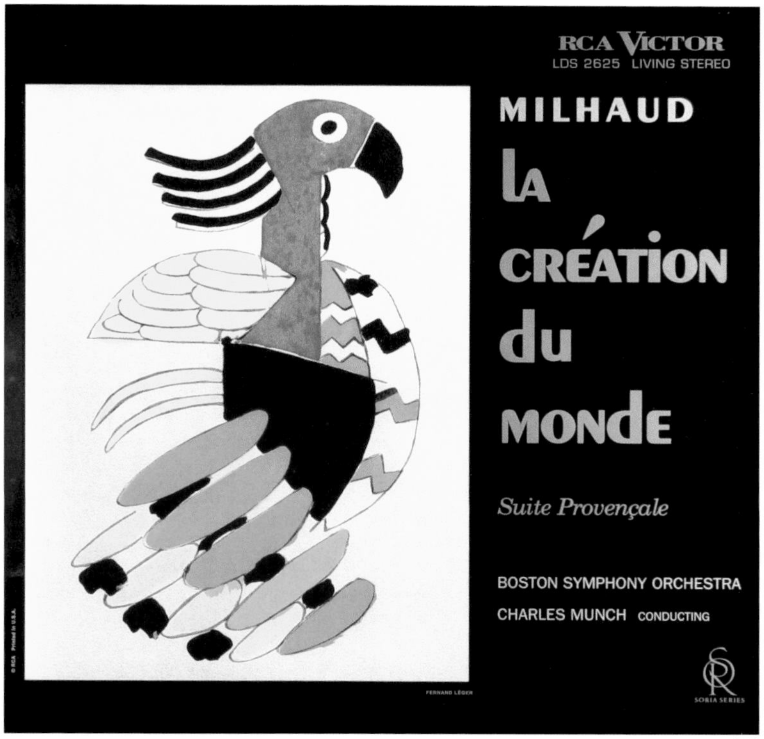

670

671

665 EMI. C063-10597, GFR 1965, CA: Clavé (Costumes for Carmen) [Design as original EMI-Columbia SAX 2566]
666 EMI. ASDF807, F 1963, CA: Alexandre Dubois (Decor for Tsar Saltan); Ph: Luc Joubert/Mercure Ed. Paris - Atelier Joubert [Design as original EMI ASD582]
667 LONDON. CS6368, USA 1963, CA: Keneth Rowell (Preliminary design for the Royal Ballet production of Le Baiser de la Fee)
668 DECCA. SXL2017, GB 1958
« (opposite page)

669 DECCA. SMD1118, D ca 1970, Ph: Axel Strencioch
670 RCA. LDS2625, USA 1962, CA: Fernand Léger
671 DECCA. SXL6488, GB 1970, CA: Leon Bakst (Design for Daphnis et Chloé; from a Diaghilev album in the William Beaumont Morris collection in the British Theatre Museum)

672

673

674

675

676

672 VANGUARD. VCS10037, USA 1968, CA: David Wilcox
(after Picasso's design for the curtain of the original performance of the Ballet Parade)
673 PHILIPS. 6580093, GB c. 1971, Ph: Michael Evans (Covent Garden Production)
674 EMI. ASD3444, GB 1978, CA: Fernand Léger
(Stage design for La Creation du Monde, copyright S.P.A.D.E.M, Paris1977)
675 EMI. C069-16302, F 1978, CA: André Hellé
(Desins d'André Hellé pour le Ballet Images; Bibliotheque de l'Opera, Paris); Ph: Jean Mainbourg
676 VARESE VC81097. USA 1979, CA: Scetches for Les Facheux by Marie Laurencine

SIR WILLIAM WALTON
Scapino, A Comedy Overture The Quest-Ballet Suite
Sinfonia Concertante (PETER KATIN piano) Capriccio Burlesco
LONDON SYMPHONY ORCHESTRA

677

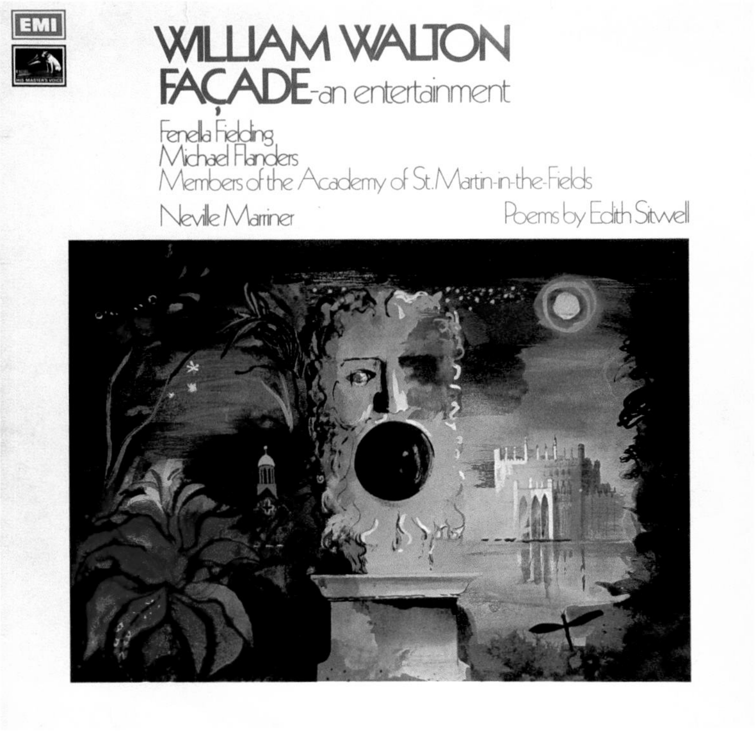
EMI
WILLIAM WALTON
FAÇADE-an entertainment
Fenella Fielding
Michael Flanders
Members of the Academy of St. Martin-in-the-Fields
Neville Marriner
Poems by Edith Sitwell

678

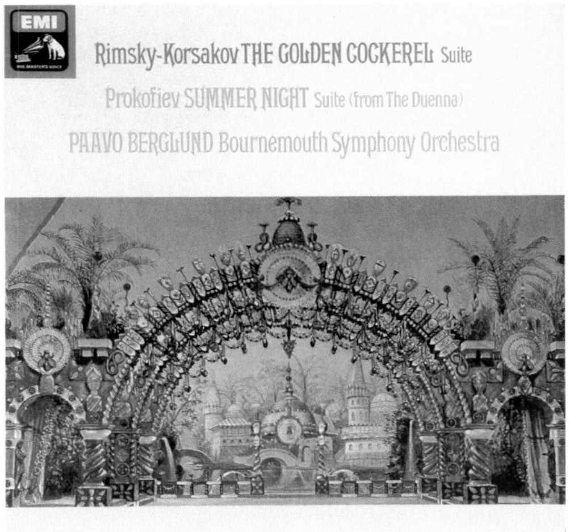
EMI
Rimsky-Korsakov THE GOLDEN COCKEREL Suite
Prokofiev SUMMER NIGHT Suite (from The Duenna)
PAAVO BERGLUND Bournemouth Symphony Orchestra

679

680

FRANK BRIDGE
Overture 'Rebus'
Dance Poem
Dance Rhapsody
Lyrita
STEREO
London Philharmonic Orchestra · Nicholas Braithwaite

681

677 LYRITA. SRCS049, GB 1971, CA: John Piper
(Design for Act III for The Quest ballet; by kind permission of artist and owner)

678 EMI. ASD2786, GB 1972, CA: John Piper
(Design for the 1942 Curtain of Facade; courtesy of the artist)

679 EMI. ASD3141, GB 1975, CA: Stage design for Act 2 of the 1892 Maryinsky Theatre production of Coq d'or; Ph: Ken Veeder

680 EMI. 270322, GB 1985, CA: Front gauze design by Peter Farmer for the Northern Theatre presentation of Othello

681 LYRITA. SRCS114, GB 1982, CD: Keith Hensby; CA: Hein Heckroth
(Design for the Tales of Hoffmann; National Film Archive, reproduced by kind permission of Mrs Ada Heckroth)

13.2 From the Old Days (682 - 691)

This category is very wide-ranging in both a temporal and geographic sense. The artwork on these covers are self-explanatory. They are not always reproductions of historic originals. Two have been especially made for the cover in question (686, 691).

— Both of the LPs with music by Alan Hovhaness signalise the oriental reference to the music of the composer (690, 691).

13.3 Ornaments (692 - 697)

— The Russian Melodiya record (693) has one of the most beautiful covers in my collection. Among my other Melodiya record covers, there is not one that can compete with this fabulous decoration.

682

683

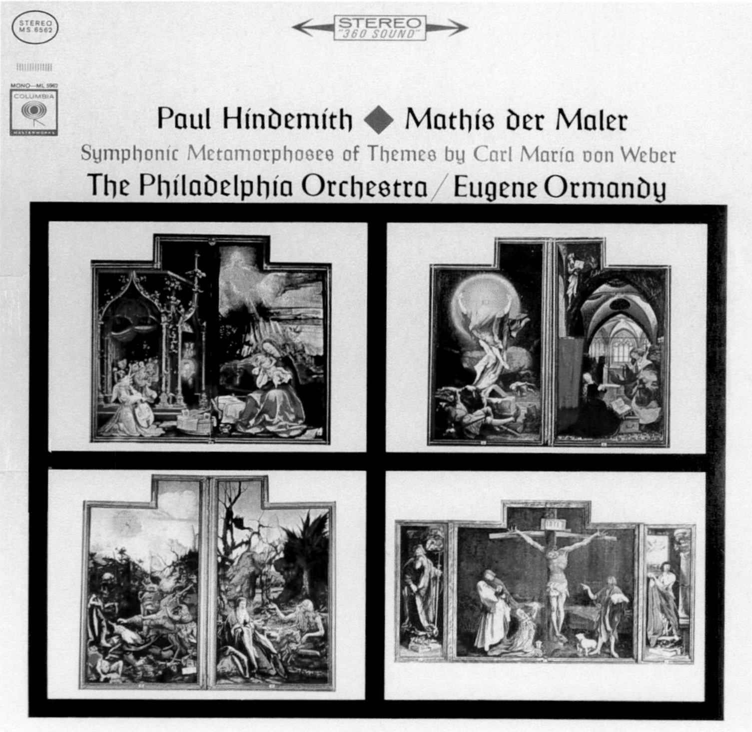

684

685

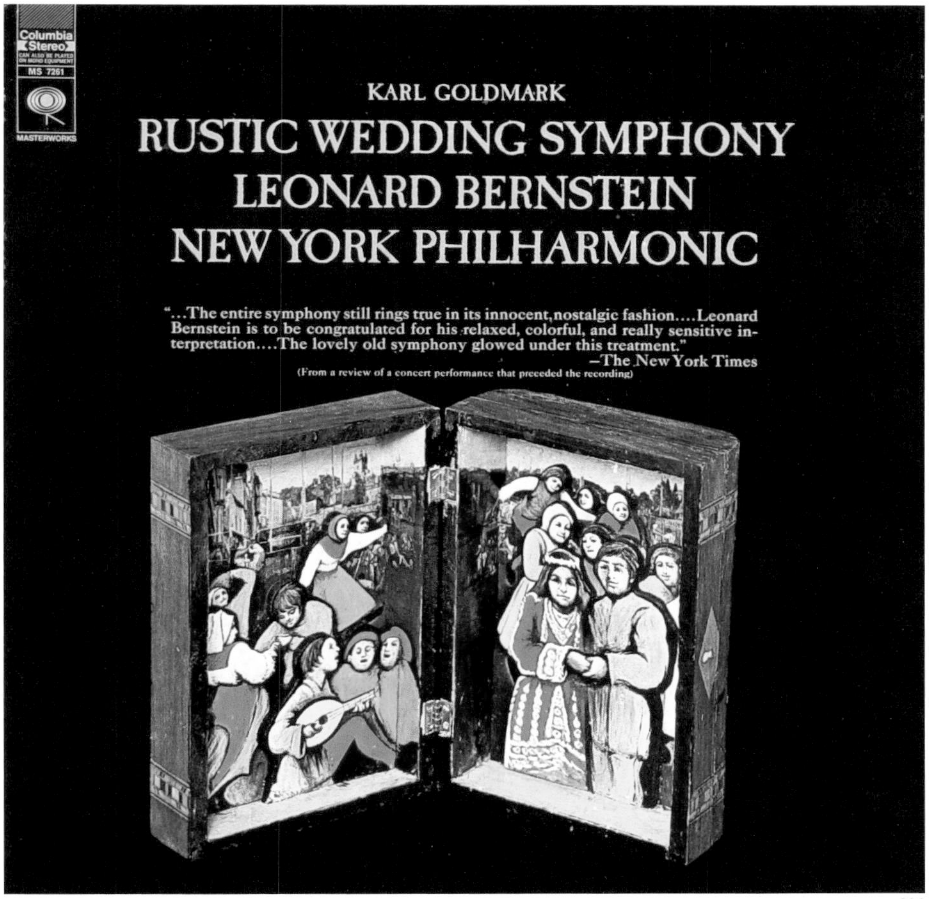

686

687

682 BALKANTON. BCA10799, Bulg 1981
683 NORSK KULTURFOND. NKF30006, N 1975, CA: Gerhard Munthe/Augusta Christensen
684 COLUMBIA. MS6562, USA 1964, CA: Mathias Grünewald (Altarpiece in Colmar, France)
685 HYPERION. A66039, GB 1981, CD: Terry Shannon; Illustration taken from Hildegard's book of Visions. Scivias, part 2, Vision 2. It shows her vision of the Creation, the Fall and the Advent of Christ (reproduced by kind permission of Otto Müller Verlag, Salzburg)
« (opposite page)

686 COLUMBIA. MS7261, USA 1968, CD: Ira Friedländer; CA: Theresa Fasolino
687 EMI. SLS807, GB 1971, CA: Akseli Gellen-Kallela *"Kullervo goes to Battle"* (Music Hall of the Old Student House, Helsinki; kind permission of the Student's Union of the University of Helsinki)
688 FINLANDIA. FA909, Fin 1982, CA: Pauline Baynes *"Map of Middle Earth"* (copyright George Allen and Unwin 1971)

688

ARTHUR
GRUMIAUX
VIEUXTEMPS
Violinkonzert Nr. 4
Chausson Poème
Ravel Tzigane
Orchestre
des Concerts Lamoureux
Manuel Rosenthal
PHILIPS
STEREO AUCH MONO ABSPIELBAR
PHILIPS
Indische Miniatur, um 1800

689

689 PHILIPS. 802708LY, EU 1967,
CA: Indian miniature *"Awaiting the Lover"*,
around 1800 (Victoria and Albert Museum, London)
690 UNICORN. RHS317, GB 1973,
CA: Miniature from a Persian manuscript,
dated 1541 (Victoria and Albert Museum,
London; courtesy British Board)
691 COLUMBIA. M34537, USA 1976,
CD: Antony Maggiore & John Berg

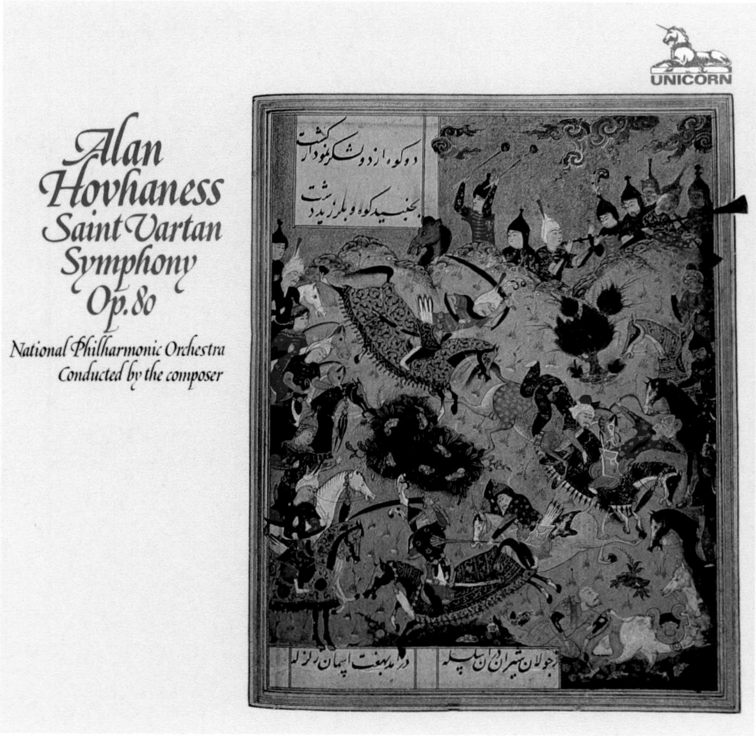
UNICORN
Alan
Hovhaness
Saint Vartan
Symphony
Op.80
National Philharmonic Orchestra
Conducted by the composer

690

Andre Kostelanetz
Conducts The Music Of Alan Hovhaness
The Rubaiyat Of Omar Khayyam Narrated by Douglas Fairbanks, Jr.
World Premiere
Sunrise, Meditation On Orpheus, And God Created Great Whales,
Fantasy On Japanese Woodprints, Floating World
Columbia

691

692 NEW WORLD. NW375, USA 1988, CD: Bob Defrin
693 MELODIYA. C04211, SU ca 1975, CA: N. Parilov (Sketches for the opera The Golden Cockerel)
694 ODYSSEY. Y33230, USA 1974, CD: Henrietta Condak; Lettering: Andy Engel; Airbrush: Fred Swanson & Danny Wong

692

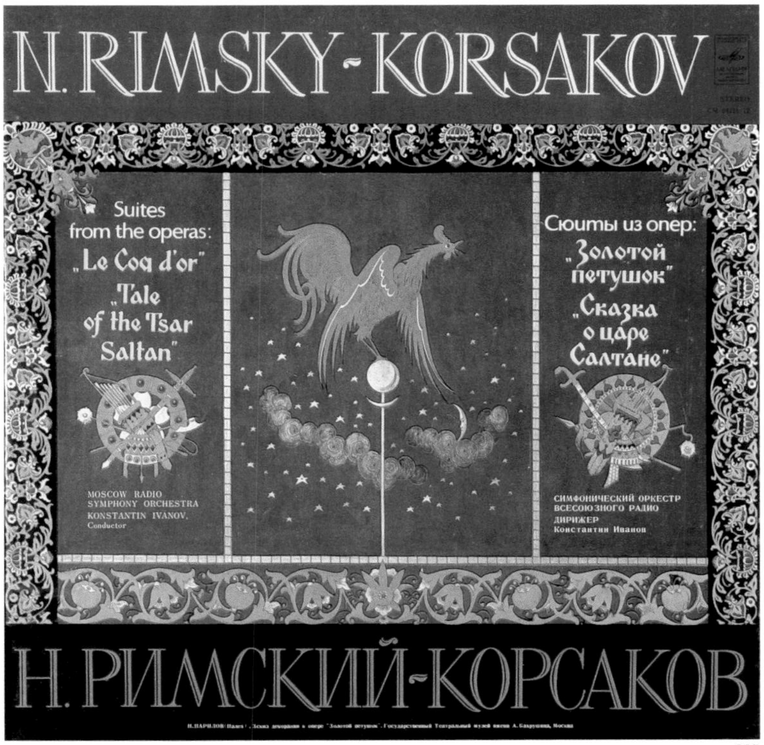

693

694

695

696

697

698

695 DECCA. SDD168, GB 1967, CD: DPAD
696 COLUMBIA. MG31078, USA, CA: Teresa Alfieri; Ph: Hank Parker
697 DECCA. SXL6588, GB 1973
698 SUPRAPHON. 1101129, CS 1972, CA: Leos Konás

13.4 Folk Art (698 - 712)

It was primarily the East European producers who drew on the medium of folk art design. Here are some particularly lovely examples, including one from an Aboriginal artist from Australia (702), and two from Azerbaijan (708, 711) and the Ukraine respectively (709, 710).

699

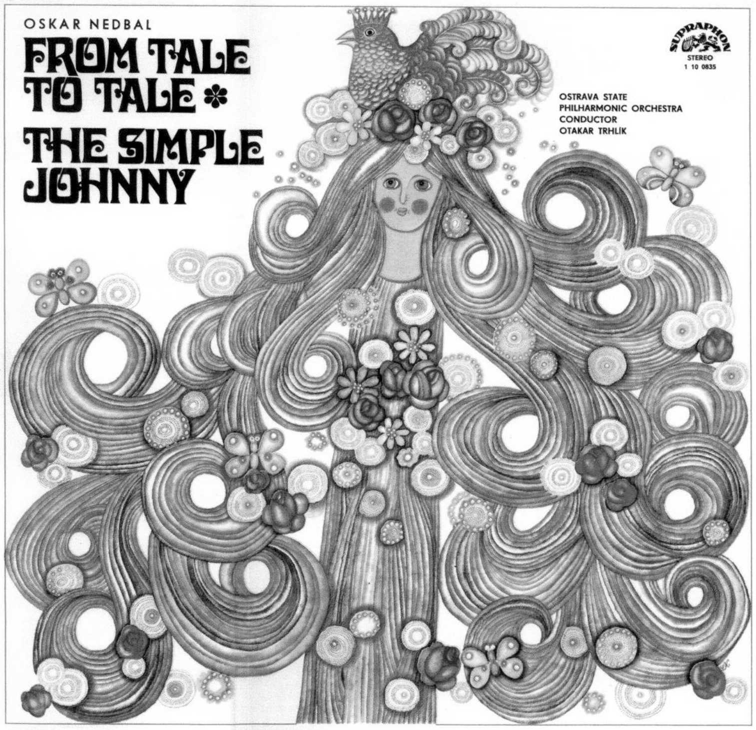

700

701

702

699 SUPRAPHON. 1100648, CS 1970, CA: Leos Konás
700 SUPRAPHON. 1100835, CS 1972, CA: Leos Konás
701 MERCURY. AMS16046, USA 1958
702 EMI. OASD7603, Aus 1977, CA: Bark painting by *"Spider"*, Malay tribe, Western Arnhem Land, depicting the Mimi, a spirit people dancing accompanied by didgeridoo players and song men with clapping sticks. Purchased by Dr. Stuart Scougall from Beswick Creek Settlement in 1960 and presented to the Art Gallery of New South Wales, by whose permission it is reproduced. [(c) Estate of the artist Spider Mamirriki Nabunu Mamarnyilk licensed by Aboriginal Artists Agency 2007]

703 ELECTRECORD. ECE01344, Rum 1971, CA: Nicolae Constantin
704 DECCA. 6.41964AS, GFR 1975, CA: Heather Payne
705 CANDIDE. CE31054, USA 1973
706 TURNABOUT. TV34440, USA ca 1972
707 COLUMBIA. MS7144, USA 1968, CD: John Crocker

703

704

705

706

707

708 MELODIYA. D031305, SU
709 MELODIYA. C03943, SU
710 MELODIYA. C03833, SU
711 MELODIYA. C09855, SU
712 EMI. ASD3108, GB 1975

708

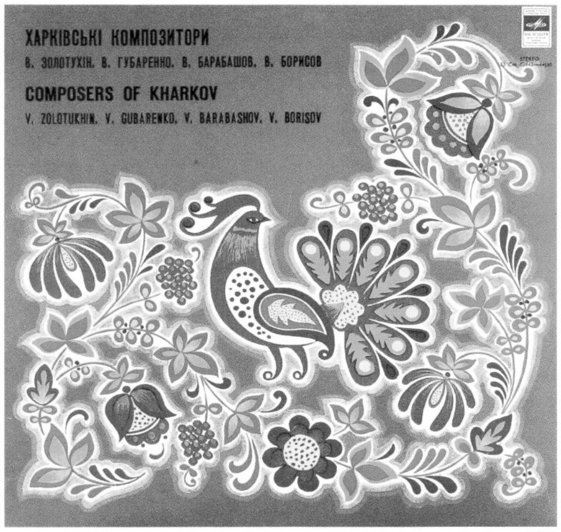

709

710

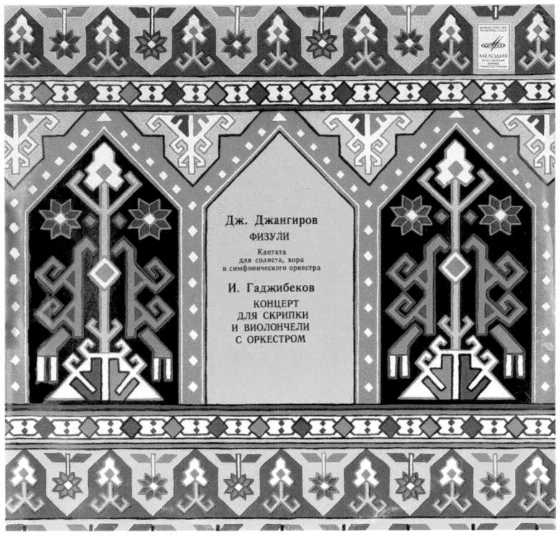

711

712

713

714

715

13.5 Variations on Notes (713 - 717)

Notes, both as a separate theme and in conjunction with other graphic elements, can help create interesting, aesthetic covers.

— The cover from the Nova record album (715) shows one of the "graphic structural sketches which were produced by the composer of the Third Symphony before the beginning of the musical detail development (musical score). [...] By colouring them differently, the individual instruments and instrument groups ... are respectively emphasised and indicated in their musical sequence." (Quote from the accompanying text)

— Cover 717 probably pretends to do something similar. In reality, the graphic artist thereby only expresses her artistic inspiration.

716

717

713 LYRITA. SRCS044, GB 1970, CD: Keith Hensby
714 MELODIYA. C30231, SU 1990
715 NOVA. 885126, GDR 1977, CD: Bernd Meier
716 MELBOURNE. SMLP4039, Can 1982, CA: Robert Daigneault
717 WESTMINSTER. WG8357, USA 1978, CD: Tim Ritchie; CA: Anne Garner

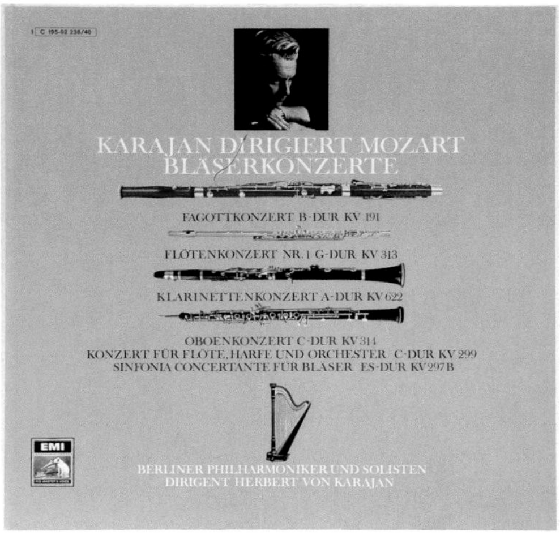

718

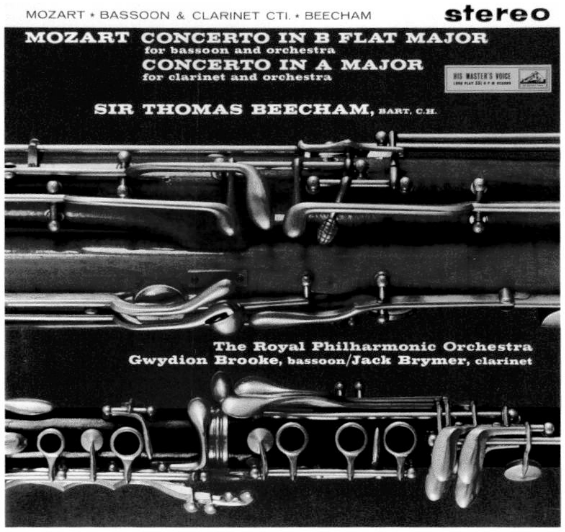

719

720

13.6 Instruments (718–733)

The artistic presentation of instruments on the packaging of a product containing music is self-evident. Thus, the standard covers in particular often portray musical instruments with nothing more than the works and the names of the artists printed on them. The ones shown here are exemplary of especially artistic processes, particularly cover 720. Cover 731, on the Columbia album with Bartok's *Concert for Orchestra,* advertises a four-channel quadraphonic recording: the instruments are all shown in position – the aim is that the listener feels in the middle of the orchestra. To achieve this, an additional stereo amplifier and two loudspeakers behind the listener are required.

721

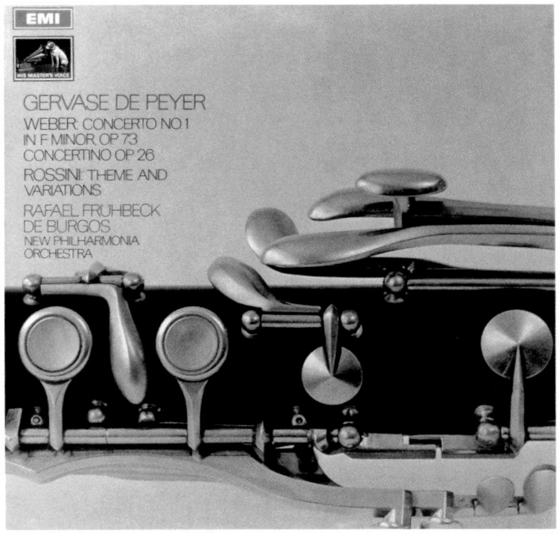

722

718 EMI. C195-02238, GFR 1972
719 EMI. ASD0344, GB 1960
720 PANTON. 110318, CS 1972, CA: Josef Hvozdensky; Ph: Stanislav Marsál
721 RCA. VICS1402, GFR, Ph: Bob Ritta
722 EMI. ASD2455, GB 1969

723

724

725

726

727

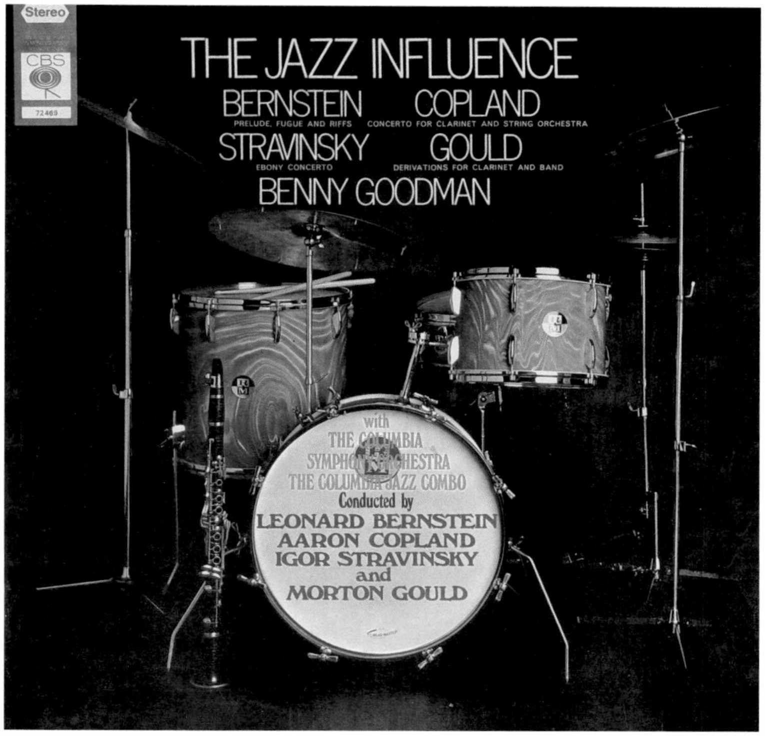

728

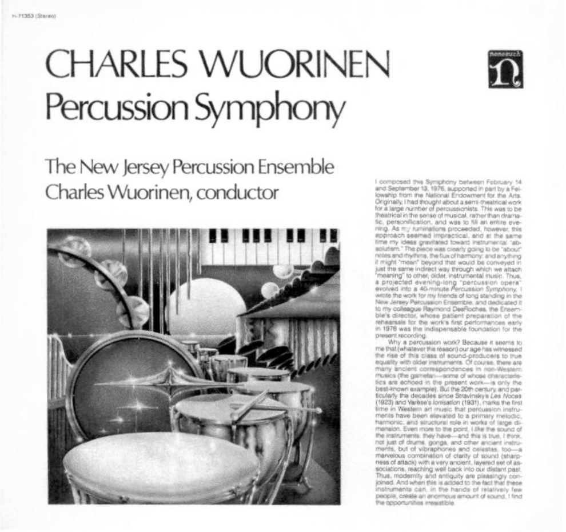

729

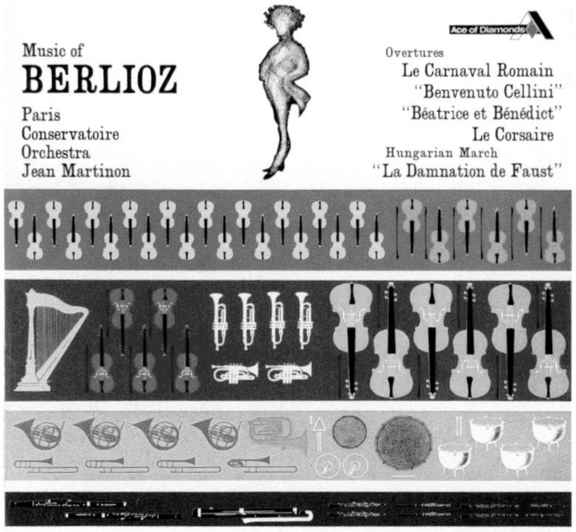

730

731

732

733

723 VANGUARD. VSD2094, USA before 1967
724 RCA. LSC3243, USA 1972, Cover sculpture Nick Aristoval
725 SERAPHIM. S60174, USA c. 1975
726 EMI. SLS 5080, GB 1977
727 SUPRAPHON. 1101680, CS 1976,
CD: Miloslav Zacek; Ph: Pavel Vácha
« (opposite page)

728 CBS. 72469, GB 1965. CD: John Hays; Ph: Bob Dowling
729 NONESUCH. H71353, USA 1978, CD: Paula Bisacca;
CA: Ron Walotsky
730 DECCA. SDD217, GB 1969, CD: DPAD
731 COLUMBIA. MQ32132, USA 1973.
CD: Hiroshi Morishima;
CA: Hiroshi Morishima & Keith Sheridan
732 COLUMBIA. M32874, USA 1975,
Airbrush rendering: Roger Huyssen
733 COLUMBIA. MQ33208, USA 1974, CA/CD: Teresa Alfieri

panton
Kalabis – Hanuš
Česká filharmonie
řídí V. Neumann / J. Bělohlávek
J. Chuchro - violoncello, J. Panenka - piano

734

13.7 Dominant Typography (734–757)

One repeatedly encounters long-playing records that have an aesthetically pleasing and interesting cover which has been created through the use of typographic stylistic devices and colours. The reference to the music is rarely indicated.

— The LP with the most interesting cover in this category is with the composers of the "New Viennese School" (Berg, Webern, Schoenberg) in picture 737. The artistic design indicates "modern" music.

— In *Dream of Gerontius,* Edward Elgar worked a religious text from Cardinal Newman into an oratorio. The cover refers to the dream scene (739).

— The Art Nouveau design on the box set with Scriabin's symphonies corresponds well with the nostalgic-sensual music of the composer (741).

— The cover on the Columbia record album (743) is illustrated with type from a type case.

— The RCA album with the Boston Pops Orchestra should no doubt inspire those classical music-lovers who enjoy a joke to buy the record (744).

— The Hebrew characters on cover 745 refer to the biblical origin of the story *Belshazzar's Feast.*

— Two covers present hand-drawn sketches (752, 753). The first is certainly by the designer of the cover. The rough sketches on the Toch record illustrating his "geographic fugue" could be from the composer himself, though the drawings can't.

735

736

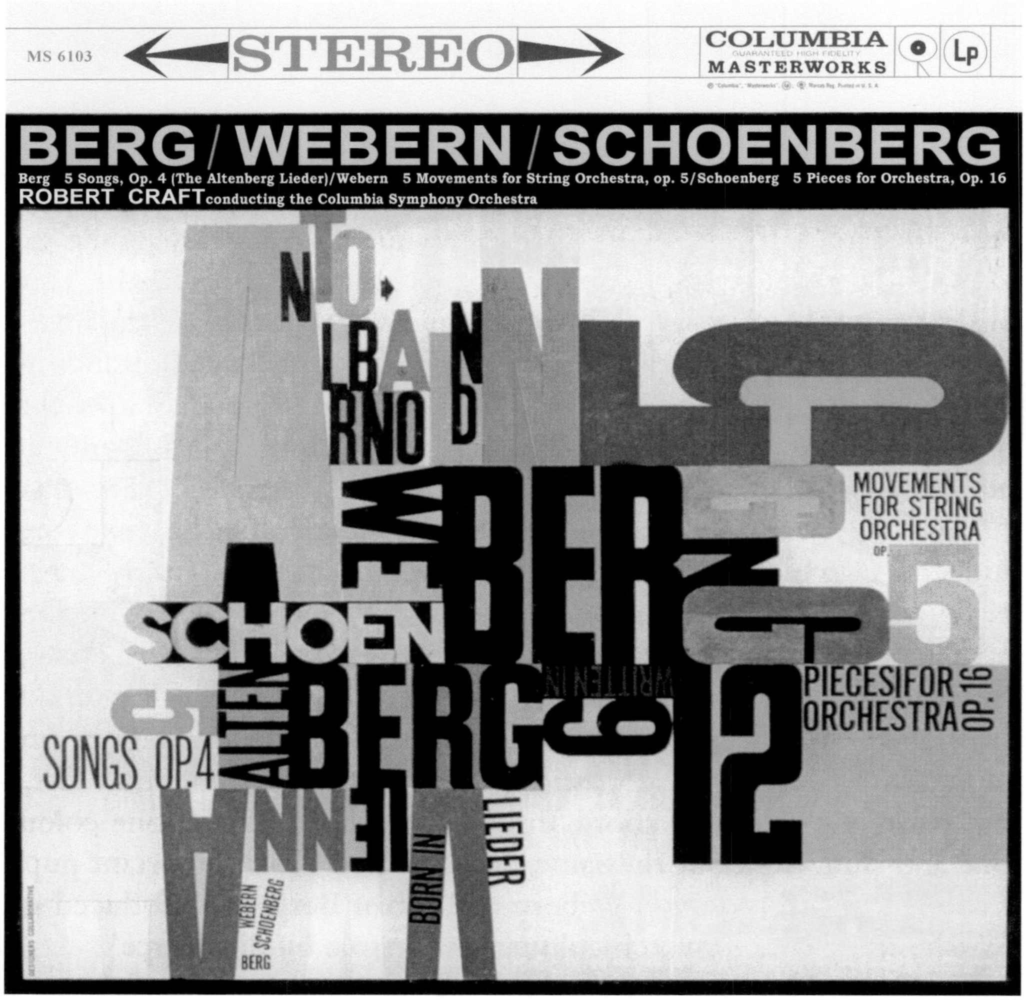

737

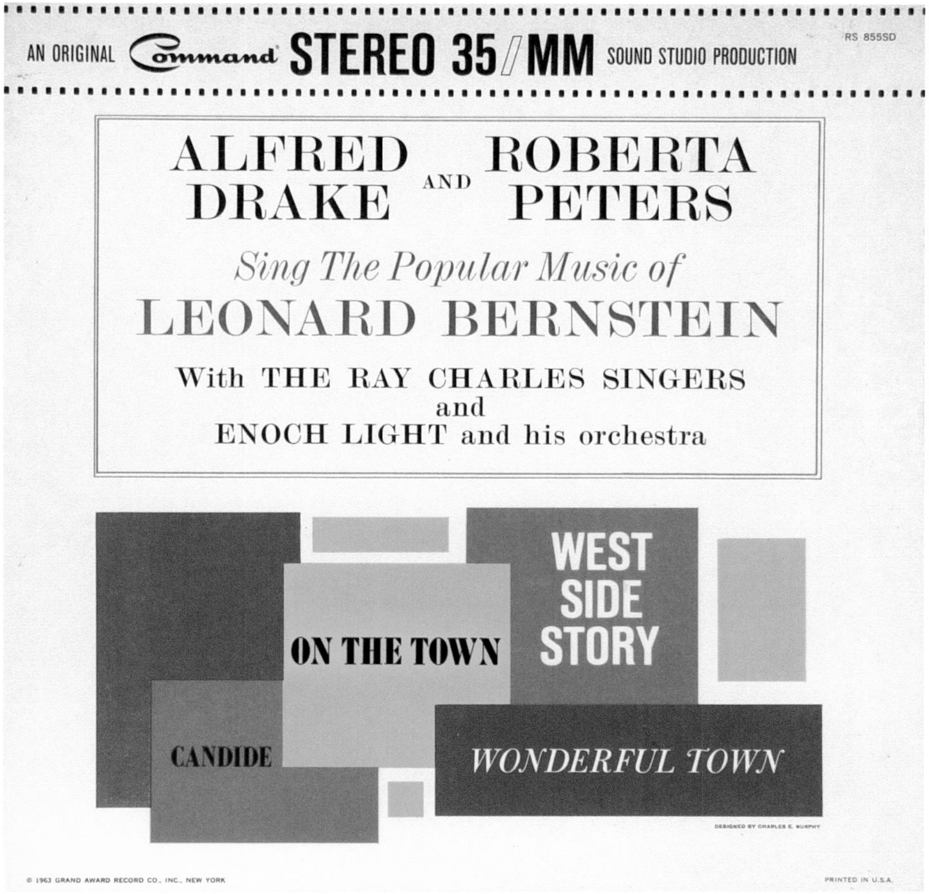

738

739

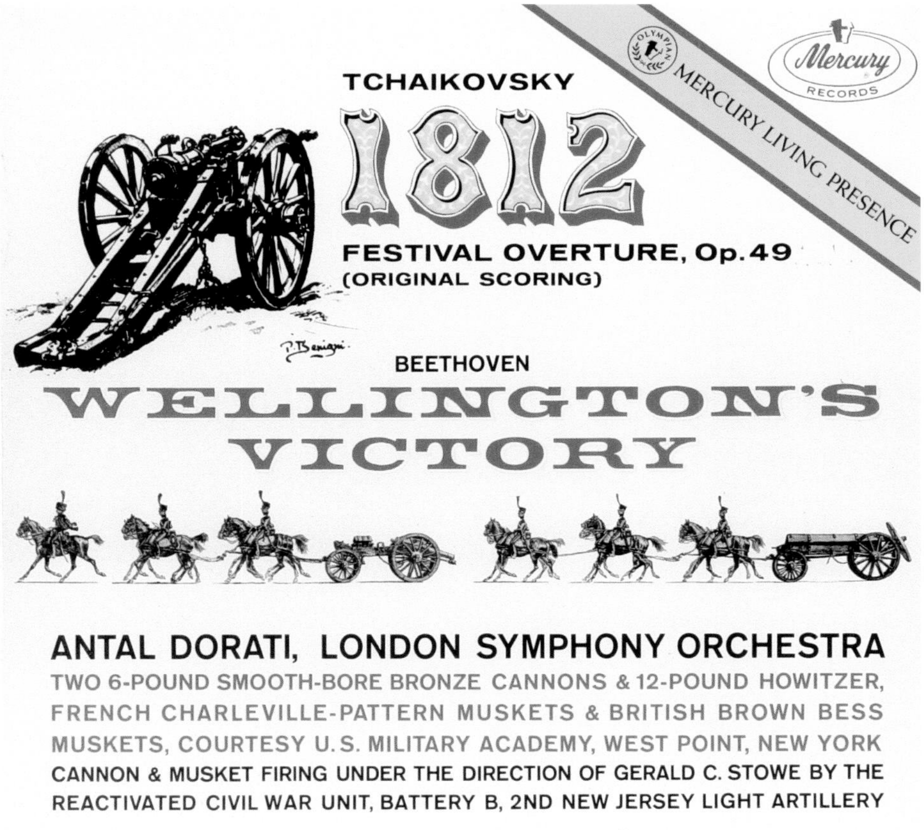

740

741

734 PANTON. 110349, CS 1972, CD: Jaroslav Fiser
735 ODYSSEY. Y32226, USA 1973, CD: Henrietta Condak
736 CONCERTEUM. CF326, F 1950s,
CA: IKA-Paris - Manquette Planet
737 COLUMBIA. MS6103, USA 1959,
CA: Designers Colloborative
« [opposite page]

738 COMMAND. RS855SD, USA 1963. CA: Charles E. Murphy
739 EMI. SLS987, GB 1976, CD: Roland Piper
740 MERCURY. 130514MGY, USA 1956
741 EURODISC. 80030XHK, D c. 1970. CD: M. Vormstein

742

743

744

745

742 FINNLEVY. SFX34, Fin 1976,
CD: Li Englund & Toivo Niiranen
743 COLUMBIA. MQ31076, USA 1971,
CD: John Berg; Ph: Don Hunstein
744 RCA. LSC2773, USA 1965
745 EMI-COLUMBIA. SAX2319, GB 1959,
CA: Atelier Joubert, Paris

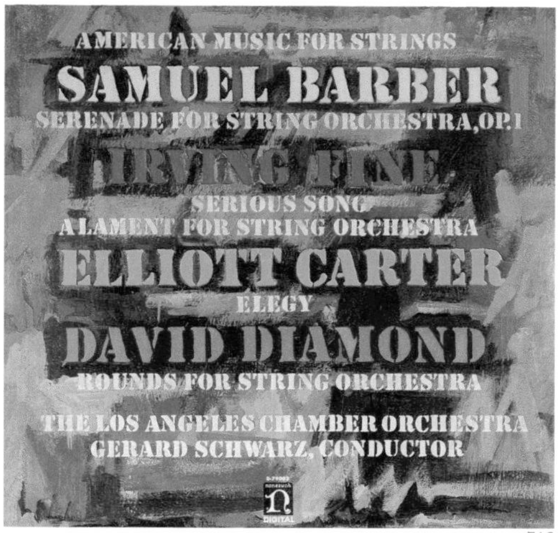

746

748

747

749

746 NONESUCH. D79002, USA 1980, CD: Jim Morphesis
747 EMI-COLUMBIA. SMC80890, GFR 1960
748 MERCURY. 130501MGY, USA 1962
749 COMMAND. CC14001SD, USA 1960s

750

751

752

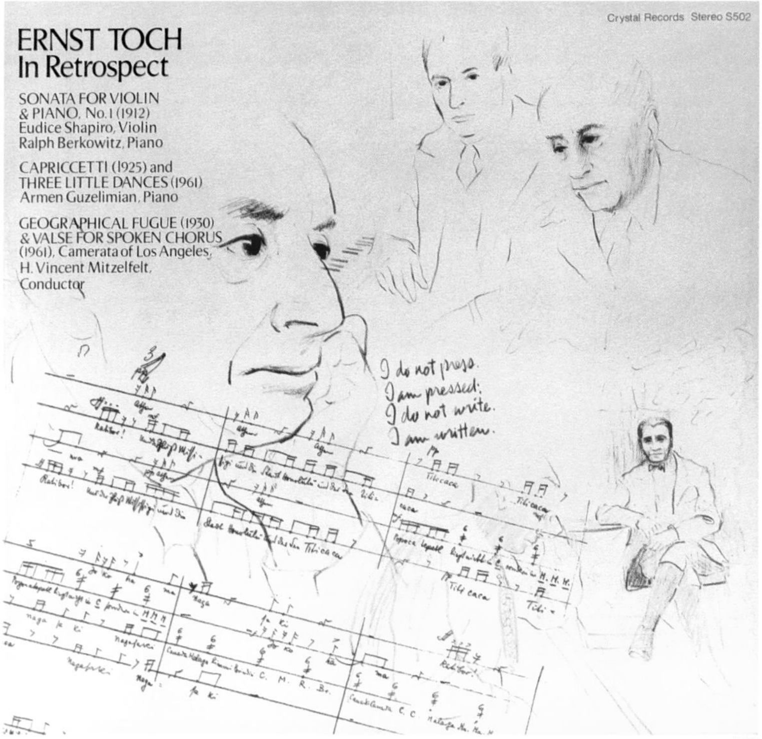

753

754

750 EURODISC. 87468XGK, D c. 1978, CD: M. Vormstein
751 RCA. SB6690, GB 1966
752 NONESUCH. 979108, USA 1985, CD: Henrietta Condak; Ph: Joel Meyerowitz
753 CRYSTAL. S502, USA 1975, CD/CA: Ed Mitchell
754 ANGEL. S35754, USA 1959.

13.8 Caricatures (755 - 767)

Caricatures on LP covers are a rarely used stylistic device for classical music.

— Hector Berlioz' works are considered to be too loud by many of his contemporaries (757).

— On the RCA record (762), the conductor Fritz Reiner (left) is drawn together with the jazz musicians Eddie Sauter and Bill Finegan.

— Arthur Sullivan's humorous operettas just beg to be portrayed as amusing caricatures (761, 763, 765, 767).

— The caricature of Anton Bruckner is not very flattering (766).

755

756

758

757

759

755 CBS. SPR25, GFR 1968, CA: Olga Koussevitzky
756 DECCA. SET617, GB 1976, CA: Laurie Richards DPAD
757 EMI. ESD290030, GB 1976, CA: A. Geiger *"Berlioz in Concert in 1846"* (Vienna State Museum)
758 SERENUS. SRS12014, USA ca 1975, CD: Sam Alexander; CA: Irwin Rosenhouse
759 HARMONIA MUNDI. C165-99721, GFR 1978. CA: Paul Hindemith (self-portrait)

760

761

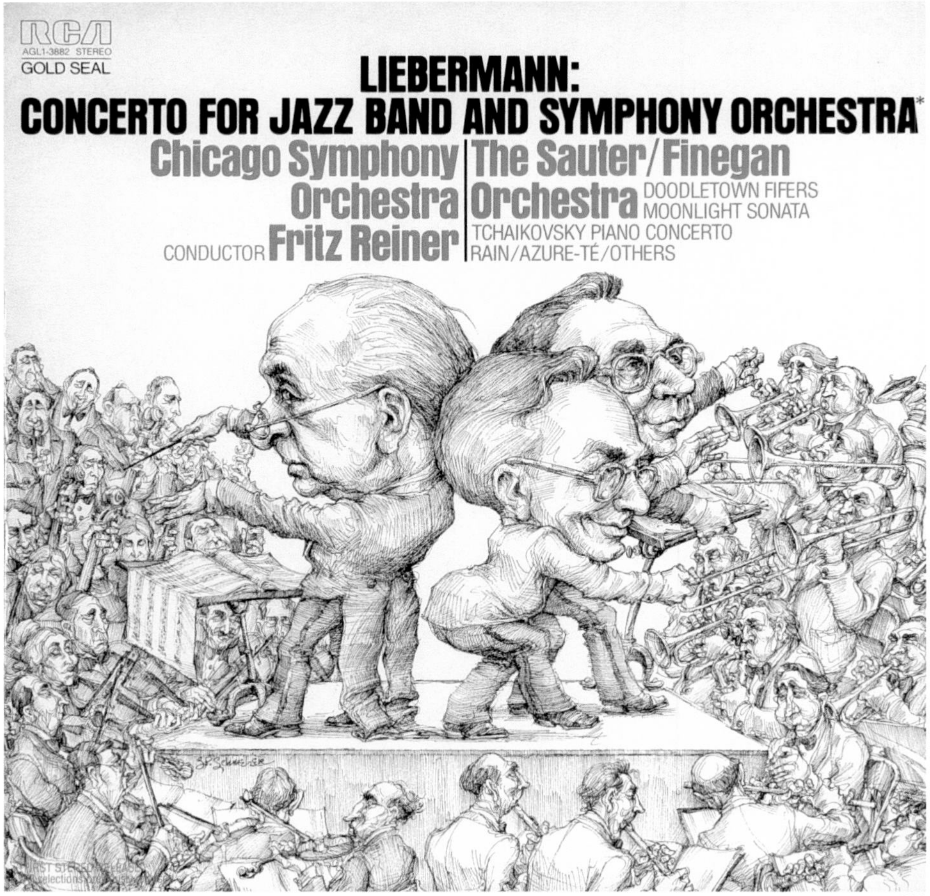

762

763

760 ANGEL. S35993, USA 1962,
CA: Francis Poulenc by Jean Cocteau (Edition Stock)
761 EMI. SXDW3034, GB 1978, CA: Jelliffe
762 RCA. AGL1-3832, USA 1981, CA: John Schmelzer
763 EMI. SXDW3029, GB 1976, CA: Jelliffe

764

765

766

767

764 EMI. 290189, F 1969, CA: Sem
765 EMI. SXDW3041, GB 1979, CA: Jelliffe
766 EMI. SXDW3047, GB 1978, CA: Jelliffe
767 CBS. 61194, GB, CA: Aubrey Schwartz

768

769

13.9 Standard Covers (768 - 775)

The standard covers of some producers testify to their explicit frugality. A standard and simply designed layout was only supplemented by the summary of contents. In the beginnings of the LP era, this was the rule, at least with the German producers, as demonstrated by the covers from DGG, Telefunken, Decca, EMI-Electrola and Philips. The standard cover was frequently implemented for use in the domestic market by the Russian Melodiya throughout the entire LP epoch. Among the two covers shown here, there is one with a printing error: a piano concert is advertised in title and image as a violin concert (774).

770

771

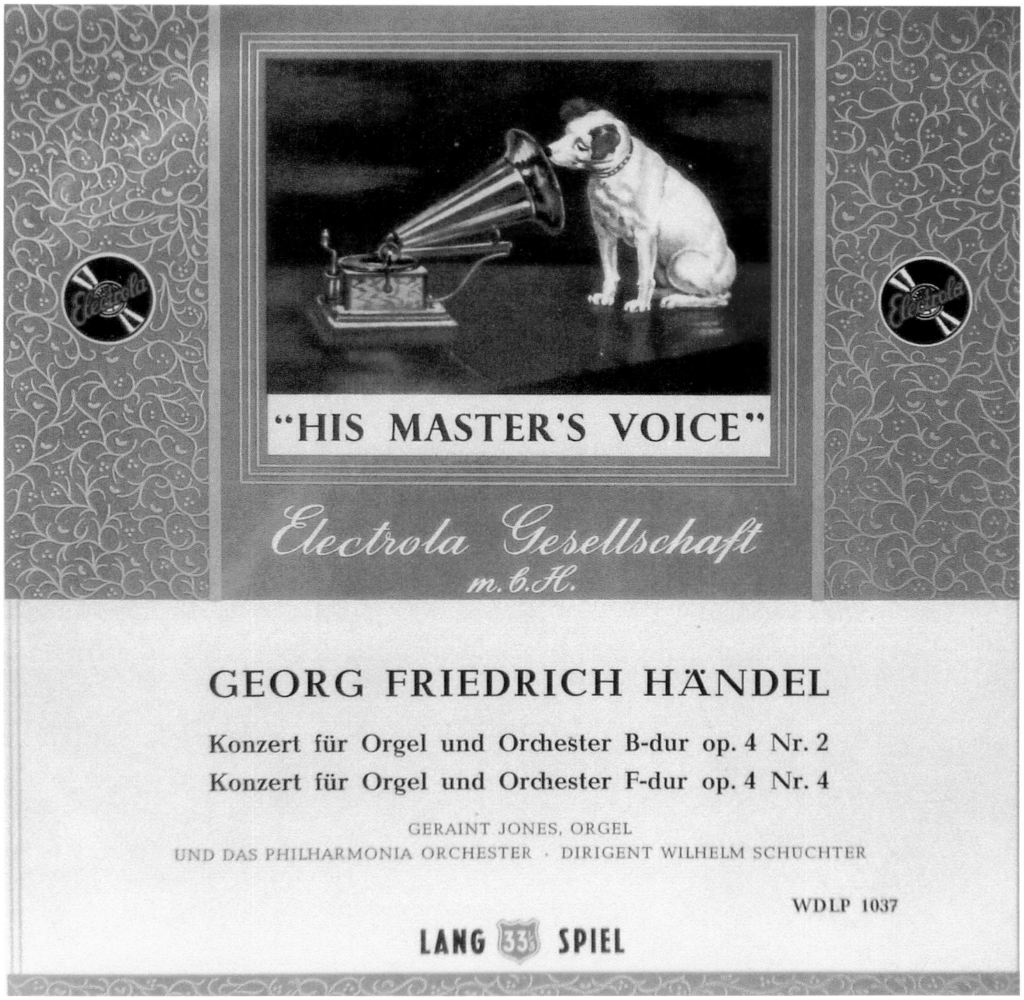

772

775

768 DGG. LPM 18520 HIFI, GFR 1950s
769 TELEFUNKEN. LT6517, GFR 1951
770 DECCA. LX3010 (25 cm), GFR 1950s
771 DECCA. LXT5178, GFR 1956
« (opposite page)

772 ELECTROLA. WDLP1037 (25 cm), GFR 1950s
773 PHILIPS. 835000AY, GFR 1960s
774 MELODIYA. C08117, SU 1978
775 MELODIYA. C12551, SU 1979

773

774

PART TWO
A BRIEF HISTORY OF LABELS

Introduction

The label, that round sticker in the centre of the LP is of interest here for two reasons: first, the label with the company logo can be aesthetically appealing – although most of them are not – and secondly, it reveals something about the time at which the record was pressed. This is due to the fact that the producers continuously changed the layout of their labels. In the *Living Stereo* Collection from the American-based RCA, for instance, this led to records with several releases having up to four different labels for the very same recording with an identical cover. The dedicated collector will always make sure to preferably find a pressing with a label that was current at the time of the recording. The effect of the increased demand for early pressings drives prices up on the second hand market. If the recordings are re-issued, not only will the label be changed, but the cover will as well.

The label is not the only value-determining factor of a record for the very same recording. Collectors also know how to interpret the letter and number combinations located in between the trail-off grooves in the vinyl. Conclusions about the value of the pressing can be made from this, at least for Decca and RCA. Then, even press matrices get outworn and subsequently, the records that they produce have inferior sound quality.

In this second part, the labels of the legendary major record companies Decca, EMI and RCA are presented in particular detail. These companies also employed the most significant order numbers to identify a series. Important here is the respective prefix.

In the following, all records from the *Living Stereo* Collection of RCA America have the prefix LSC, followed by a four-digit number. Even the country of origin is of significance. For identical recordings, the record that has been produced from the original soundtrack has a higher value than the one that has been engraved by a press matrix. As a rule, companies did not loan original soundtracks to their foreign subsidiaries, only copies.

The list of record companies is by no means complete. It only takes those into consideration which are represented in my collection and of these, only those which in my opinion might be of interest to collectors of classical LPs. There is also no guarantee that all of the labels of the producers covered here are mentioned or shown.

The Decca, EMI and RCA labels that are sought-after by audiophile collectors are, however, shown with nearly all the key labels. All interlinking among companies is based on the status at the time of the LP era. Ownership structures today are, to some extent, completely different. Detailed information, particularly with regard to the order number system and the production year can be found in the book by von Witteloostuyn (see Literature).

The same country abbreviations apply as in Part 1.

Angel - USA

Angel belongs to the English EMI Group, the American branch of which is called Capitol Records. The company primarily released English EMI recordings and as a licensee, recordings from the Russian Melodiya company. Angel only produced very few of their own recordings with American orchestras and soloists. The logo depicts a *writing angel* – an angel that is perched on top of a record and "writes" in the grooves with a quill pen. The layout of the main label and the colours have been changed three times during the lifespan of the stereo LP (1-4). Licensed editions from Russian Melodiya have their own label (5, 6).

There were re-issues under the Seraphim label (7, 8). Recordings from England were marketed under the Angel label in many other countries, especially in South America and Japan.

1 ANGEL. (S), USA. L:1 "Red Label"
2 ANGEL.(S), USA. L:2 "Blue Label"
3 ANGEL. (S), USA. L:3
4 ANGEL. (S), USA. L:4
5 ANGEL. (SR) *Melodiya,* USA. L:1
6 ANGEL. (SR) *Melodiya,* USA. L:2
7 ANGEL. (S-1) *Seraphim,* USA. L:1

Argo - GB

Argo is a division of Decca and released both old and modern works that were relatively unknown. A Beethoven symphony, for example, would have been absolutely uncharacteristic for Argo. The records have the same excellent recording quality as those from Decca. The standard prefix of the stereo records is ZRG (9, 10). In Germany, some of the Argo recordings that were released in England were published under the Decca label.

1

2

3

4

5

6

7

Capitol - USA

Capitol Records is a subsidiary of the English EMI in the USA. They only produced classical records, however, up until the late 1960s. The focus here is on the rather lighter works from the classical repertoire, often conducted by Carmen Dragon or Felix Slatkin. In the early days of stereo, Capitol also released recordings from the English EMI in the USA. This was done later on the Angel label, a division of the Capitol Group (see above). The order numbers for LPs with English EMI recordings begin with the prefix SG, American recordings with the prefix SP. Re-issues from Capitol are released on *Seraphim* (see *Angel)*. The layout was changed many times over. Capitol used five different labels in the USA, including the label for the mono records. The label for mono records and the first stereo label (11, 12) still display the "FDS" logo *(Full Dimensional Sound)*, followed by the *side label* (13) and the *centre label* (14). During the age of the FDS label, recordings of the English EMI were furnished with the *EMI* label (15). The Capitol covers of that time are some of the most beautiful, providing that they were painted and not designed with photos. They have been extensively acknowledged in the first part. The press quality leaves much to be desired. With the introduction of stereophony, Capitol packaged the records in technically informative inner sleeves (17).

8 ANGEL. (S-1) *Seraphim*, USA. L:2
9 ARGO. (ZRG), Decca GB. L:1 "Oval Label"
10 ARGO. (ZRG), Decca GB. L:2
11 CAPITOL. (P) *FDS*, USA. L:Mono
12 CAPITOL. (SP) *FDS*, USA. L:1
13 CAPITOL. (SP) *Side Logo*, USA. L:2
14 CAPITOL. (SP) *Center Logo*, USA. L:3

8

9

10

11

12

13

14

15

16

THE FULL SPECTRUM OF SOUND

Capitol STEREO THE FULL SPECTRUM OF SOUND

. . . YOUR ASSURANCE OF THE FINEST STEREO ON RECORDS Capitol Records, long the leader in high-fidelity recording, has constantly maintained the highest standards in audio-engineering and quality control. These standards, combined with the finest performances by outstanding artists, have made the Capitol name synonymous with artistic and technical excellence. Capitol stereo records benefit from that excellence in every respect. They afford the optimum in stereophonic fidelity.

The eight questions most often asked about stereo records

■ First of all, what is stereophonic sound?

Stereo is, most simply, the difference between what you hear from the best monaural recordings and what you hear "in person."

Even the finest monaural sound (the single-source sound heard on all previous records) cannot equal the best stereo sound. The reason is quite simple. Our sense of direction, perspective, and depth in sound depends on one phenomenon: we hear the same sound slightly differently with each ear. A sound coming from our right is louder and more distinct to our right ear than to our left. Thus, we automatically place that sound to our right. A system of home listening that could reproduce this phenomenon would finally bring "in person" listening into the home. Stereo is that system.

■ What is a stereo record?

MONAURAL — SINGLE CHANNEL; STEREO — FIRST CHANNEL, SECOND CHANNEL

Again, we must go back to the monaural record. On a monaural record the *same* sound is engraved on both sides (walls) of the groove. No matter how many speakers or amplifiers we use, we cannot get away from a single, point-source effect. And since our ears demand at least two "points of view" to establish real perspective, we are left with a good representation of sound, but one that lacks natural, all-around-us realism. This stereo record recreates the needed perspective. Sounds are recorded from two points of view and, ultimately, engraved one on each side of the groove.* Thus, the stereo record, when properly played, gives a realistic "display" of sound. All that is needed to produce this three-dimension effect is the stereo record, two amplifier-speaker systems, a turntable, and a stereo cartridge.

■ Why a stereo cartridge?

A cartridge is the device which transforms into an electric signal the vibrations picked up by the needle as it travels the record groove. But the important fact about a *stereo* cartridge is that with one needle, two sound messages can be kept separate.

NEEDLE — FIRST CHANNEL — SECOND CHANNEL

■ Do I need both monaural and stereo cartridges to play both kinds of records?

No. Stereo cartridges play both monaural and stereo records. And monaural records play just as well with a stereo cartridge.

STEREO TAPE RECORDER — FIRST MICROPHONE — SECOND MICROPHONE

■ Why can't I play stereo records with my old cartridge?

Because most ordinary cartridges are too stiff to follow the vertical movements caused by the varying depth of the stereo groove. Since ordinary cartridges are capable of only slight vertical movement, they cut into stereo grooves, seriously damaging the record. When an improper cartridge is used, you hear distorted sound and your needle may skip from one groove to another.

*Since the two sounds are engraved at 45° angles from the record surface, this system of cutting a record is often called the 45/45 system.

■ Why do I need two audio systems?

Probably you already have one system: a turntable, cartridge, amplifier, and speaker. To keep the two audio channels separate until they are reproduced in your living room, you need a stereo cartridge and an additional amplifier and speaker. Only with this equipment can the two audio channels be kept separate until they are presented as stereo sound.

■ Why must the two audio channels be kept separate when they mix again before we hear them?

Just as in a concert hall the sound is not kept separate for each ear, the sound need not be kept separate in your living room. The two necessary "points of view" discussed earlier are recreated by your speakers.

RECORD PLAYER WITH STEREO DISC — FIRST AMPLIFIER — SECOND AMPLIFIER — FIRST SPEAKER — SECOND SPEAKER — LISTENER

Although proper speaker placement depends on each room's characteristics, a critical element in proper stereo performance is this: the two speakers should be separated as far as possible without creating a "hole" (drop-off of sound) between them. Good stereo equipment is perfectly capable of creating an even, natural display of sound all across the "stage" in front of the listener.

■ Are stereo records more delicate than ordinary high-fidelity records?

No. The precautions you take to preserve the life of monaural long-playing records are sufficient to protect stereo records.

Capitol albums are recorded with the RIAA standard recording characteristic

17

18

Columbia and Epic - USA, CBS - Europe

Along with RCA, Columbia is one of the leading companies in the USA, founded in 1888 as the Columbia Phonograph Company. In 1956, Columbia developed its own stereo cutting process. However, it didn't find acceptance. With Columbia, artists such as Isaac Stern, Glenn Gould, Leonard Bernstein, Bruno Walter, George Szell and Eugene Ormandy became world-famous. The older stereo pressings up to 1963 are the so-called "six eyes" (18), succeeded by the "two eyes" label (19). In the USA, there were re-issues on the *Odyssey* label (21).

CBS. In Europe, Columbia recordings were released under the CBS *(Columbia Broadcasting Systems)* label, because in Europe the name *Columbia* had already been claimed by the English EMI. This early label, which was of great relevance to collectors, existed in Europe until about 1975. The colour for first releases was blue (22).

Re-issues on *CBS Classics* (Series 61nnn) had a red label and the same layout. Starting around 1976, the European label differs from the American label (20) only in terms of the "CBS Masterworks" logo instead of "Columbia" (23).

Epic is also a division of Columbia USA. Recordings of Dutch-based Philips were primarily offered in the USA on this label (24, 25). In return, Philips marketed Columbia recordings in Europe under its own name, since the brand mark "Columbia" was owned by the European EMI Group.

15 CAPITOL. (SG) *EMI Side Logo,* USA. L:1
16 COLUMBIA. (ML) Masterworks USA. L:mono
17 CAPITOL. USA. Inner sleeve
18 COLUMBIA. (MS) Masterworks, USA. L:1
"Six Eyes" (label designed by Alex Steinweiss)

19

20

21

22

23

24

Command Classics - USA

19 COLUMBIA. (MS) *Masterworks*, USA. L:2 "Two Eyes"
20 COLUMBIA. (M) *Masterworks*, USA. L:3
21 COLUMBIA. (Y) *Odyssey*, USA.
22 CBS. GFR. L:1
23 CBS. *Masterworks*, Eu. L:2
24 EPIC. (BC), USA. L:1
25 EPIC. (BC), USA. L:2
26 COMMAND CLASSICS. (CC), USA. L:1 "Gold"
27 COMMAND CLASSICS. (CC), USA. L:2

The leading artists under contract on this label were first and foremost the conductor William Steinberg with the Pittsburgh Symphony Orchestra.
Command Classics used the 35 mm magnetic film recording process. The same applied to Everest and Mercury (see below). The fold-out record covers contain related information (30). As with Mercury, Robert Fine was also responsible for the recordings here. The catalogue is quite modest, with fewer than 100 records. The early pressings with the gold label are collector's items (26). The later pressings were produced by ABC.

25

26

27

28

29

31

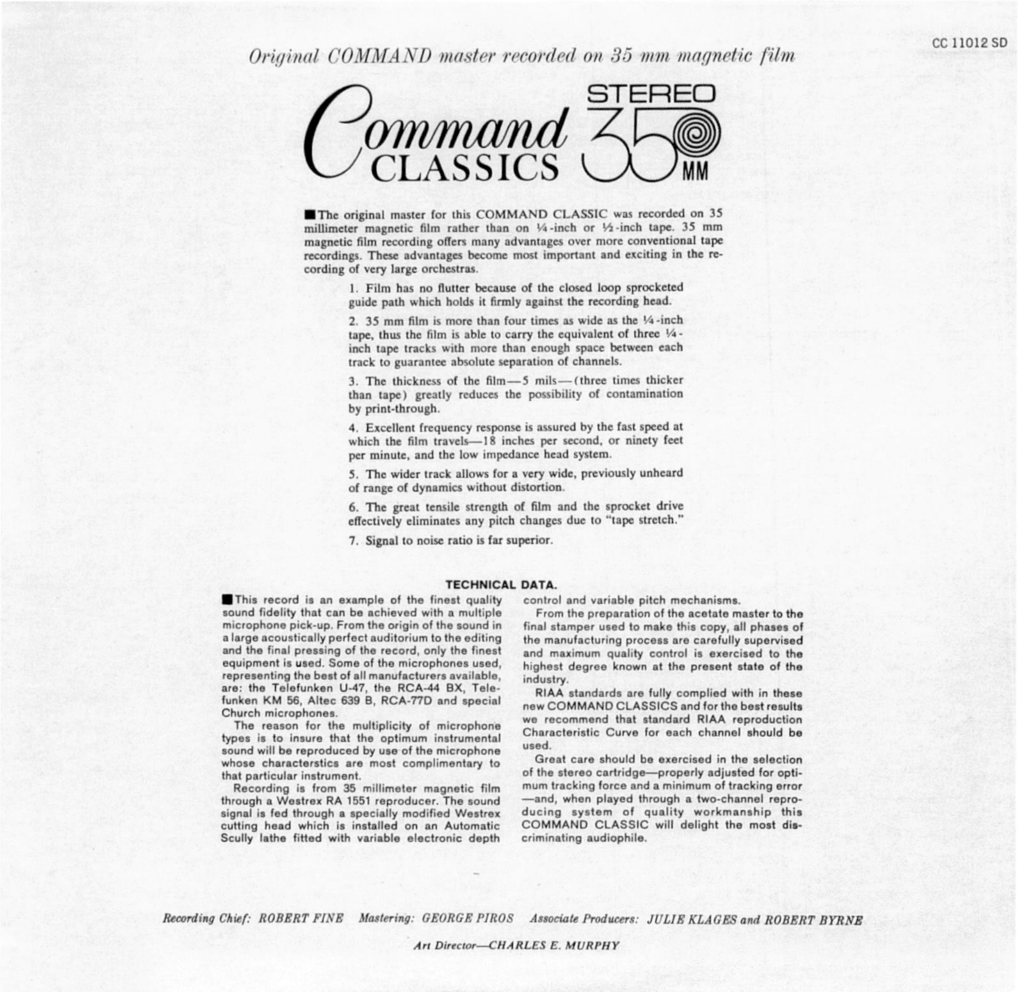

CC 11012 SD

Original COMMAND master recorded on 35 mm magnetic film

Command CLASSICS STEREO 35 MM

■ The original master for this COMMAND CLASSIC was recorded on 35 millimeter magnetic film rather than on ¼-inch or ½-inch tape. 35 mm magnetic film recording offers many advantages over more conventional tape recordings. These advantages become most important and exciting in the recording of very large orchestras.

1. Film has no flutter because of the closed loop sprocketed guide path which holds it firmly against the recording head.
2. 35 mm film is more than four times as wide as the ¼-inch tape, thus the film is able to carry the equivalent of three ¼-inch tape tracks with more than enough space between each track to guarantee absolute separation of channels.
3. The thickness of the film—5 mils—(three times thicker than tape) greatly reduces the possibility of contamination by print-through.
4. Excellent frequency response is assured by the fast speed at which the film travels—18 inches per second, or ninety feet per minute, and the low impedance head system.
5. The wider track allows for a very wide, previously unheard of range of dynamics without distortion.
6. The great tensile strength of film and the sprocket drive effectively eliminates any pitch changes due to "tape stretch."
7. Signal to noise ratio is far superior.

TECHNICAL DATA.

■ This record is an example of the finest quality sound fidelity that can be achieved with a multiple microphone pick-up. From the origin of the sound in a large acoustically perfect auditorium to the editing and the final pressing of the record, only the finest equipment is used. Some of the microphones used, representing the best of all manufacturers available, are: the Telefunken U-47, the RCA-44 BX, Telefunken KM 56, Altec 639 B, RCA-77D and special Church microphones.

The reason for the multiplicity of microphone types is to insure that the optimum instrumental sound will be reproduced by use of the microphone whose characterstics are most complimentary to that particular instrument.

Recording is from 35 millimeter magnetic film through a Westrex RA 1551 reproducer. The sound signal is fed through a specially modified Westrex cutting head which is installed on an Automatic Scully lathe fitted with variable electronic depth control and variable pitch mechanisms.

From the preparation of the acetate master to the final stamper used to make this copy, all phases of the manufacturing process are carefully supervised and maximum quality control is exercised to the highest degree known at the present state of the industry.

RIAA standards are fully complied with in these new COMMAND CLASSICS and for the best results we recommend that standard RIAA reproduction Characteristic Curve for each channel should be used.

Great care should be exercised in the selection of the stereo cartridge—properly adjusted for optimum tracking force and a minimum of tracking error—and, when played through a two-channel reproducing system of quality workmanship this COMMAND CLASSIC will delight the most discriminating audiophile.

Recording Chief: ROBERT FINE Mastering: GEORGE PIROS Associate Producers: JULIE KLAGES and ROBERT BYRNE

Art Director—CHARLES E. MURPHY

30

Decca and London - Great Britain

Decca is one of the really big traditional companies with a huge repertoire. Famous conductors from the stereo era included, among others, Ernest Ansermet, Peter Maag, Zubin Mehta, Pierre Monteux and Sir Georg Solti. The company was founded in London in 1929.

English Deccas and Londons. English Decca pressings (in the USA under "London") are sought after by audiophile collectors. In 1941, the *full frequency range recording* (fffr) was developed from a procedure that was used to locate submarines. In 1958, the *full frequency stereophonic sound* (ffss) followed. The original English full price records carry the prefix SXL. The number series SXL2nnn constitutes the early age of stereo technology and pressings with the "Wide Band" (WB) label (28), which runs to SXL6448, are especially coveted. The box sets with the prefix SET are on par with SXL. English re-issues are the series *Ace of Diamonds* (SDD and GOS), *Eclipse* (ECS) and *The World of...* (SPA). These series are largely of equal significance. The Jubilee (JB) set appeared later to mark the 25th anniversary of the coronation of Queen Elizabeth II.

Decca recordings were marketed in the USA under the name London (prefix CS) and are technically identical with the Decca records, due to the fact that they were both simultaneously pressed in England. Only the labels and the covers vary.

The brand name Decca was previously used in the USA by another record producer. This was originally a subsidiary of English Decca and was supposed to distribute their recordings in the USA. They became independent in 1938 and ever since, recordings from Decca are sold under the name "London" in the USA. Even London records had an early and a later label at the same time as the "Wide Band" and "Narrow Band" from Decca. There were also London re-issues in the *Stereo Treasury Series* (STS). The most significant Decca and London series are listed together with the prefix in chart 1.

Phase 4 Stereo is a recording technique and was first employed for classical music in 1963.

28 DECCA (SXL). GB. L:1 "Wide Band"
29 DECCA (SXL). GB. L:2 "Narrow Band"
30 COMMAND CLASSICS. USA. Inner sleeve
31 DECCA. (PFS) *Phase Four Stereo,* GB

Twenty channels were mixed on "four phases" (twice left, twice right) and these were then distributed over two channels. The aim was to create particularly atmospheric recordings, although these are not appreciated by today's collectors.

German Decca pressings (36-38) were pressed in Hanover at Teldec, the pressing plant of which had an excellent reputation. Teldec quickly abandoned the SXL numbering procedure and introduced a numerical code, which is not as easily remembered as the letter combination on the English original. German re-issues have been released on the labels *Meister der Musik* and later on *Noblesse* and *Aspekte.*

32

Chart 1 – Prefixes for English Decca long-playing albums

SXL	First edition in England at full price (28, 29).
SET	First edition in England in a boxed set, mainly operas.
PFS	Phase 4 Stereo recordings (31).
ECS	Eclipse. Re-issue in the mid-price category, in part with Decca recordings that had been released in the USA under RCA (32).
SDD and GOS	Ace of Diamonds. Re-issue in the mid-price category (33, 34).
SPA	The World of ... of Re-issue of recordings that had been previously re-issued under SDD or ECS.
JB	Silver Jubilee (of Queen Elizabeth II). Late re-issues in the mid-price category (35).
London CS	Like SXL, but produced in England for the US market (39, 40).
London CSA	Like SET, but produced in England for the US market.
London STS	Stereo Treasury Series. Re-issue produced in England for the US market, otherwise like SDD (41).
London SP and SPC	Phase 4 Stereo. Produced in England for the US market.

33

32 DECCA. (ECS) *Eclipse*, GB
33 DECCA. (SDD) *Ace of Diamonds;* GB. L:1
34 DECCA. (SDD) *Ace of Diamonds;* GB. L:2
35 DECCA. (JB) *Jubilee*, GB. L:2
36 DECCA. (SXL), Teldec GFR. L:1

34

35

36

37 DECCA. (SXL), Teldec GFR. L:2
38 DECCA. Teldec GFR. L:3
39 LONDON. (CS) *FFSS*, USA. L:1
40 LONDON. (CS) *FFRR*, USA. L:2
41 LONDON. (STS) *Stereo Treasury Series*, USA
42 EMI. (ALP) *HMV*, GB: L:mono
43 EMI. (ASD) *HMV*, GB. L:1 "White and Gold"

37

38

39

40

41

42

43

EMI - Great Britain

EMI (Electrical and Musical Industries) is the top ranking traditional company in England next to Decca. EMI proudly boasted that it was the "greatest recording organisation in the world", even printing this slogan on its record sleeves.

It was founded jointly by the Gramophone Company Ltd. and the Columbia company. EMI has international subsidiaries, such as Electrola in Germany, Pathé Marconi in France and Capitol Records in the USA. The logo portrays the dog Nipper and bears the title "His Master's Voice" (HMV), which is how EMI referred to itself in the beginning. The name EMI was mentioned on the back of the cover, if at all. Use of the famous trademark is not permitted in the USA. The rights there belong to the RCA record company. Many famous conductors were on long-term contract with EMI: Sir Thomas Beecham, Sir John Barbirolli, Sir Adrian Boult, Otto Klemperer, André Previn, and others.

English pressings have a prefix incorporated into the order number. These are summarized in chart 2. In comparison with German and European editions, the English editions are more highly valued by collectors. This depends on the time of the pressing, particularly in the case of the important ASD prefix, especially for older recordings from the late 1950s and 1960s. The oldest ASD stereo label is "White and Gold" with Nipper the dog in front of a shaded background (43). It was in use until ASD575. The subsequent label "Red and Black Dog" (44) portrays Nipper in a semicircle, similar to the mono label (42). It was used up to ASD2478. Later label versions depict Nipper on a "stamp" (45,46).

The English EMI was also licensee of the Russian Melodiya and released their recordings almost exclusively in the ASD series (48, 49). As a result, a highly interesting repertoire of Melodiya recordings was released in Great Britain. These included recordings with famous conductors such as Vladimir Fedoseyev, Boris Khaikin, Yevgeny Mravinsky, Gennady Rozhdestvensky, Yevgeny Svetlanov and Kiril Kondrashin.

Although the colouring is different, the first CSD label (50) is similar to the "White and Gold". The second CSD label shows a smaller Nipper (51).

Another division of the EMI Group was the English Columbia with the "Magic Notes" logo: two semiquavers (sixteenth notes). The first "Black and Silver" stereo label was in use up to SAX2538 (62).

German pressings were produced by the Electrola company. Earlier full price records have the prefix SME (EMI Electrola), SMC (EMI Columbia), and subsequently the codes C063-nnnnn and C065-nnnnn (52-54). There was no longer a differentiation made between HMV and Columbia. Previous to the C, there is a one-digit number which indicates the country of origin. The one stands for Germany. Later productions from the end of the LP era start with the prefix EL or have no prefix. For these records, the country of production (in this case Holland) does not affect the collector value. The series *Das Meisterwerk* (The Masterpiece), is a German re-issue series (prefix C037 or C051). Please note: all records with "Cnnn-" are not English, but rather German or continental European in origin.

Other pressings. EMI is a multinational corporation. All major countries have produced EMI editions with the aid of band copies, in part under the *Angel* label. We'll show some of these labels later in the section "Selected Pictures from Around the World".

44

45

46

Chart 2 - Prefixes for English EMI long-playing albums

ALP	The most important HMV label from the mono era (42), followed by ASD for stereo. In the interim period, there were both variants.
ASD	The key HMV full price classical series, including many English composers (43-46). Russian Melodiya recordings had a separate ASD label (48, 49).
CFP	Classics for Pleasure. Re-issue in the lower price category (60).
CSD	Full price. Rather light classical and ballet music (50, 51).
ESD	Greensleeves. Re-issue in the mid-price category (55).
HQS	Vocal and choir works, chamber music. Mid-price category.
MFP	Music for Pleasure. Re-issue in the mid-price category (59).
SAN	Angel series. Full price, mainly operas and choir works (47).
33CX	Columbia label from the mono era (61), succeeded by SAX for stereo. In the period of transition there were both variants.
SAX	Columbia at full price, primarily popular classic and romantic (62-63).
SLS	Box sets at varying prices. Layout like the corresponding ASD label from the same time.
SREG	Regal. Very early re-issue series in the mid-price category (56).
SXLP	HMV Concert Classics. Re-issue from the ASD and SAX series in the mid-price category (57-58).
TWO	Promenade series or Studio Two. Full price. Studio recordings with particularly spatial acoustics (64, 65).
33CX	Columbia label from the mono era (61), succeeded by SAX for stereo. During the transition period there were both variants.
SAX	Columbia at full price, primarily pragmatic Classic and Romantic (62-63).
SLS	Box set at varying prices. Layout like the corresponding ASD label from the same time.
SREG	Regal. Very early re-issue series of the mid-price category (56).
SXLP	HMV Concert Classics. Re-issue from the ASD and SAX series in the mid-price category (57-58).
TWO	Promenade series or Studio Two. Full price. Studio recordings with particularly spatial acoustics (64, 65).

44 EMI. (ASD) *HMV*, GB: L:2 "Red and Black"
45 EMI. (ASD) *HMV*, GB. L:3
46 EMI. (ASD) *HMV*, GB. L:4

47 EMI. (SAN) *Angel Series;* GB. L:1
48 EMI. (ASD) *Melodiya,* GB. L:1
49 EMI. (ASD) *Melodiya,* GB. L:2
50 EMI. (CSD), GB. L:1
51 EMI. (CSD), GB. L:2
52 EMI. (SME) *Electrola,* GFR. L:1 (until ca. 1967)
53 EMI. (SME) *Electrola,* GFR. L:2 (until ca. 1974)
54 EMI. (1C065), GFR. L:3
55 EMI. (ESD) *HMV Greensleeve,* GB
56 EMI. (SREG) *Regal,* GB

47

48

49

50

51

52

53

54

55

56

57

58

59

60

61

62

63

64

65

66

57 EMI. (SXLP) *HMV Concert Classics*, GB. L:1
58 EMI. (SXLP) *Concert Classics*, GB. L:2
59 EMI. (MFP) *Music for Pleasure*, GB
60 EMI. (CFP) *Classics for Pleasure*, GB
61 COLUMBIA. (33CX), GB. L:mono
62 COLUMBIA. (SAX) , GB. L:1 "Blue and Silver"
63 COLUMBIA. (SAX) , GB. L:2 "Red and Black"
64 COLUMBIA. (TWO) *Studio 2 Stereo*, GB. L:1
65 COLUMBIA. (TWO) *Studio 2 Stereo*, GB. L:2
66 COLUMBIA. (SMC) *Electrola*, GFR. L:2

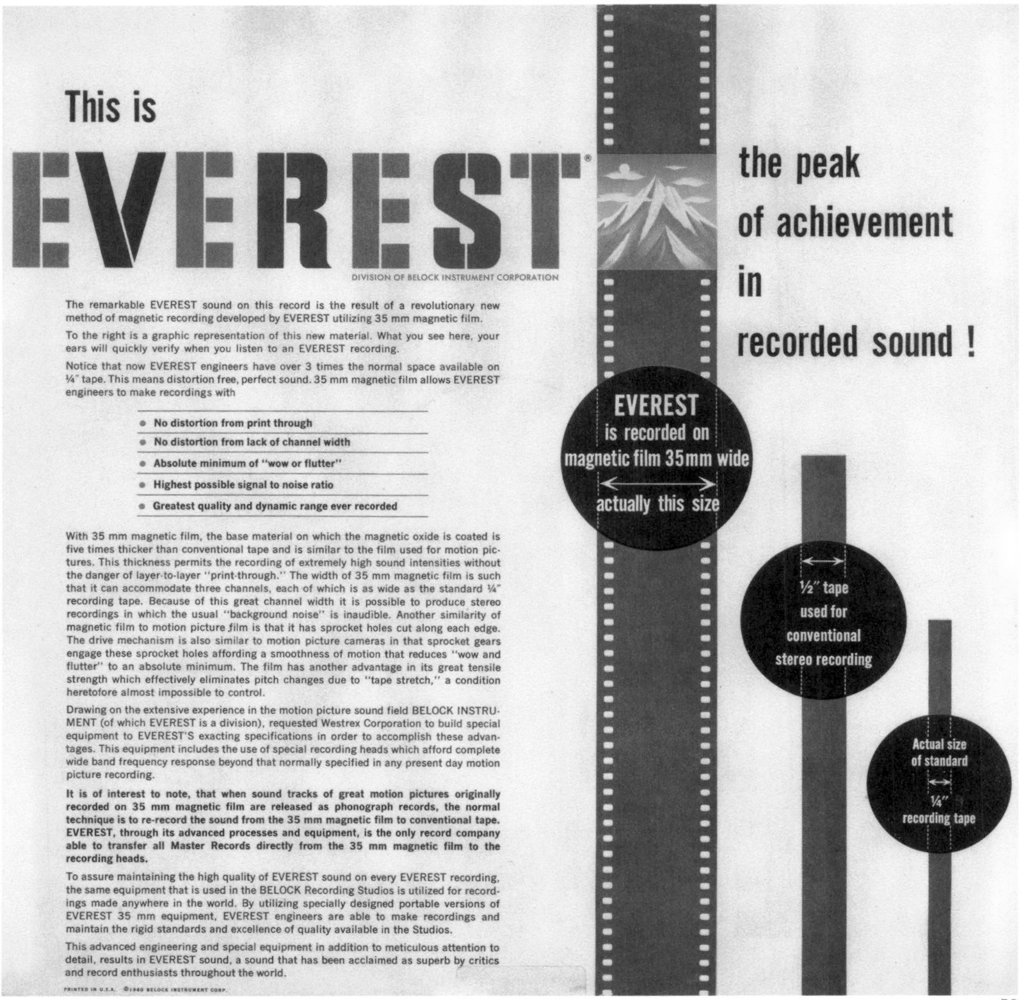

This is

EVEREST®

DIVISION OF BELOCK INSTRUMENT CORPORATION

the peak of achievement in recorded sound !

The remarkable EVEREST sound on this record is the result of a revolutionary new method of magnetic recording developed by EVEREST utilizing 35 mm magnetic film.

To the right is a graphic representation of this new material. What you see here, your ears will quickly verify when you listen to an EVEREST recording.

Notice that now EVEREST engineers have over 3 times the normal space available on ¼" tape. This means distortion free, perfect sound. 35 mm magnetic film allows EVEREST engineers to make recordings with

- **No distortion from print through**
- **No distortion from lack of channel width**
- **Absolute minimum of "wow or flutter"**
- **Highest possible signal to noise ratio**
- **Greatest quality and dynamic range ever recorded**

With 35 mm magnetic film, the base material on which the magnetic oxide is coated is five times thicker than conventional tape and is similar to the film used for motion pictures. This thickness permits the recording of extremely high sound intensities without the danger of layer-to-layer "print-through." The width of 35 mm magnetic film is such that it can accommodate three channels, each of which is as wide as the standard ¼" recording tape. Because of this great channel width it is possible to produce stereo recordings in which the usual "background noise" is inaudible. Another similarity of magnetic film to motion picture film is that it has sprocket holes cut along each edge. The drive mechanism is also similar to motion picture cameras in that sprocket gears engage these sprocket holes affording a smoothness of motion that reduces "wow and flutter" to an absolute minimum. The film has another advantage in its great tensile strength which effectively eliminates pitch changes due to "tape stretch," a condition heretofore almost impossible to control.

Drawing on the extensive experience in the motion picture sound field BELOCK INSTRUMENT (of which EVEREST is a division), requested Westrex Corporation to build special equipment to EVEREST'S exacting specifications in order to accomplish these advantages. This equipment includes the use of special recording heads which afford complete wide band frequency response beyond that normally specified in any present day motion picture recording.

It is of interest to note, that when sound tracks of great motion pictures originally recorded on 35 mm magnetic film are released as phonograph records, the normal technique is to re-record the sound from the 35 mm magnetic film to conventional tape. EVEREST, through its advanced processes and equipment, is the only record company able to transfer all Master Records directly from the 35 mm magnetic film to the recording heads.

To assure maintaining the high quality of EVEREST sound on every EVEREST recording, the same equipment that is used in the BELOCK Recording Studios is utilized for recordings made anywhere in the world. By utilizing specially designed portable versions of EVEREST 35 mm equipment, EVEREST engineers are able to make recordings and maintain the rigid standards and excellence of quality available in the Studios.

This advanced engineering and special equipment in addition to meticulous attention to detail, results in EVEREST sound, a sound that has been acclaimed as superb by critics and record enthusiasts throughout the world.

EVEREST is recorded on magnetic film 35mm wide actually this size

½" tape used for conventional stereo recording

Actual size of standard ¼" recording tape

PRINTED IN U.S.A. ©1960 BELOCK INSTRUMENT CORP.

30

Everest - USA

67 EVEREST. (SDBR), USA. L:1 (label designed by Alex Steinweiss)
68 EVEREST. (SDBR), USA. Inner sleeve
69 EVEREST. (SDBR), USA. L:2
70 EVEREST. (SDBR), USA. L:3

Like Command Classics and Mercury, Everest used the 35 mm magnetic film recording process (68). The records have a certain image with audiophile collectors, since technically they were ahead of their time. Nearly all of the recordings are from the 1950s. Particularly the recordings with the conductor Leopold Stokowski have high collector's value. The records that don't have a silver label (67) are later pressings. They were sold at a reasonable price up until the 1980s. As can be seen in the first section, Everest covers are quite attractive.

67

69

70

RCA - USA

The Radio Corporation of America is, after Columbia, the second major American company of long-standing tradition. Famous artists such as Arthur Rubinstein or Jascha Heifetz and composers such as Erich Leinsdorf, Jean Martinon, Charles Munch and especially Fritz Reiner achieved world fame on this label. Certain series of RCA records are highly valued by audiophile collectors. These include the recordings from the *Living Stereo* series with the prefixes LSC and LDS. In this regard, see the information on the inner sleeve (78). An additional appreciated value occurs when the recordings are American pressings with one of the two earlier labels: "Shaded Dog" (72) and "White Dog"(73). This refers to the "His Masters Voice" trademark, for which RCA holds the rights in the USA. The rights for the trademark in Europe, on the other hand, are owned by English EMI. The credential *Dynagroove* reduces the value somewhat. The Living Stereo records produced in England with the prefix SB (74) are also collector's items, providing that they have been manufactured in the Decca pressing plant. Picture 76 depicts the German counterpart. The *Living Stereo* series was followed by the Red Seal series (75,79).

Re-issues were first introduced in the USA and Europe under the RCA *Victrola* label with prefix VICS (77) and later under *Gold Seal* (prefixes GL, AGL1 and PGL1). Victrola records are more valuable than GL records. The *Point 5* series also contains re-issues from the Living Stereo series, which were produced using the *Half Speed Mastering* process in the 1970s and released by RCA at full price. Chart 3 contains an overview of the most important RCA editions.

71

72

Chart 3 - Prefixes for RCA albums

LM	Mono record (71).
LSC	Living Stereo US first editions (72).
LDS	Soria series of the Living Stereo first editions, label like LSC.
SB and LSB	English first editions from the Living Stereo series (74).
ARL1 and RL	Later American, German and English first editions from the Red Seal series (75, 79).
VICS	Victrola. Re-issue of the LSC first editions without remastering (77).
AGL1, PGL1, GL	Gold Seal. Later European or American re-issues in analogue remastering.
ARP1,ATL1	Point 5. Re-issues from the Living Stereo Collection produced by RCA with the Half Speed Mastering process.

75

73

74

71 RCA. (LM) *New Orthophonic High Fidelity,* USA. L: mono
72 RCA. (LSC) *Living Stereo,* USA. L:1 "Shaded Dog"
73 RCA. (LSC) *Living Stereo,* USA. L:2 "White Dog"
74 RCA. (SB) *Living Stereo,* Decca GB. L:1
75 RCA. (ARL) *Red Seal,* USA. L:1

76

77

79

Enthusiastically received, as one of the finest song recitals of recent years.
MONAURAL LM-2275—STEREO LSC-2275

To his operatic laurels, Valletti adds here a beautiful bouquet of great songs.
MONAURAL LM-2280—STEREO LSC-2280

Definitive reading by a master conductor and a virtuoso orchestra. Thrilling sound.
MONAURAL LM-2201—STEREO LSC-2201

Spectacular hi-fi and stereo show pieces, played and recorded with virtuosity.
MONAURAL LM-2251—STEREO LSC-2251

In opera, too, RCA Victor brings you the music you want, as you want it!
MONAURAL LM-6055—STEREO LSC-6141

WHAT IS STEREOPHONIC SOUND?

Stereophonic sound on records is finally here. It will be widely discussed, widely written about, and, perhaps, widely misunderstood. It cannot help but be; it is a complex achievement as well as an extraordinary one. We offer the following primer on the subject with the hope that it will both help you in understanding how and why stereo works and enhance the hours of listening pleasure stereo will offer you in your home.

Before stereo recording techniques were developed, the impulses of music were picked up by only one *microphone*. These impulses were then fed to one *tape* and from there to the conventional, monaural *record*, which you heard in your living-room through one *loudspeaker*. The conventional record offered brilliant sound and exciting sound, but, of necessity, it also offered only one-dimensional sound.

Microphone — Tape — Record — Loudspeaker

Now, the simple and obvious fact remains that we all have two ears, and we are used to hearing things dimensionally. Generally speaking, your left ear has a tendency to hear what goes on in the left side of a room, your right ear, what goes on in the right side of a room. Your brain then does two jobs. It combines both the impression received by the left ear and that received by the right ear into one total impression which we call music. At the same time, it retains the spatial or dimensional impression, music to the left and music to the right.

Let's compare hearing to seeing for a moment. You see images on your left with your left eye, images on the right with your right eye. Yet, because your brain can do two jobs at once, you get a total unified picture in its true perspective.

Stereo sound is simply the attempt to give you music as it is heard by *both* ears. Essentially, what happens is that two microphones, left and right, pick up what goes on in the orchestra at the recording session. These two microphones feed the musical impulses to two soundtracks on tape. The two soundtracks are then pressed into the grooves on a stereo record.

Microphone A — Tape A — Record — Groove — Tape B — Microphone B

The sound from a record partly depends upon how the needle moves or vibrates. For example, when Edison designed his phonograph to play cylindrical records, he made the needle vibrate up and down. This is called the "hill and dale" system, or vertical cutting.

On a conventional, monaural record, however, the needle moves from side to side, or laterally. The lateral movement has been used ever since the flat record replaced Edison's cylinder.

What about the stereo record? Each groove on the stereo record has two sound tracks containing both lateral and vertical modulation. In order to pick up the two sound tracks, a stereophonic cartridge equipped with a small diameter stylus has been developed to move both laterally and vertically simultaneously. This stylus reproduces the lateral and vertical modulations contained in each groove wall and channels the information to the proper amplifier and speaker. The information contained on the inner groove wall is fed to the right hand speaker whereas the information on the outer groove wall is fed to the left hand speaker.

The net of it is an overlapping and blending which gives music a more natural, more dimensional sound. For the first time, your ears will be able to distinguish where each instrument and voice comes from—left, right or center. In short, enveloped in solid sound, you will hear music in truer perspective.

Stereophonic sound is the latest step in an improvement process that began about 80 years ago. In listening to it, you will enjoy the highest achievement yet in the art of recording.

Loudspeaker A — Loudspeaker B — Amplifier A — Pickup Cartridge — Amplifier B — Record — Groove

When you "go Stereo"—either by acquiring a new stereo phonograph, or by converting your present set—your library of "monaural" recordings does not become obsolete. Quite the contrary—stereo reproducing equipment brings out the best in any recording, monaural or stereo.

RCA Victor now offers an already large—and rapidly growing—selection of the music you want, performed by the world's greatest artists, on LIVING STEREO long play records.

RCA VICTOR
RADIO CORPORATION OF AMERICA

Gwen Verdon and the Original Cast take you to hear Broadway's smash musical.
MONAURAL LOC-1048—STEREO LSO-1048

Belafonte and Horne are "dream" stars in Gershwin's gorgeous musical masterpiece.
MONAURAL LOP-1507—STEREO LSO-1507

Howard Keel and Gogi Grant star in this perennial Jerome Kern melodic gem.
MONAURAL LOP-1505—STEREO LSO-1505

The illustrious mood music conductor makes the Strauss Waltz his very own.
MONAURAL LPM-1757—STEREO LSP-1757

A delightful new interpretation of arias. Deft, tasteful piano "Feyer-works."
MONAURAL LPM-1926—STEREO LSP-1926

78

Mercury - USA

Mercury was a rather modest company in the classical sector. After Decca, EMI and RCA, however, LPs by Mercury records were some of the most sought-after by audiophile collectors. Among the long-standing conductors, Antal Dorati was the most famous. Original Mercury recordings with the prefix SR (80) are the most-wanted records ever. Even the Mercury records pressed by EMI in England with the prefix AMS (81) and the editions released in France (82) and Germany (83) are collector's items. In Europe, re-issues of the Mercury series *Golden Imports* produced for the US market were given the prefix SRI (84) by Philips. These have far less groove noise than the originals.

80

81

76 RCA. (LSC) *Stereo Orthophonic High Fidelity,* Teldec GFR. L:1
77 RCA. (VICS) *Victrola,* Decca GB. L:1
78 RCA. (LSC), USA. Inner sleeve
79 RCA. (RL) *Red Seal,* GFR. L:2. This layout was used on all RCA series since the mid- sixties
80 MERCURY. (SR) *Living Presence,* USA
81 MERCURY. (AMS) *Living Presence,* EMI GB

82

83

84

85

86

87

88

Deutsche Grammophon Gesellschaft

The Deutsche Grammophon Gesellschaft (DGG) is one of the major international companies with a long-standing tradition. For many decades, Herbert von Karajan was the top-seller among the conductors. Among the earlier artists, Wolfgang Schneiderhan, Wilhelm Kempf, and many others advanced to world class status. DGG didn't achieve the collector image of the major English and American companies. The number system was introduced in the 1950s and encompasses the series 138nnn and 139nnn for full price records – first indicated by the prefix SLPM. The series 136nnn consists of early re-issues. Around 1970, the numbering was changed. Up until that time, DGG used the earlier stereo label with the tulip border (85). In the 1960s, a series for "early music", called *Archiv,* was introduced (87). *Heliodor* was an independent label (88). There were re-issues under *Privilege, Resonance* and *Collectors Series.*

Philips - The Netherlands

Philips is a globally operating traditional company with headquarters in the Netherlands. The repertoire encompasses all types of classical music, including an excellent chamber music series with the Quartetto Italiano and the Beaux Arts Trio.

Highly recommended is the complete edition of Mozart symphonies with Neville Marriner at the conductor's stand. The series *Fontana, Universo, Grandioso* and *Sequenza* are re-issues. Some Mercury recordings were also re-issued on Universo and Fontana. Pictures 89 and 90 depict the label for the first editions.

82 MERCURY. *Magie du son,* F
83 MERCURY. NL
84 MERCURY. *Golden Imports,* Philips NL
85 DGG. (SLPM), GFR. L:1 "Tulips"
86 DGG. (139), GFR. L:2
87 DGG. *Archiv,* GFR
88 DGG. *Heliodor,* GFR

89 PHILIPS. NL. L:1 (Hi-Fi Stereo Label)
90 PHILIPS. NL. L:2
91 MELODIYA. (D) *Dolgoigrayuchtchaya*, SU. L:1
92 MELODIYA. (D) *Dolgoigrayuchtchaya*, SU. L:2
93 MEZHDUNARONAYA KNIGA. MK (33C), SU
94 MELODIYA. (C10), SU. L:1
95 MELODIYA. (C10), SU. L:2

Melodiya and the Forerunners - USSR

All sound carrier products in the USSR were published by the Ministry of Culture. During the early stages of the long-playing record, the label used was *Dolgoigrayuchtchaya*, which means simply "long-playing record" (*91*, *92*). Picture *93* depicts probably the first format for an export record. For record collectors, the recordings of the works of Russian and Soviet composers are of primary interest, including composers from Armenia, Azerbaijan, Georgia, the Ukraine, Uzbekistan and the Baltic Republics Estonia, Latvia and Lithuania.

Among the Russian conductors there are many famous names such as Kondrashin, Rozhdestvensky and Svetlanov. A differentiation is made between mono recordings (prefix Д, the Russian D), stereo recordings (prefix C, the Russian S for stereo) and digital recordings (prefix A).

Melodiya labels generally have a blue background, but other colours exist as well (for example red, yellow or white), without any recognisable system. Better designed covers with texts in English and French were produced for export. Together with licensed editions of Western recordings, the scope of the classical programme is probably unique the world over. The quality of the pressing is, on the average, only a trifle worse than the "western" pressings from major producers. Orchestral recordings sometimes have a slight reverberation. Melodiya has produced many superb piano recordings.

89

90

91

92

93

94

95

96

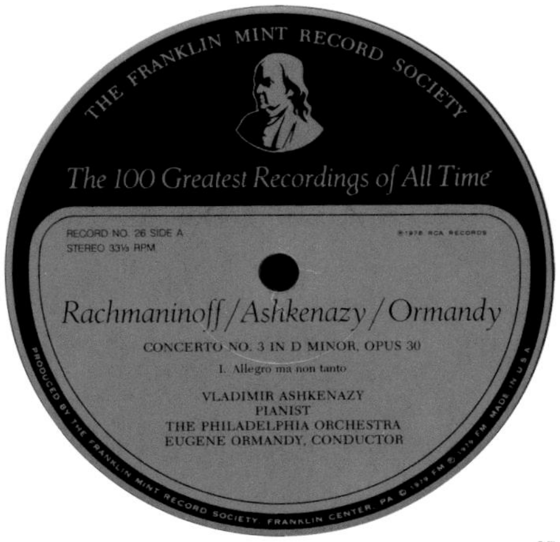

97

98

99

100

101

102

Other American Companies

Chesky produced new, re-worked RCA *Living Stereo* recordings which are by no means inferior to the originals in terms of sound quality and offer an inexpensively priced alternative (no image).

Composers Recordings Inc (CRI). Since around 1955, this label has been releasing modern American compositions exclusively (no image) in the same way as Louisville (see below).

Decca USA was founded as a subsidiary of the English Decca for the distribution of their recordings in the USA (96). During the LP era, Decca USA was an independent label. For this reason, English Deccas were sold in the USA under the London label.

Eastman Rochester Archive (ERA). The Eastman Rochester Orchestra was under contract with Mercury and produced a series with works of American composers, all conducted by Howard Hanson. These were released a second time under the ERA label (no image).

Franklin Mint produced a series of luxury albums around 1980 with the title “The 100 Greatest Recordings of All Time”. For this purpose, they procured licenses from other record companies. The records were pressed on transparent, red vinyl (97).

Louisville First Edition Records. In over 100 editions of first editions, the Louisville Orchestra and the Louisville Philharmonic Society Inc. have published works by contemporary American composers under the name “First Edition Records”. The first recordings were still in mono (98-100).

Musical Heritage Society (MHS) specialised in less popular works by European composers. The recordings were licensed by Europe, for example from Lyrita or Erato (101).

New World is supported by a foundation and publishes works from American composers. The first records in the early 1980s were still analogue recordings (no image).

Nonesuch focused on modern composers, particularly those from the USA (102).

Quintessence only produced re-issues of older EMI and RCA recordings with excellent sound quality (no image).

96 DECCA. (DL) *Gold Label Series*, USA
97 FRANKLIN MINT RECORD SOCIETY. *The 100 Greatest Recordings of All Time*, USA
98 LOUISVILLE ORCHESTRA. (LOU) *First Edition Records*, USA. L: Mono
99 LOUISVILLE ORCHESTRA. (LS) *First Edition Records*, USA. L:2
100 LOUISVILLE ORCHESTRA. (LS) *First Edition Records*, USA. L:3
101 MUSICAL HERITAGE SOCIETY. (MHS), USA
102 NONESUCH. (H), USA. L:1

Reference Records is the record company belonging to Professor Johnson with an outstanding purist recording technology (no image).

Turnabout is a division of the Vox Production Group and produced records in the mid-price category. The repertoire consists mainly of less popular works from the Romantic period and orchestral works by US composers (103,104).

Aside from soundtracks, United Artists only produced very few classical records in the early days of the LP, including orchestral recordings with conductor Leopold Stokowski (105).

Vanguard. There are three key series worth mentioning here: *Everyman Classic* with prefix SRV, favourably priced, but no re-issues; the *Stereolab* series with prefix VSD; the *Cardinal* series with prefix VCS (106-108).

Varese produced LPs with early analogue recordings from other companies such as Remington, Urania and Decca USA from the early days of the long-playing record, many also in stereo. Visually, the albums are very attractively designed and have better sound quality than the originals. The label portrayed here shows a remarkable logo – an inkblot (109).

Vox and Turnabout were labels of Vox Productions and both produced for the mid-price category. The repertoire was wide-ranged with a focus on Classic and Romantic (110-112).

Westminster. Original Westminster records have collector value. The majority of the recordings are in mono. There are also about 250 stereo records. Famous conductors have made recordings for Westminster: Rodzinski, Scherchen, Leinsdorf, Leibowitz and others (113).

103

104

105

106

107

103 TURNABOUT. (TV-S), USA. L:1
104 TURNABOUT. (TV), USA. L:2
105 UNITED ARTISTS. (AUS) *High Fidelity Stereo*, USA. L:1
106 VANGUARD. (SRV) *Everyman Classics*, USA
107 VANGUARD. (VSD), USA

108 VANGUARD. (VCS) *Cardinal Series,* USA
109 VARESE. (VC) *Sarabande,* USA
110 VOX.(STGBY) *Candide,* Decca GB
111 VOX. (STDL), USA. L:1
112 VOX. (QSVBX) *Vox Box,* USA. L:2
113 WESTMINSTER. (WST), USA. L:1
114 LYRITA. (SRCS) *Recorded Edition,* GB

108

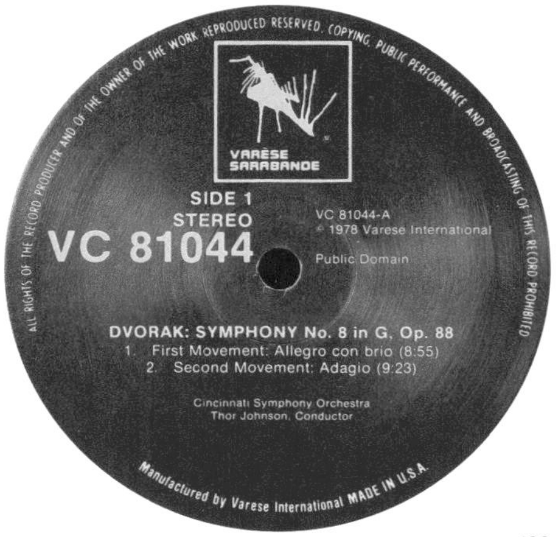

109

110

111

112

113

114

Other English Companies

Lyrita produced 130 records with outstanding sound quality which were recorded by the Decca team and to a great extent also pressed at Decca. Later re-issues were pressed by Nimbus in England or Philips in Holland. Decca pressings have the highest collector's value. There are exclusively English composers from the first half of the 20th Century on Lyrita: English Late Romantic and Neo-Classical by Alwyn, Bax, Bliss, Ireland, Moeran, Rawsthorne, Walton and many others. Most of these are orchestral works. The collector's value is therefore limited, since the composers are less popular outside England. (114).

L'Oiseaux Lyre is a label of the English Decca. Its origin, however, is French. The repertoire consists primarily of chamber music (115).

Unicorn. This is a broad repertoire with a focus on 20th Century English composers (116, 117).

French Companies

Erato concentrated its repertoire on 20th Century French composers and on Baroque and early classical works during the LP era. There are two prefix series for original French stereo records: STE50... and STU70... (118).

Inedits devoted itself to the release of French works from the 20th Century. The recordings were produced by French broadcasting companies (119).

Carthagène produced only about a dozen records. Similar to Inedits, the repertoire encompasses contemporary French works recorded by French broadcasting company orchestras or soloists (no image).

Scandinavian Companies

BIS (Sweden) has been in existence since the 1970s and produced mainly works from Scandinavian composers, primarily as digital recordings with excellent sound quality, during the LP age. Highly recommended here are the symphonies of Eduard Tubin (no image).

Caprice specialises in Swedish composers. The LPs were pressed by the German Teldec (120).

Finlandia produced almost exclusively the works of Finnish composers of the 20th Century. Analogue recordings carry the prefix FA, otherwise FAD (no image).

Finnlevy published – as did Finlandia – primarily 20th Century Finnish composers (no image).

NKF (Norsk Kultura Fond) is a foundation of the Norwegian Cultural Council for the promotion of works by Norwegian composers. The records were probably pressed at DGG in Germany (no image).

Swedish Society Discofil exclusively produced recordings of Swedish composers. The LPs were pressed by Teldec, Germany (121).

115 L'OISEAUX LYRE. (SOL), Decca GB
116 UNICORN. (UNS), GB. L:1
117 UNICORN. (UNS), GB. L:2
118 ERATO (STU), F
119 INEDITS. F
120 CAPRICE. S
121 SWEDISH SOCIETY. (SLT), S

115

116

117

118

119

120

121

122

123

124

125

126

122 BALKANTON. (BCA), Bulg
123 ELECTRECORD. (ST-ECE), Rum
124 HUNGAROTON. (SLPX), Hu. L:1
125 HUNGAROTON. (SLPX), Hu. L:2
126 MUZA. (SX), PL. L:15

East European Companies

Balkanton (Bulgaria). The state-owned manufacturer produced records since the beginning of the 1960s. The compositions of Pancho Vladigerov have high repertory value (122).

Electrecord (Rumania). From this state-owned company, the otherwise hardly acquirable works from Rumanian or Rumanian-German composers such as Berger, Feldman and Herman are primarily of interest. Among the Rumanian composers, particularly Enescu, Constantinesu and Dumitrescu are worthy of mention. Rumania was and is a very poor country. Due to the lack of suitable adhesives for the manufacture of LP covers, they were occasionally sewn together (123)!

Hungaroton is also a state-owned label. In the West, Hungaroton is particularly known for the recordings of works of 20th Century Hungarian composers. Hungaroton also released a complete edition of works by Bela Bartok (124, 125).

Muza (Poland) is the traditional Polish company. Specifically the recordings with works by 19th and 20th Century Polish composers are interesting for collectors (126, 127).

Opus (CSSR). The Bratislava-based Slovakian manufacturer is the smallest of the three Czechoslovakian record companies. Repertory focus is on composers from Slovakia (128).

Panton (CSSR) is the second largest record company in Czechoslovakia after Supraphon. The repertoire focuses on Czechoslovakian composers, many from the 20th Century (129). I became familiar with the Czech composer Lubomír Železný (1925-1979) on the Panton label. He is one of my most significant discoveries from East Europe.

Supraphon (CSSR) is the largest Czechoslovakian producer with long-standing tradition and in possession of a vast catalogue of recordings. Famous conductors from the time of the LP were Václav Talich, Karel Ancerl and Václav Neumann. The collector is specifically interested in Czech works (for example the composers Flosmann, Janácek, Martinu, Novák). Records with the prefix SUAST (red label) and SV (blue label) are older than those with a code consisting only of digits. The labels depicted here are all on Czechoslovakian pressings (130-132). In Germany there were numerous Supraphon recordings that were marketed by Ariola Eurodisc and by Bärenreiter Music Publishing under their own label.

Additional German Companies

Eterna was the classical music label of the nationally-owned enterprise (VEB) of the former German Democratic Republic (133).

Nova was another label of the nationally-owned enterprise German Records and concentrated on contemporary GDR composers, for example Hanns Eisler, Paul Dessau, Ernst H. Meyer, Paul Kurzbach, Otto Reinhold (no image).

Eurodisc released numerous recordings with GDR orchestras and Russian Melodiya recordings during the division of Germany. (134, 135).

Telefunken only played a role as a German traditional company with their own recordings in the early age of the stereo LP (136-138).

127 MUZA. (SX), PL. L:2
128 OPUS. CS
129 PANTON. CS
130 SUPRAPHON. (SUAST), CS. L:1
131 SUPRAPHON. (SV), CS. L:2
132 SUPRAPHON. CS. L:3
133 ETERNA. GDR
134 EURODISC. GFR. L:1
135 EURODISC. GFR. L:2

127

128

129

130

131

132

133

134

135

136

137

138

139

140

141

142

Selected Highlights from around the World

China Record Company is the national Chinese record producer. The label depicted has been taken from a recording of the revolutionary Peking opera *Fighting on the Plain* (139).

Concert Hall (Concert Hall Society). This company has an international base. It was active up until the 1960s (140). Records from Concert Hall have a certain collector's value.

Kiwi is New Zealand's national record manufacturer. The focus is in the works of composers from New Zealand. Worthy of mention here are David Farquhar and Douglas Lilburn in particular. The label shows a stylised kiwi bird (141).

Lyrichord was an American speciality label (142).

Pathé (Pathé Marconi) operated under this name until the beginning of the stereo era and then became – like Electrola for Germany – the French branch of English EMI. Pathé Marconi had

136 TELEFUNKEN.(LT), GFR. L:Mono
137 TELEFUNKEN. (SLT), GFR. L:1
138 TELEFUNKEN. (SL), GFR. L:2
139 CHINA RECORD COMPANY. China
140 CONCERT HALL.
141 KIWI PACIFIC RECORDS. (SLD), NS

recorded a vast catalogue of works by French composers such as Ibert, Magnard, Roussel, Dukas, Pierné, Ravel and Debussy and distributed them internationally via EMI. The label shown here was manufactured during the period when Pathé records still didn't have a connection with EMI (143).

Philips had production facilities in many countries. Here we see a French label from the early days of stereophony (144). This is a recording from Columbia USA which was produced for France from the licensee Philips.

Serenus was an American speciality label (145).

Remington and Urania (146, 147) were both manufacturers in the USA during the mono era. Urania also made a few dozen stereo records.

Telefunken records were pressed for the English market by Decca. Picture 148 depicts an early label from the Everyman Classics series.

Toshiba is a major Japanese manufacturer. However, they mainly produced pressings for Angel/EMI (the famous "quiet" Japan pressings). Also of interest to the collector is the Toshiba-produced Modern Japanese Composers series with Japanese orchestras (149).

The EMI Group had local subsidiaries around the world. Pictures 150-153 are of EMI and Angel labels from France, Portugal, Brazil (Angel) and Germany (Electrola). From Spain and France we see here labels from EMI Columbia (154, 155). On the *Odeon* label, EMI preferably produced light operas and operettas (156, 157).

From Australia, the World Records Club pressed and marketed many EMI recordings that were made in Great Britain (158). These included some very choice records, particularly those that had been manufactured with original English pressing matrices.

A label from Brazil on an LP with works by the Brazilian composer Hekel Tavares (159) contains no reference to the manufacturer and was perhaps produced on behalf of the composer. The label probably portrays Pedro Alvares Cabral (1467-1524), the man who discovered Brazil. 143

143

144

145

146

147

148

149

143 PATHÉ MARCONI. FR. L:Mono
144 PHILIPS. Hi-Fi Stereo, F
145 SERENUS. (SRE) Recorded Edition, USA
146 REMINGTON. (R-199), USA
(label designed by Alex Steinweiss)
147 URANIA. (URLP), USA
148 TELEFUNKEN. (SMA) Everyman Classics, GB
149 TOSHIBA. (JSC) Modern Japanese Composers Series, Jap

150

151

152

153

154

155

156

157

158

159

150 EMI. (ASDF) La Voix de son maitre, F
151 EMI. A voz do dono, Port
152 ANGEL. (33SCBX), Brazil
153 ELECTROLA. (WDLP), GFR. L:mono
154 EMI. Columbia (CS), SP
155 EMI. Columbia (SAXF), F
156 EMI. Odeon (PTWO), GB
157 EMI. Odeon (STO), GFR
158 WORLD RECORDS CLUB. Aus
159 PRIVATE. Brazil

APPENDIX

Literature

Bibliography

Pop and jazz records and a few classical records, primarily from the age of the shellac record

Eric Kohler. *In the Groove – Vintage Record Graphics 1940-1960.* Chronicle Books, San Francisco, 1999

Jennifer McKnight-Trontz and Alex Steinweiss. *For the Record – the Life and Work of Alex Steinweiss.* Princeton Architectural Press, New York, 2000

Pop and jazz records only

Nick de Ville. Album: *Style and image in sleeve design.* Mitchell Beazley, London 2003

Barry Miles, Grant Scott and Johnny Morgan. *The Greatest Album Covers of All Time.* Collins & Brown, London 2005

The standard work on the classical long-playing record, also containing a chapter on Cover Culture and approx. 400 cover images

Jaco van Witteloostuyn. *The Classical Long Playing Record: Design, Production and Reproduction.* A.A. Balkema, Rotterdam/Brookfield, 1997 (also available from www.polyphonlp.nl/book.html)

The following illustrated books depict jazz album covers

Graham Marsh and Glyn Callingham (Editors). *California cool – West coast cover art.* Edition Olms, Zurich, 1992

Graham Marsh and Glyn Callingham (Editors). *East coasting – the cover art of New York's Prestige, Riverside and Atlantic Records.* Edition Olms, Zurich, 1993 (also available from Collins and Brown, London)

Graham Marsh, Glyn Callingham and Felix Cromley (Editors). *The Cover Art of Blue Note Records.* Edition Olms, Zurich, 1992 (also available from Chronicle Books, San Francisco)

Websites

For more information on recordings or labels shown in the book, please refer to the following websites:

Angel, Capitol, Classics for Pleasure, Music for Pleasure, Electrola, EMI, EMI-Columbia, Regal, Seraphim, United Artists, Virgin ____________ / *www.emiclassics.co.uk , www.emiclassics.de , www.emiclassics.com*

Archiv, DGG, Heliodor, Westminster ____________ / *www.deutschegrammophon.com, www.klassikakzente.de, www.deutschegrammophon.de*

Argo, Decca, London, Philips, Mercury, L'Oiseau Lyre ____________ / *www.universalclassics.com*

BIS ____________ / *www.bis.se*

Canadian Music Center, Melbourne ____________ / *www.musiccentre.ca*

Chandos ____________ / *www.chandos.co.uk/*

Chesky ____________ / *www.chesky.com*

Columbia, CBS, Conifer, Epic, Eurodisc, Harmonia Mundi Deutschland, Odyssey, RCA ____________ / *www.sonybmgmasterworks.com/, www.sonybmgclassical.de/*

Columbia, Everest, RCA *(audiophile LP re-issues)* ____________ / *www.classicrecords.com*

Crystal, Poseidon ____________ / *www.crystalrecords.com*

Decca, London, Deutsche Grammophon, Mercury, Philips, Westminster *(audiophile LP re-issues)* ____________ / *www.speakerscorner.de*

EMI, EMI-Columbia *(audiophile LP and CD re-issues)* ____________ / *www.testament.co.uk*

Erato, Finlandia, Telefunken ____________ / *www.warnerclassicsandjazz.com*

Hungaroton ____________ / *www.hungaroton.hu*

Hyperion ____________ / *www.hyperion-records.co.uk*

Kiwi ____________ / *www.kiwipacific.com*

Lyrita ____________ / *www.lyrita.co.uk*

Melodiya ____________ / *www.melody.su/eng*

New World Records, Composers Recordings ____________ / *www.newworldrecords.org*

Nonesuch ____________ / *www.nonesuch.com*

Supraphon ____________ / *www.supraphon.com*

Swedish Society Discofil ____________ / *www.swedishsociety.se*

Turnabout, Vox ____________ / *www.voxcd.com*

Unicorn ____________ / *www.regisrecords.co.uk*

Varese ____________ / *www.varesesarabande.com*

Labels for collectors: ____________ / *www.mikrokosmos.com/labelography.html*

Important American labels (Ron Penndorf): ____ / *www.ronpenndorf.com/contents.html*

Labels from around the world: ____________ / *www.collectable-records.ru*

Mercury Covers and Labels, from Kohji „Shaolin" Matsubayashi: ____________ / *http://microgroove.jp/mercury*

Remington Covers, from Rudolf A. Bruil: ____ / *www.soundfountain.com*

Register of cover images

Copyrights

Acknowledgement

Many thanks go to

Günther Braus, Rudolf A. Bruil, Harald Bussemer, Glenn Koppel, William Alan Landes, Henrik Jungaberle, Kohji Matsubayashi, Wolf-Rüdiger Rubien, Michael Steiner, Alex Steinweiss and Rolf Verres

— Dedicated to Gaby and my two daughters —

CLASSIQUE Cover Art for Classical Music

By Horst Scherg (ed.)

Edited by Robert Klanten
Layout and Cover by Floyd Schulze for Gestalten
Typefaces: LaPolice BP by François Rappo; Belwe™ Mono by Linotype

Project management by Julian Sorge for Gestalten
Production management by Janni Milstrey for Gestalten
Translation by Patricia Mehnert
Proofreading by GlobalSprachTeam
Printed by Offsetdruckerei Grammlich, Pliezhausen
Made in Germany

Published by Gestalten, Berlin 2008
ISBN 978-3-89955-228-7

Bibliographic information published by the Deutsche Nationalbibliothek.
The Deutsche Nationalbibliothek lists this publication in the Deutsche Nationalbibliografie;
detailed bibliographic data is available on the internet at http://dnb.d-nb.de.

This book was printed according to the internationally accepted FSC standards for environmental protection, which specify requirements for an environmental management system.

FSC Mixed Sources
Product group from well-managed forests and other controlled sources
www.fsc.org Cert no. IMO-COC-028001
© 1996 Forest Stewardship Council